RHETORICAL RECEPTION

STUDIES IN RHETORICS AND FEMINISMS
Series Editors: Jessica Enoch and Sharon Yam

The series promotes and amplifies the inter/transdisciplinarity of rhetorics and feminisms by connecting rhetorical inquiry and criticism with vital academic, sociopolitical, and economic concerns. Books in the series explore enduring questions of rhetoric's rich and complex histories (globally and locally), as well as rhetoric's relevance to current public exigencies of social justice, power, opportunity, inclusion, equity, and diversity. This attention to interdisciplinarity, gender, and power has transformed the rhetorical tradition as we have known it (white, Western, upper-class, public, powerful, mostly political, antagonistic, and delivered by men) into regendered, inclusionary rhetorics (democratic, deliberative, diverse, collaborative, private, and intersectional). Our cultural, political, and intellectual advancements continue to be enriched by explorations into the varied ways rhetorics and feminisms intersect and interanimate each other at the same time that they take us in fresh political, cultural, scientific, communicative, and pedagogical directions.

Cheryl Glenn and Shirley Wilson Logan served as series editors for *Rhetorical Reception: One Hundred and Fifty Years of Arguing with Sex in Education* by Carolyn Skinner, guiding it through review, providing feedback, and shaping its development. They thank the current series editors, Jessica Enoch and Sharon Yam, for supporting its publication.

BOOKS IN THE SERIES

Rhetorical Reception: One Hundred and Fifty Years of Arguing with Sex in Education by Carolyn Skinner (2025)

City Housekeeping: Women's Labor Rhetorics and Spaces for Solidarity, 1886–1911 by Liane Malinowski (2025)

Not Playing Around: Feminist and Queer Rhetorics in Videogames by Rebecca S. Richards (2024)

Inclusive Aims: Rhetoric's Role in Reproductive Justice edited by Heather Brook Adams and Nancy Myers (2024)

A Rhetoric of Becoming: USAmerican Women in Qatar by Nancy Small (2022)

Rhetorical Listening in Action: A Concept-Tactic Approach by Krista Ratcliffe and Kyle Jensen (2022)

RHETORICAL RECEPTION

One Hundred and Fifty Years of Arguing
with *Sex in Education*

Carolyn Skinner

Parlor Press
Anderson, South Carolina
www.parlorpress.com

Parlor Press LLC, Anderson, South Carolina, USA
© 2025 by Parlor Press.
All rights reserved.

SAN: 254-8879

Library of Congress Cataloging-in-Publication Data

Names: Skinner, Carolyn, 1977- author
Title: Rhetorical reception : one hundred and fifty years of arguing with Sex in education / Carolyn Skinner.
Description: Anderson, South Carolina : Parlor Press, [2025] | Series: Studies in rhetorics and feminisms | Includes bibliographical references and index. | Summary: "Rhetorical Reception traces commentary on an infamous nineteenth-century book across historical, contemporary, popular, professional, and silent sites of reception. By identifying the rhetorical practices, values, and developments that emerge in these receptive contexts, Rhetorical Reception argues for the value of reception studies to feminist rhetorical scholarship"-- Provided by publisher.
Identifiers: LCCN 2025044830 (print) | LCCN 2025044831 (ebook) | ISBN 9781643175294 paperback | ISBN 9781643175300 adobe pdf | ISBN 9781643175317 epub
Subjects: LCSH: Clarke, Edward H. (Edward Hammond), 1820-1877. Sex in education. | Women--Education | Women--Health and hygiene | Feminism and rhetoric
Classification: LCC LC1621.C7 S55 2025 (print) | LCC LC1621.C7 (ebook)
LC record available at https://lccn.loc.gov/2025044830
LC ebook record available at https://lccn.loc.gov/2025044831

2 3 4 5

Cover design by David Blakesley.
Cover images: Top, L-R: The Readers (1897, Library of Congress), Group of Young Women Reading in Library of Normal School, Washington, D.C. (1899, Library of Congress), Portrait of Lydia Maria Child (1865, Library of Congress), Middle, L-R: Dr. Anna Manning Comfort (1916, Library of Congress), Edward Hammond Clarke (1868, Harvard University Archives). Bottom, L-R: Bryn Mawr's President at Mt. Holyoke Founder's Day (1921, Library of Congress), Vassar Women Playing Basketball (1913, Library of Congress)

Parlor Press, LLC is an independent publisher of scholarly and trade titles in print and multimedia formats. This book is available in paper and ebook formats from Parlor Press on the World Wide Web at www.parlorpress.com or through online and brick-and-mortar bookstores. For submission information or to find out about Parlor Press publications, write to Parlor Press, 3015 Brackenberry Drive, Anderson, South Carolina, 29621, or email editor@parlorpress.com.

Contents

Acknowledgments   *ix*

Introduction: A Call for Feminist Rhetorical Reception Studies   *1*

1 A Physiological Education: Audience Constitution, Reception, and the Construction of Gender in *Sex in Education*   *27*

2 The Popular Reception of *Sex in Education* and the Role of Science in Public Discourse   *61*

3 The Construction of Professionalism in the Reception of *Sex in Education*   *93*

4 Silence and Indirect Reception   *130*

5 The Receptive Repurposing of *Sex in Education*, 1973–2023   *164*

Conclusion: Pathways for Feminist Rhetorical Reception Studies   *197*

Works Cited   *213*

Index   *235*

About the Author   *243*

For Graham and Miranda

Acknowledgments

I am grateful for the many forms of support—institutional, professional, and personal—that made this work possible. A Critical Difference grant from The Women's Place at Ohio State provided funding for research assistance. Jordan Haas and Tymber Hetsler both performed careful bibliographic work, compiling and checking the many citations involved in this project. A faculty professional leave, an Arts & Humanities course release, and several Mansfield campus professional development course reductions gave me time to pursue this work.

Librarian Andrea Wittmer helped me trace the publication history of *Sex in Education* and assisted in several searches for nineteenth- and early twentieth-century commentary on the book, from the unreasonably specific to the impossibly broad. Her interest in my research was reassuring and motivating. Likewise, librarian Katie Blocksidge was enormously helpful as I thought through how I could locate and access more recent instances of reception.

I had many helpful and generous readers who have contributed much to the final version of this book. My powerhouse writing group—Liz Weiser, Beverly Moss, and Kelly Whitney—carefully read every chapter, multiple times. It's no exaggeration to say that I couldn't have done this without them. I've also benefited from suggestions by Sarah Hallenbeck, Tarez Samra Graban, Elizabeth Renker, Elizabeth Zeman Kolkovich, and Anne-Marie Pedersen. All of these readers offered smart, insightful feedback, each helping just when I needed it most. Comments by Cheryl Glenn and Shirley Wilson Logan, editors of the Studies in Rhetorics and Feminisms series, helped me refine my argument and the context that I situated it in; an anonymous reader also offered a constructive and supportive response to a draft of this project. Parlor Press editor David Blakesley responded helpfully, promptly, and cheerfully to my many questions; I deeply appreciate his work in ushering this book through the revision and publication process. I also benefitted from Fran Chapman's attentive copyediting.

As always, Dan consistently heard my ideas—some of them many times through—as I worked them out aloud. He reassured me that I had something to say, making him one of the first and one of the best receivers of this work.

Introduction: A Call for Feminist Rhetorical Reception Studies

In December 1873, the *Boston Journal of Chemistry* printed a brief notice of a new publication: "No book of the day has attracted more attention than Dr. Edward H. Clarke's *Sex in Education*, as is shown by the demand for a second edition in little more than a week after the first appeared, as well as by the lively discussion it has roused among the reviewers and in educational circles" ("Literary Notes" 70). For this writer and others (see also "Sex in Education" March 26, 1874; "Editor's Literary Record"; "Sex in Education" March 1874), it was not Clarke's book alone that was significant; the prolific debate prompted by *Sex in Education* was equally worthy of the journal's notice. That debate addressed issues as wide-ranging as women's nature and women's rights, the epistemological and rhetorical features of science, the characteristics of the ideal professional, and the future of the white, middle-class, American "race." Importantly, many of these significant rhetorical, institutional, and ideological developments are not attributable to *Sex in Education* itself or to Clarke as a rhetor; instead, they emerged through the book's reception and the rhetorical efforts of those who read and responded to Clarke's ideas.

In *Rhetorical Reception: One Hundred and Fifty Years of Arguing with* Sex in Education, I demonstrate that a feminist rhetorical analysis of the various contexts in which *Sex in Education* was received can more fully account for the book not just as Clarke's own argument, but as a complex rhetorical phenomenon. "Arguing with *Sex in Education*," then, refers both to efforts to refute Clarke's book as well as to citations that use the book as evidence supporting a wide range of claims about women, science, medicine, education, history, and other topics. Using my study of the reception of *Sex in Education* as an example, I argue that reception should play a more prominent role in feminist rhetorical scholarship. Feminist analyses of reception can help us account for a wider range of human rhetorical activity by treating audience members as rhetors in their own right, not simply as people who are persuaded (or not) by a rhetorical act, but as people who also use that act as the basis for their own rhetorical activity. Because the reception that I focus on here conveys a message, with a purpose, in a context—in other words, because it exhibits the characteristics of a rhetorical act—I call it *rhetorical reception*. Broadening our analytical focus to include the systematic study of such acts of reception opens new avenues for feminist scholars to explore rhetorical practices of interest to them, including those of marginalized rhetors, those that are collective, and those that are silent. Attending to reception as a vital component of rhetorical activity can also help us better explain how rhetoric "works" to promote or resist social change by giving us a window into what people do with and in response to rhetorical activity.

In *Sex in Education; or, A Fair Chance for the Girls* (1873), Edward H. Clarke asserted that even though women could succeed in college academically, they did so at great risk to their physical health, especially if they pursued their education in the same fashion as men. Males, Clarke claimed, were physiologically capable of persistence—week after week of continuous study for up to six hours a day. Female physiology, on the other hand, was characterized by periodicity, which meant that the academic routines developed for young men were dangerous for young women. Clarke warned women to study no more than four or five hours a day and to reduce their studies further or refrain from study altogether while menstruating. Clarke's physiological arguments were built on the theory that energy expended in building mental faculties was energy diverted from reproductive development, and the complexity of the female reproductive system meant that it required a great deal of energy to develop properly. Clarke was not just concerned with the well-being of individual women; he believed that white, middle-class women who followed the "male" model of education risked the future of their entire "race" because they would be incapable of bearing healthy children.

Sex in Education was immediately popular. It sold so rapidly that in December 1874—a little over a year from its initial publication—Clarke's friend and medical colleague Oliver Wendell Holmes wrote that "about a dozen editions" of *Sex in Education* had been printed. By 1889—sixteen years after the initial publication—the eighteenth edition was published.[1] According to Maxine Seller, 12,790 copies had been printed by 1903 (18, n5). Historians David Tyack and Elisabeth Hansot report that two hundred copies were purchased in one day alone in Ann Arbor, Michigan, home to one of the earliest co-educational state universities (*Learning* 151).

Criticism of the book was also quick and prolific. In addition to publication notices, book reviews, and commentary in the periodical press, at least four entire books challenging Clarke appeared in the year following *Sex in Education*'s initial publication. Public figures in education and science

---

1. Although most scholarship on *Sex in Education* maintains that the book was published in seventeen editions, I have located eighteen editions; the eighteenth was published in 1889. Thanks to librarian Andrea Wittmer for helping me confirm the publication history of Clarke's book.

continued to write articles and books addressing Clarke's arguments in the decade or so immediately following *Sex in Education*'s publication, including Herbert Spencer (originator of the phrase "social Darwinism"), Edward L. Youmans (founder of *Popular Science* magazine), and Henry Maudsley (a leading British psychiatrist). By the early 1900s, everyone from psychologist G. Stanley Hall to educators M. Carey Thomas, John Dewey, and David Starr Jordan had weighed in on the debate about women's ability to pursue an education while maintaining physical health, often directly citing Clarke. *Sex in Education* is still with us. The book was cited in Ruth Bader Ginsburg's 1996 Supreme Court majority opinion finding that the Virginia Military Institute's male-only admissions policy was unconstitutional. It also featured in the public discourse around the 2016 US presidential election, where it was referred to in a *Slate* article attributing doubts about Hillary Clinton's health to a tradition of questioning the health of ambitious women. And, of course, this book itself extends the receptive "life" of *Sex in Education*.

In arguing that women's physiology restricted their educational potential, Clarke joined a long history of Western scientists and philosophers who asserted that women's bodies limited their intellectual and social capacities. Greek physician Galen (129–216 AD) explained sexual differences by theorizing that women's lesser "vital heat" made them imperfect men and limited their intelligence (Schiebinger 160–65). Even as scientific thinking moved away from the Galenic model, physical differences were understood to dictate intellectual and social potential. According to Londa Shiebinger's history of women and science, in the 1700s, "the medical community . . . established a clear notion of causality: physical differences produce moral, and eventually social, differences" (222). Anatomical and physiological differences, particularly the supposed weakness of the female body and mind, were cited to rationalize women's exclusion from political life (215–16); women's skulls and brains were measured, usually leading to the conclusion that they were less intelligent than men (207). By the nineteenth century, the scientific consensus on women's "nature" justified their intellectual and social inequality. Women's minds and bodies were believed to be "under the influence" of their reproductive functions, and their decisions were understood to be governed by emotion and instinct rather than reason (Rowold xvii). Throughout much of Western history, beliefs about women's physiology and the related limitations or tendencies in their intellect and temperament have denied them access to personhood, citizenship, education, and rhetorical activity, as several historians of women's rhetoric have demonstrated.

Although others had asserted women's physiological limitations for centuries before Clarke, several trends in the US around the 1870s contributed to the popularity of *Sex in Education*. Widespread anxiety about women's health coincided with women's pursuit of higher education and of political rights. Significantly, Clarke's book shifted the terms of the women's rights debate by relying on the authority of physiology rather than on traditional, religious, or metaphysical ideals about women. The public was also increasingly interested in science and the benefits it could offer individuals and society. The fact that he promised to address so sensitive a topic as women's reproductive physiology using "Great plainness of speech" no doubt piqued some readers' curiosity as well (6). We might expect, then, that the combination of the topic and Clarke's physiological approach would attract a large nineteenth-century audience.

Even after the initial *Sex in Education* controversy faded, writers over the last 150 years have used *Sex in Education* to create their own texts in their own contexts, for their own purposes, to achieve rhetorical ends such as persuasion, knowledge building, identity construction, and establishing communal values. In a sense, I am doing the same, but rather than refute, support, or even analyze *Sex in Education* itself, I examine the arguments and appeals that have been composed in response to it. My aim is to use the reception of *Sex in Education* to illustrate the potential of what I call *feminist rhetorical reception studies*, an approach that brings feminist principles to bear on receptive phenomena in order to account more fully for the rhetorical processes of making meaning, shaping patterns of power, and coordinating social action. I demonstrate that the reception of *Sex in Education* has been a site of substantial rhetorical work, including negotiating rhetorical values, contributing to the women's rights debate, articulating the nature of professionalism, and even reconstructing the meaning, value, and rhetorical function of *Sex in Education* itself.

In addition to the ongoing presence of *Sex in Education* in US culture, its reception is relevant to modern readers because it demonstrates that reception can enact feminist values, serve the goals of members of marginalized groups, and complicate the principles of traditional rhetorical theory. Applying feminist rhetorical reception studies to the arguments produced in response to *Sex in Education* over the past 150 years illuminates

- How audiences contribute to the rhetorical construction of gender.
- How audiences use texts for purposes other than those intended by the rhetor, sometimes even subverting those intentions.

- How women were not merely victims of but also actively contributed to significant rhetorical shifts, such as the emergence of science and professionalism as persuasive resources for collective and personal decision-making.
- How rhetorical change is accomplished collectively, rather than through the efforts of autonomous "great" speakers and writers.
- How silence is an important component of reception, one that can highlight rhetorical opportunities and constraints that might not be visible by looking at rhetorical production in isolation.
- How reception is crucial to understanding how rhetoric works to support, challenge, and revise worldviews; rhetoric's social and material effects cannot be attributed to production alone.

In focusing our attention on what audiences do with (and to) texts, we can identify and theorize rhetorical processes that not only enact feminist principles but also more fully account for the variety of human rhetorical activity. By examining the reception of *Sex in Education* in particular, we can recognize women's historical and contemporary efforts to shape how science and professionalism were understood, the racist underpinnings of the nineteenth century's "separate spheres" gender ideology, and contemporary scholars' use of Clarke as a shorthand for a constellation of nineteenth-century attitudes toward women.

In the remainder of this introduction, I first illustrate what a reception-focused rhetorical analysis might yield with a brief contemporary example. Then, I survey the scholarship in reception studies that I have found to be most helpful in my research, foregrounding the points at which reception studies speaks to the commitments and interests of feminist rhetorical scholarship. Next, I review work in feminist rhetorical studies that decenters the autonomous rhetor, identifying existing projects that engage with receptive concepts, even if they don't always refer directly to reception. Building on that background, I elaborate on my earlier description of feminist rhetorical reception studies, detailing how the combination of feminist, rhetorical, and reception studies research can open new pathways for scholarship. Feminist rhetorical reception studies raises some challenging methodological questions, so after outlining the key features of this approach, I discuss the major methodological decisions I made in the process of researching and writing this book. Finally, I outline the scope of *Rhetorical Reception* by previewing the chapters that follow this introduction.

Reception-Focused Rhetorical Analysis: A Brief Example

As an example of what a rhetorical analysis of reception might yield, consider the case of the writing program administrator (WPA) who emailed the instructors in the first-year writing (FYW) program to inform them that everyone would need to teach at least one evening class each year. A production-focused rhetorical analysis might ask about the context in which the email was drafted and sent, how the WPA anticipated her audience's reactions, and the affordances or limitations of the genre—an email—that the WPA selected for communicating her message. It might also look at the rhetorical choices she made while composing the email: the reasons she offered to explain her decision; the tone she adopted; any emotional appeals she made; how she referred to her own authority or expertise; and how she characterized students, college teaching, or the role of FYW in the university. In other words, much of the analysis would consider decisions that the writer made in the process of composing the email.

In contrast, a reception-focused rhetorical analysis would examine choices the audience made in receiving or as a result of receiving the WPA's email. It might ask who responded and who didn't respond, and what that might suggest about power within the program, about various people's conceptions of the program as a collaborative or a hierarchical entity, and about the degree to which people were bothered by the new policy. It might also ask how instructors who did respond chose to respond (did they "reply all" to the initial email, write or speak to the WPA privately, or complain in the hallway?) and what effect that choice had on the reputation of the WPA, the morale of the program, or any revisions to the evening-teaching policy. It might focus on what the instructors who received the email did with it rhetorically: for instance, some might have picked up on one phrase that suggested flexibility and referred to it in an effort to avoid an evening class; others might have acknowledged that the WPA was well-intentioned in her concern for students but suggested alternative ways that the program might better serve students; and some might have forwarded the email to the department chair along with praise for the WPA's decision. A reception-focused analysis might also ask about the collective and individual receptive contexts (a night owl's response likely differed from an early bird's; people in different caregiving situations might welcome or resist evening classes; someone who just received some bad news and who dislikes evening classes might read the email as another sign that nothing is going his way). The receptive context might extend well beyond the time the email was sent: the WPA might reread it months later while organizing her email folders, her successor might find it in a file he inherited from her, or an instructor might come across it years later and (even though she complained strongly at the time) look fondly on it as a product of "the good old days." Each of these questions would help illuminate what the audience did with the email, what purposes they used it for, and how the responses shaped others' perceptions of the policy, the WPA, and/or the writing program.

RECEPTION STUDIES AND THE CENTERING OF TEXTUAL EFFECTS

As suggested by the brief example above, I believe that analyzing and theorizing reception has the potential to contribute to the feminist goal of more fully accounting for a wide range of human rhetorical activity. *Rhetorical Reception* draws from several concepts developed by reception studies, an interdisciplinary exploration of the ways that audiences receive texts and of the effects that texts and audiences have on one another. Literary scholar Ika Willis characterizes *reception* as covering three interrelated approaches: "reception study, which analyses how readers and audiences interpret and use texts; reception history, which tracks the afterlives of texts and/or investigates the history of reading and the history of books; and reception theory, which explores the nature of interpretation, language and meaning itself" (1). *Rhetorical Reception* engages in all three of these approaches to varying degrees. In this section, I discuss some of the reception scholarship that has influenced my work here, foregrounding the points of correspondence with feminist rhetorical interests.

Although audiences have always played a prominent role in rhetorical theory and practice, with rhetors frequently instructed to adapt their speeches and texts to their audiences, that advice does not meaningfully account for reception. Instead, because it is generally intended to support the crafting of an effective text, the advice to consider one's audience foregrounds production rather than reception (Ratcliffe, *Rhetorical* 20). In contrast, analyses of reception examine the effects of rhetorical activity: how audiences encounter, absorb, take up, revise, and repurpose texts. In "Audience Analysis and Reception Studies of Rhetoric," rhetorician Jens Kjeldsen asserts that, despite the centrality of audiences to rhetorical decision-making, rhetorical scholars have not sufficiently attended to what audiences do as receivers of rhetoric:

> Without audiences, there would be no rhetoric. Understanding audiences, therefore, is essential for understanding rhetoric. If we do not understand when, how and why audiences are influenced

> by communication, or see how they negotiate and reject rhetorical messages, then we do not understand rhetoric. In light of this, it is surprising that rhetorical scholars have paid so little attention to audiences—or to be more precise: to empirical audiences. (1)

After surveying recent rhetorical scholarship focused on audience, Kjeldsen concludes that this work, rather than describing and analyzing how actual audiences received acts of rhetoric, engages in "speculative, theoretical constructions of the audience." Without accounting for reception in practice, Kjeldsen contends, we will not be able to fully explain "the workings, influence and effects of rhetoric" (4; see also Jasinski and Mercieca; Blair). My call for feminist rhetorical reception studies echoes Kjeldsen's assertion that a thorough understanding of rhetoric requires attending to how real audience members receive rhetorical acts; however, I maintain that the political and scholarly commitments of feminist rhetorical scholarship make attention to reception especially relevant to this subfield of rhetoric.

Feminist researchers have long questioned the stereotypical alignment of action and masculinity in contrast to the linkage of passivity and femininity. This complication of the gendered nature of activity accords with reception scholars' insistence that reception is an active process, not a passive event (Willis 44; Martindale 11; Kallendorf 2). Like any rhetorical act, reception involves discursive choices reflective of the receiver's context and purpose; it is as intentional and dynamic as rhetorical production. Because the act of reception is a meaning-making process, reception theory acknowledges that audiences exert power over texts just as texts exert influence over audiences. Kjeldsen and Ida Andersen articulate what this principle means for the purposes of rhetorical scholarship that investigates reception:

> The aim [of reception studies] is not to establish a single source effect and connect this to the discourse or sender, or to establish strict, causal links between rhetorical utterances and changes in opinions or behaviour. The aim is to understand the complex interaction between the rhetorical situation, the characteristics of the utterances, and the audience uptake and its negotiation of the rhetoric. (311)

Exploring the complex and oftentimes continuously evolving interaction among context, text, and audience is key to identifying the processes involved in rhetoric and social change. Because understanding how rhetorical action promotes reform or maintains existing power structures is at the heart of feminist rhetorical scholarship, analyses of reception align with our interests in connecting rhetoric and praxis (for a similar argument in the context of literary studies, see Schweickart, "Reading Ourselves" 39).

Especially relevant to my study of *Sex in Education*, a book that "succeeded" by some measures, but "failed" by others, is work that adds nuance to the ideas of rhetorical success or effectiveness. Such projects complement feminist scholarship that decenters persuasion as the primary purpose of rhetoric (discussed below). One call to complicate our understanding of rhetorical success comes from Danette Paul, Davida Charney, and Aimee Kendall, who encourage rhetoricians of science "[t]o move beyond the moment" of a text's initial publication (374). They observe that rhetorical success is often a tautological concept:

> Too frequently, texts are chosen [for analysis] because they have been acclaimed for their contributions to the world's knowledge; they are deemed great works in the canon of scientific literature. Their contemporary status as revolutionary texts is attributed backward into their histories without sufficient examination of their initial effect on their original audiences and how that effect may have changed over time. In such acclaimed cases, the contemporary status of the texts serves as a self-fulfilling prophecy for the effectiveness of particular rhetorical strategies: If a work is successful, then any aspect of it may be assumed to be effective a priori. (373–74)

Paul, Charney, and Kendall remind us, furthermore, that "the status of a text is never static" (375); therefore, "pinning down when success occurs or gauging relative success is difficult" (376). A text may be unsuccessful with its immediate audience and only gradually achieve acceptance; or it may be immediately successful but later fall out of favor.[2] Acknowledging that a text's status can evolve requires adapting our analytical processes to account for different audience responses over time (Frow 15–16; Kallendorf 3–4). This phenomenon is likely familiar to feminist rhetorical historians, who have long engaged in "rescue, recovery, or (re)inscription" of women's rhetorical practices that may have "failed" in their initial contexts but are today viewed as effective responses to the constraints inherent in those contexts (Royster and Kirsch 14).

As the example of feminist recovery work suggests, the various values and meanings attributed to texts through successive processes of reception can accumulate over time and within communities of readers. Writing of

---

2. Responding to Paul, Charney, and Kendall, Randy Allen Harris argues that attention to reception is already incorporated into research in the rhetoric of science, in part through scholarship on scientific controversies, which by their nature involve a broader view than attention to a specific text (250).

the reception of classical texts, Charles Martindale explains that "our current interpretations of ancient texts, whether or not we are aware of it, are, in complex ways, constructed by the chain of receptions through which their continued readability has been effected. As a result we cannot get back to any originary meaning wholly free of subsequent accretions" (qtd. in Kallendorf 2). For historians of women's rhetoric, Martindale's use of *accretions* might call to mind the concept of *rhetorical accretion* as defined by Vicki Tolar Collins (Burton). Collins describes rhetorical accretion as the addition of texts (such as an introduction, a dedication, or other separate works) surrounding a woman's text; in the process, "the speaker of the core text is respoken" (548). Although Martindale and Collins refer to different rhetorical processes with the term *accretion*, they share an interest in how later interpretations affect the reception of an earlier text (see also Watson). In feminist rhetorical studies, the history of recovery work, which can be viewed as the effort to alter the reception of previously dismissed or overlooked texts, makes the entwined nature of past and present in reception not just a theoretical matter for us, but a practical one, too.

Another practical implication of rhetorical activity that interests many feminist scholars (and one that I take up in chapter one) is the discursive construction of gender. Existing reception scholarship understands the text and the reader as mutually constitutive, a concept that helps explain but also raises questions about gendering as a rhetorical process. Classicist William W. Batstone writes about "how our reading always changes the text and how the text always changes us" (18), and literary scholar John Frow asserts that "Readers are formed by texts as much as texts are formed by readers. What matters is precisely the relationship between the two" (15). These models present reception as constitutive of both the reader and the text, as grounded in the specifics of positionality (rather than an objective stance), and as an interpersonal and emotional process. The situated reciprocity between text and reader has a counterpart in feminist scholarship's recognition of the role of positionality and connectedness in rhetorical practice (for example, Ede, Glenn, and Lunsford 412). Such theorizations, moreover, prompt questions about how the rhetorical construction of gender might function reciprocally, affecting texts as it affects readers.

Although I have highlighted a few features of feminist rhetorical studies (praxis, recovery work, constructions of gender) that coincide with concepts articulated by reception scholarship in this admittedly brief overview, I believe that many more potential connections exist. Most importantly, what Martindale calls an "egalitarian politics of reception" (11) suggests a wealth of collective and sometimes collaborative rhetorical activity that might not be accessible through analyses of rhetorical invention and delivery. Investigating reception may open pathways through which more differently positioned people (not just the affluent and powerful) can be recognized as rhetors. Because reception often does not require the rhetorical and material resources that initial production does, reception can be a more accessible avenue for discursive activity for many people. Identifying and theorizing that receptive activity constitutes important work for feminist rhetorical scholars, work that extends prior feminist efforts to expand notions of rhetoric beyond the image of the autonomous rhetor who seeks to persuade an audience.

FEMINIST RHETORICAL STUDIES AND THE DECENTERING OF THE AUTONOMOUS RHETOR

Although much of the research foregrounding reception has occurred outside of feminist scholarship, some feminists have found reception to be a means of exploring questions associated with feminist priorities and even to identify feminist practices in action. For example, literary reception scholar Patrocinio Schweickart acknowledges the collective and collaborative nature of reception, illustrating the intrinsically collaborative nature of any rhetorical act that reaches a large audience. As she puts it, "The 'test of time' that great works have supposedly passed convincingly is really an abstraction for the energy and time generations of readers have devoted to the careful understanding of such works" ("Understanding an Other" 20, n11). Feminist media scholars also have a strong tradition of pursuing reception analysis to explore women's interpretation of a range of texts (including soap operas, romance novels, and tabloids), often concluding that women have found these genres to be a form of escape from their gendered drudgery, while they also resisted some of the patriarchal assumptions featured in such texts. Later feminist reception analyses broadened their scope to consider queer audiences of color, the gendered nature of forms of media engagement (including with new and social media), and challenges to public/private and gendered binaries.[3]

Although feminist rhetorical scholarship (like rhetorical scholarship more broadly) has not engaged with reception to the extent that research in classics, literature, and media studies has, feminist rhetorical theorists have sought to refigure rhetorical activity and rhetorical contexts in ways that decenter persuasion as the primary goal of rhetoric and the autono-

---

3. For more on feminist reception research in media studies, see the 2017 special issue of *Feminist Media Studies* focused on reception, edited by Andre Cavalcante, Andrea Press, and Katherine Sender, which I drew on for this very brief summary.

mous deliberate rhetor as its primary actor (Foss and Griffin; Royster and Kirsch 98–109; Ede and Lunsford, *Singular*; Buchanan; Hallenbeck, "Toward a Posthuman"; Fredlund, Hauman, and Ouellette). These theoretical challenges to traditional rhetorical values establish points of compatibility between feminist rhetorical studies and reception studies, even if feminist scholarship rarely adopts reception as a conceptual framework.

Among the rare examples of feminist scholarship focused on reception in rhetorical history is Tarez Samra Graban's exploration of irony as a paradigm through which to read historical texts. Ultimately, irony as a resource for moving beyond recovery requires awareness of what I might call the receptive nature of rhetorical scholarship: "Irony *as a whole discourse* draws historians' attention to the interstices of language, history, memory, and archive, embroiling while also liberating a present political problem in a past political narrative each time it is read. Whatever is liberatory about women's political irony is only fully realized in our interactions *with it* and *with them*" (175). What Graban says about irony as a historiographic paradigm applies to reception more broadly: rhetorical scholarship is inherently an act of reception, one that participates in what may be a long history of "ordinary" reception. Although scholarly and non-scholarly reception may reflect different purposes, the contrasts between them should not be overstated; all kinds of reception foreground interconnections among people, language, materiality, and positionality.

Listening, too, is a form of reception that has been explored by feminist rhetoricians. In her foundational work on the subject, Krista Ratcliffe presents listening as "a trope for interpretive invention" (*Rhetorical* 17), challenging the tendency to treat reception and production as separate rhetorical acts: "[R]hetorical listening turns hearing (a reception process) into invention (a production process), thus complicating the reception/production opposition and inviting rhetorical listening into the time-honored tradition of rhetorical invention" (46). This blurring of the supposed boundary between production and reception, as well as the re-valuing of reception, contributes to the feminist effort to better account for the full range of human rhetorical activity by decentering the autonomous rhetor.

Without referring directly to reception, other feminist scholarship has argued for expanding the frame of reference for women's rhetorical activity. Much of this work builds on Karlyn Kohrs Campbell's observation that immediately achieving persuasive goals is not an appropriate measure of success for rhetors for whom simply speaking was an accomplishment, especially when the purpose of the speech was a social change that was unthinkable for many in their culture (2). For example, in her study of contemporary women's childbirth rhetorics, Kim Hensley Owens articulates the necessity of a broader view to fully grasp the scope and effects of women's rhetoric: "[F]eminist rhetorical agency can be understood as a series of disparate, collective assertions over time and space . . . , potentially effective for future women even when those individual assertions do not end with success for individual rhetors" (138). Hensley Owens suggests that women's rhetorical effectiveness is perhaps best viewed from a distance: "[F]eminist rhetorical agency cannot be understood solely in terms of success or at a particular moment frozen in time. Feminist rhetorical agency . . . can also be understood in terms of women's shaping of events for their own and others' understanding and reassessment across time and space" (10). Like Graban, Hensley Owens suggests that rhetorical scholarship could better explain women's rhetorical practices if it methodologically accounted for more voices, including voices that emerge across time and that build on earlier expressions. I believe that attending to reception offers one means of accounting for women's voices in these ways.

Although it foregrounds circulation rather than reception, Jaqueline Jones Royster and Gesa E. Kirsch's "Social Circulation," one of their "Terms of Engagement" for feminist rhetorical scholarship (see also Royster, "'Ain't I a Woman'") also suggests a broader scale for the analysis of women's rhetorical activity. They write that they chose the term "social circulation" to serve as a metaphor to explain how women's rhetorical activity operates dynamically, "how such performances ebb, flow, travel, gain substance and integrity, acquire traction, and not" (23). Royster and Kirsch seek to "disrupt the public-private divide" by "mak[ing] more visible the social circles within which [women] have functioned and continue to function as rhetorical agents" (24; see Briggette for an application of social circulation). The theory and methods of reception studies could help feminist rhetoricians articulate how and why audience members' uptake, revision, repurposing, or reframing of women's rhetorical acts are mechanisms by which these texts and these women have rhetorical and social relevance beyond their initial contexts.

Feminist rhetorical scholarship that foregrounds reception is still relatively rare. Indeed, Sarah Hallenbeck observes that our attention to "discrete, organized locations" of rhetorical activity has limited our ability "to capture the broadest possible range of rhetorical practices, including the embodied and material rhetorics emerging both from individual women and men and from the larger systems of power in which they are enmeshed" ("Toward a Posthuman Perspective" 14). Attention to reception offers one means of complementing studies of individuals and bounded groups with research into more diffuse, though no less significant, rhetorical activity. While studies that focus narrowly on women's rhetorical acts are vital to identifying, describing, and analyzing how women have communicated, studies that focus on women's engagement in "mainstream" discourses—as producers and receivers in a multilayered, dynamic exchange—are crucial to seeing women's contributions to social change (or to social conservatism) and to rhetorical innovation (or to reinforcing the rhetorical status quo). In the case of *Sex in Education*, an examination of the book's reception reveals that it is not just a discredited, misogynistic book from the late nineteenth century, but that it has also been the site of substantial social and rhetorical work, by women and men, over the course of 150 years, work that participated in changing public rhetorical values and expectations.

Existing feminist scholarship that decenters the role of the autonomous rhetor suggests that feminist rhetorical studies and reception studies already share important perspectives on how texts operate at the intersections of producers, receivers, and material contexts. The commonalities between the two fields also point to ways that bringing their scholarship together could prompt new research and new theories to better explain human rhetorical activity. For instance, Ronisha Browdy's discussion of Black Women's Rhetoric(s), which highlights the importance of self-definition in Black feminist theory, interconnects with and enhances understandings of reception as constitutive of the audience. Browdy describes self-definition as "an interrogation of power—the possession of power and authority to interpret one's own reality." One site for such an interrogation might be in the act of reception. Browdy also highlights "multi-conscious and multi-voiced representations" as a theme in Black Women's Rhetoric(s) that reflects their intersecting identities. This rhetorical practice might be productively explored in studies of reception and might in turn enrich existing theories in both feminist rhetorical studies and reception studies, by asking such questions as: How can reception be a form of self-definition, perhaps in ways that challenge the definition offered by the original text? How might reception, which is already understood to involve multiplicity, be an effective rhetorical site for recognizing intersectionality?

Although several rhetoricians have called for greater attention to reception, I want to add to those calls a focus on feminist rhetorical studies. As the reception and feminist scholarship discussed above demonstrates, some commonality already exists in the research interests of the two fields, but I see much more potential along these lines, particularly in intentionally applying feminist commitments to analyses that foreground reception. Attending to reception broadens the sites in which we can identify people, genres, purposes, and arguments that have been overlooked. It also offers opportunities for new theorizations based not on dominant rhetors, situations, and forms, but on what may be the more numerous and diverse instances of rhetorical action that, while not recognized as "the statement" on a subject, may well be collectively more powerful in their work confirming, undermining, or revising such a statement. In exploring the audience's participation in a text's effects, attending to reception illuminates the collective processes by which rhetoric works to achieve social change or to maintain the status quo. Rather than focusing primarily on the crucial text that represented and mobilized a social change, reception highlights the often contradictory and uneven rhetorical efforts through which people share the work of deciding on social values. In sum, studies of reception offer sites in which to explore several questions of longstanding interest to feminist rhetorical scholarship.

FEMINIST RHETORICAL RECEPTION STUDIES

Although my overview of the connections between feminist rhetorical studies and reception focuses on the scholarship with the most bearing on my work in *Rhetorical Reception*, even this partial characterization suggests that attention to reception can enhance the project of feminist rhetorical scholarship. Doing so would yield what I call *feminist rhetorical reception studies*, a feminist, rhetorical approach to reception studies and theory. Its scope and purposes might best be characterized through definitions of its component parts:

It is feminist in several of the senses outlined by Lindal Buchanan and Kathleen J. Ryan in their definition of *feminist rhetorics*: as "an intellectual project dedicated to recognizing and revising systems and structures broadly linked to the oppression of women"; as a theoretical enterprise interested in "the shaping powers of language, gender ideology, and society"; as "a practice" invested in "regendering rhetorical histories and traditions"; as a "scholarly endeavor capable of transforming the discipline of rhetoric through gender analysis, critique, and reformulation"; and as "a political agenda directed toward promoting gender equity within the academy and society" (xiii). As Buchanan and Ryan conclude, such feminist work "encourages [people] to think, believe, and act in ways that promote equal treatment and opportunities for women" (xiii–xiv). Notably, research need not examine texts by women to be feminist; neither are studies of women's rhetoric inherently feminist. In the context of reception studies, engaging in feminist research means both capitalizing on existing features of reception scholarship that align with feminist commitments (for example, notions of the text and audience as mutually constitutive, of reception as situated, and of the egalitarian potential of reception) and bringing feminist prerogatives to bear on the receptive phenomena under study (for example, by exploring silence and listening as meaningful rhetorical forms of reception or by contending with the risk of re-centering dominant voices by naming them as "producers" who are being "received" by sometimes marginalized rhetors).

It is rhetorical. Feminist rhetorical reception studies complements the reception scholarship occurring in classics, literary studies, media studies, and other fields by foregrounding the rhetorical characteristics and consequences of reception. In other words, it attends to the epistemic features of symbol use; the ways communicative acts create, resist, or maintain certain patterns of power; and the ways symbols (including words) coordinate social action. *Rhetoric* names a study and a practice; as such, feminist rhetorical reception studies possesses (and continues to develop) a set of theories and concepts that can be used to name and explain the features and effects of receptive acts, and it also recognizes reception itself as a rhetorical process. The rhetorical nature of reception is evident in the fact that reception occurs within its own rhetorical situation—with its own audiences, constraints, and exigencies—one that might be quite different from the situation for which the received text was originally produced.

It explores reception from the standpoints of rhetorical practice and rhetorical theory. Of course, whether a text is considered an instance of rhetorical production or reception is a matter of perspective; many texts could be interpreted through both frameworks. Willis categorizes approaches to reception as primarily "text-to-text," which focuses on the texts audience members produce in response to other texts, or "text-to-reader," which examines how a reader interprets a text and the effects the text has on the reader; she also suggests the possibility of "reader-to-reader" processes of reception, which foregrounds the conversations readers have about texts (102).[4] Feminist rhetorical reception studies might adopt any of these approaches to exploring reception practices and developing theories that explain reception, though researchers engaged in historiography might find text-to-text reception most accessible. A reception-centered approach to rhetorical historiography may require substantial revisions to our notions of "the archive."

Rhetorical Reception engages in feminist rhetorical reception studies, demonstrating the methodology's potential to identify a wider variety of women

---

4. According to Willis, the text-to-text approach is common in studies of classical and Biblical reception, medievalism, as well as in research on creative texts produced in fan communities. She identifies media and film studies as well as traditional literary studies as disciplines interested in text-to-reader reception (35).

rhetors, to locate them in mainstream discourses and identify their contributions to rhetorical innovations, to reveal the functions of silences, and to explore how rhetoric works to influence social change over time.

METHODS AND METHODOLOGY

Feminist rhetorical reception studies may require historians to adopt research practices that differ from research that focuses on rhetorical production. For instance, in this case study of the reception of *Sex in Education*, I developed methods for making the most of the "archival abundance" offered by some digital archives (Enoch and Bessette). I also created practices that allowed me to pursue an analysis across the diffuse phenomenon of rhetorical reception. I sought approaches that would help me answer questions especially appropriate to reception, questions that differ from those usually asked in studies of rhetorical production. Instead of foregrounding the rhetorical choices Clarke made in order to persuade his readers, I asked how other writers used references to *Sex in Education* to serve their own rhetorical purposes, how the debate around *Sex in Education* participated in significant social and rhetorical developments, and how reception has altered the meanings of *Sex in Education* itself. Finally, because of the expansive nature of the reception of *Sex in Education*, I made decisions about setting boundaries, representing the corpus of responses, and accounting for receptive silences. The process of developing these research methods (how I gathered evidence) and methodology (the theory or rationale informing how I analyzed the evidence that I gathered) was recursive. As my "dataset" of texts accumulated, I considered (and reconsidered) how to refine my search and analysis processes. Because the research practices that I pursued for this study might be new to many readers, in this section I describe some of the decisions that I made as I collected and analyzed the texts that participated in the reception of *Sex in Education*.

I located many of the instances of the reception of Clarke's book using research databases that search for words and phrases in the body of texts. This allowed me to identify receptive texts in places that weren't obviously connected to questions of women's rights, health, or education, such as articles about architecture, books about the Supreme Court, and a local newspaper in Texas. Keyword searches, primarily using "sex in education," "Clarke," or "Clark" (to account for inconsistent spelling) in databases like *American Periodicals Series*, *America's Historical Newspapers*, *African American Newspapers*, and *Gerritsen Women's History Collection* allowed me to locate most of the nineteenth- and early twentieth-century sources, while I found many of the instances of reception occurring between 1973 and 2023 using *JSTOR* and *Project Muse*. I supplemented these searches by tracing references made by nineteenth-century writers in the texts that I had already located as well as by checking the indexes and citations in contemporary books and articles discussing women's history, women's health, nineteenth-century US history, the history of education, and other related topics. Notably, my search for the recent reception of *Sex in Education* led me to many of the texts that I also read and cited to provide historical context. Consequently, some texts appear at one point in this book as secondary sources providing background information and at other times as primary sources that I analyze as instances of the recent reception of *Sex in Education*.

I soon realized that the volume of texts that I was collecting would require me to make some decisions about the boundaries of my research and about how to represent my findings. Although different approaches to navigating archival abundance will be appropriate for different research topics and questions, a researcher's decisions should reflect an ethical, thorough, and systematic approach to the situations and people being studied, as well as to the audience for the scholarship. With that in mind, as I gathered and analyzed the corpus of texts participating in the reception of Clarke's book, I sought to

- Synthesize, as accurately as possible, the full scope of the relevant evidence. Even though I knew that I would need to focus my analysis on selected aspects of the available evidence, I did not want that analysis to appear to be the whole story; instead, I wanted it to be clear that the evidence presented was situated within a larger rhetorical ecology.

- Reflect the variety of rhetors who appear across the evidence. This meant looking beyond the most prolific or famous rhetors, looking beyond mainstream rhetorical sites, and looking beyond conventional characterizations of what makes someone an important contributor to a rhetorical exchange. Including perspectives that might otherwise be dismissed is vital to accurately describing the rhetorical work and effects of reception as a collective rhetorical phenomenon.

- Resist the temptation to privilege the texts and the rhetors who seemed, from my vantage point, to be the most accurate or effective. Studying reception can reveal the messiness of real human reading and writing, including misinterpretations, self-interested responses, and reliance on facts and principles that have been discredited. These imperfect rhetorical acts and the rhetors who produced them are at least as important to understanding how rhetoric functions in society as the texts and rhetors we admire and identify with.

- Organize the evidence and analysis in ways that foster ethical and useful research. This meant developing systems for storing and sorting texts in the process of researching and writing. I also considered how best to present to readers the wealth of information that I had collected: What citational and organizational principles would be most useful to readers? How could those principles be made transparent? How could I help readers make sense of what might feel like an overwhelming flood of names, titles, and quotations?

Working according to these principles involved decisions that bridged method and methodology. For example, attempting to "reflect the variety of rhetors who appear across the evidence" sent me back to look for more texts and to ask who might be missing, while also prompting me to consider how my categories of analysis might inadvertently foreground some rhetors and overlook others.

Additional decisions, values, and research interests likewise required moving back and forth between gathering and analyzing texts. For example, my decision to examine only those texts that explicitly engaged with *Sex in Education* was a matter of both method (affecting the texts I collected) and methodology (affecting and reflecting my approach to analysis). The vast discussion of co-education and women's education in the late nineteenth century often seemed to imply reference to Clarke's work (sometimes even using the title "Sex in Education" for articles without mentioning the book by the same title, sometimes using the phrase "sex in education" to suggest the questions around co-education or of the role of physiology in women's education, but again, without clearly referring to Clarke or his book). Although other studies of reception might include texts that refer to ideas or key terms rather than only those that cite a specific text, the prolific debate around *Sex in Education* made a focus on texts that overtly engaged with that book possible. I also chose to examine only the reception of *Sex in Education* in the US; although the book was debated in the British press, Clarke's repeated concern for "our American women" (31, 88, 89, 90) and my own need to set manageable limits on my dataset led me to make this decision. By their nature, studies of reception are likely to have boundary issues, and I tried to be purposeful and consistent in the selections I made to establish the parameters of my research.

Other decisions about how to focus my analysis responded to existing scholarship on *Sex in Education*. For example, I set aside a stack of nineteenth-century articles that would have served as evidence that writers emphasized Clarke's authority, experience, and expertise as a physician, because other scholars have thoroughly assessed Clarke's ethos and readers' perceptions of it (see, for example, Douglass; Bateman). I also opted to discuss Clarke's debts to Charles Darwin, Herbert Spencer, Hermann von Helmholtz, and others only briefly, because those too have already been traced (see, for example, DeLuzio; R. Rosenberg).

Although some methodological decisions resulted in a narrowing of the sources I collected, others prompted me to expand my search for texts. In the midst of evidentiary abundance, it can be tempting to believe that all the receptive rhetoric one has collected accurately and completely covers the range of responses to the text. It is very important, however, to pause to ask who is absent from that evidence. When I stopped to ask this question, I located several key silences in the reception of *Sex in Education*, silences that revealed that Clarke relied not only on sexism, but also on racism, classism, and anti-immigrant sentiment to make his argument. By their nature, analyzing silences can be difficult (What does the silence mean? Was it intentional or incidental? Did anyone notice the silence?), but silence is a form of reception rich with rhetorical meaning.

As I worked back and forth between collecting evidence and interpreting it, I also recursively experimented with processes for studying reception as a rhetorical phenomenon. I eventually developed a set of analytical practices that overlapped with and extended those I was familiar with from previous studies of rhetorical production. I read the sources multiple times, not only identifying rhetorical choices within individual texts but also asking what the writers were *doing* with *Sex in Education* and how their references to the book served rhetorical purposes, purposes that might be consistent with or quite different from Clarke's own purposes. I also read across texts to trace the receptive patterns that emerged, particularly those that participated in significant social and rhetorical developments, like the women's suffrage movement and the articulation of rhetorical values for scientific writing. For the nineteenth- and early twentieth-century texts, I found it helpful to sort them first by context (popular or professional) and then chronologically, so that I could observe the book's reception as it unfolded over time.

As I collected the texts published from 1973–2023, which were less likely to take *Sex in Education* as their primary topics than the nineteenth-century texts were, I copied and pasted, typed out, or summarized the passages that referred to Clarke and his book. I also documented bibliographic information and identified the overall purpose or argument of the book, chapter, or article so that I had a record of the context in which Clarke was cited. Later, I read through those notes (eventually comprising a 130-page single-spaced document) and color coded passages according to patterns that emerged in the purposes for which contemporary writers cited *Sex in Education*. For example, I highlighted the references to *Sex in Education* that were part of a discussion of nineteenth-century historical context in turquoise, those that argued that ideas like Clarke's still circulate today in yellow, passages that asserted that Clarke had failed to achieve his goals in teal, etc. As I learned more about the recent reception of *Sex in Education*, I subdivided and regrouped some categories to better reflect the rhetorical purposes that references to Clarke and his book served for late-twentieth- and early-twenty-first-century writers.

Finally, in drafting the chapters that follow, I determined that I should try to convey the scope of the reception of *Sex in Education*. In part, I wanted to provide readers with a sense of how frequently some arguments recurred in the debate. It was also important to me, however, to foreground the collective nature of reception; although I selected some texts and rhetors to represent the features of the reception of *Sex in Education*, these should be understood less as independent exemplars and more as one instance in a larger rhetorical phenomenon. Consequently, I have made extensive use of *see also* citations in the analysis of *Sex in Education*'s late-nineteenth- and early-twentieth-century reception. Although the *see also* lists should not be read as exhaustive, they do suggest the range of the rhetorical acts participating in the book's immediate reception. Because of the volume of receptive texts published in the late twentieth and early twenty-first centuries, I decided to present the evidence of recent receptive patterns in tables rather than in parenthetical citations, to improve readability and to provide readers with a visual representation of how often some forms of reception occurred. More importantly, grouping the texts according to receptive pattern conveys the collective discursive effort involved in achieving rhetorical effects through reception.

The Reception of *Sex in Education*: A One-Hundred-and-Fifty-Year History

Before Clarke published *Sex in Education*, he first presented his ideas in a lecture. In December 1872, Clarke was invited by the New England Woman's Club in Boston to speak on the topic of "the higher education of Women as influenced by Physical Conditions" (Blackwell, "Sex in Education"). Clarke had earlier expressed his support for women's medical education, so club members were surprised when he argued that female students risked their health in pursuing rigorous education. Immediately, contributors to the suffrage periodical the *Woman's Journal*, many of whom had attended Clarke's address, criticized his position. In his preface to *Sex in Education*, Clarke noted the interest in his argument:

> The essay excited an unexpected amount of discussion. Brief reports of it found their way into the public journals. Teachers and others interested in the education of girls, in different parts of the country, who read these reports, or heard of them, made inquiry, by letter or otherwise, respecting it. Various and conflicting criticisms were passed upon it. This manifestation of interest in a brief and unstudied lecture to a small club appeared to the author to indicate a general appreciation of the importance of the theme he had chosen, compelled him to review carefully the statements he had made, and has emboldened him to think that their publication in a more comprehensive form, with added physiological details and clinical illustrations, might contribute something, however little, to the cause of sound education. (5–6)

In October 1873, Clarke published the first of eighteen editions of his book *Sex in Education; or, A Fair Chance for the Girls*.

Rhetorical Reception picks up with the publication of Clarke's book. Chapter one, "A Physiological Education: Audience Constitution, Reception, and the Construction of Gender in *Sex in Education*," situates Clarke's book in the context of nineteenth-century Americans' popular and scientific interest in evolution, the rise of scientific professionalism, and women's rights activism. After providing some background on Clarke to explain his motivations and purposes in publishing *Sex in Education*, I analyze the book's rhetorical construction of gender as grounded in physiology and the related audience constitution of his readers as people who were scientifically inclined. Audience constitution is the point of contact between the rhetor's inventive choices and the audience's receptive choices. In this case, Clarke invoked an audience with characteristics favorable to his argument, and audience members variously accepted and resisted that position as they received *Sex in Education*. I examine the challenges to Clarke's gender construction and audience constitution posed by a few of the responses to his book. In addition to providing the basis for the chapters that follow, this analysis demonstrates the value of looking beyond individual texts (even when those texts are as influential as *Sex in Education*) when studying the rhetorical construction of gender in order to better understand the contested and multi-layered nature of how gender is collectively constructed through discourse. Ultimately, I argue that audience constitution, gender construction, and reception—as inter-related and mutually-determining rhetorical processes—should be examined together to gain a clearer picture of how gendering is accomplished, reinforced, and at times resisted through rhetoric.

After exploring how Clarke attempted to set the terms for the reception of *Sex in Education* through audience constitution, I turn to the immediate reception of Clarke's book by the public. The second chapter, "The Popular Reception of *Sex in Education* and the Role of Science in Public Discourse" discusses the hundreds of reviews, editorials, articles, and letters to the editor that appeared in newspapers and magazines across the country in the first fifteen months after the publication of *Sex in Education*. The reception of Clarke's book reveals the efforts of commentators to shape who read the book and how those readers interpreted it. The meaning of *Sex in Education* was certainly not set by Clarke alone or at the moment of its publication. Instead, the meaning of the book was contested through its reception.

Taking a broader view, this chapter demonstrates that the men and women involved in the debate over Clarke's book also worked to determine the epistemological and discursive expectations for science used in public decision-making (in this case, in the debates about women's education) and to articulate the kinds of authority that could be deployed by physicians, teachers, and members of other professions who claimed specialized expertise. Nineteenth-century writers frequently noted the move that Clarke initiated from arguments about women based in sentiment, theory, or abstract ideas of rights to arguments based in science. Both supporters and opponents of higher education for women believed that science would uphold their positions, although women, because of their long exclusion from science and medicine, also insisted that other forms of expertise and experience (particularly that of teachers and mothers) could contribute valuable insights to the debate. As the public looked to science for answers to the social dilemma of women's roles, it also developed expectations for rhetorical uses of science. What counted as sufficient evidence? How should writers demonstrate their expertise and objectivity? What standards of logic should apply to public scientific reasoning? What tone and style should the scientific professional adopt when writing for public audiences? In chapter two, I argue that the analysis of the reception of *Sex in Education* illuminates the intersections between the emergence of science as a popular rhetorical resource and women's rights discourses. Furthermore, I demonstrate that in those intersections, women were intensely involved in the process of articulating the rhetorical values that would be associated with the invocation of science in public discussions.

Following my analysis of the popular reception of *Sex in Education*, I examine the professional discussions around Clarke's book, focusing especially on the two fields most closely related to the issues it raised—medicine and education. Chapter three, "The Construction of Professionalism in the Reception of *Sex in Education*," demonstrates that the professional reception of *Sex in Education* not only participated in the debate about co-education but also involved an articulation of the nature of professionalism. In fact, very few professional responses to Clarke's book engaged with his argument by reporting on research into women's reproductive physiology (in medicine) or on studies of the effects of alternative pedagogical practices on women (in education). In other words, these writers did not often take up the kinds of rhetorical and epistemological work one might expect of professionals, such as performing research, outlining best practices, or advising the public. Instead, they discussed the values and characteristics of science-informed professionalism for physicians and teachers and encouraged their colleagues to engage in behaviors that they believed would improve the perceptions of their fields.

Although most histories of the emergence of the professions in the late nineteenth-century US describe professionalization as a process of masculinization and the concomitant exclusion of women, the professional reception of *Sex in Education* suggests that medicine was inconsistent in how it constructed and invoked gender as a feature of the professional. In fact, physicians often encouraged their colleagues to adopt epistemological and rhetorical values that supported women's capacity for professional training and work. The reception of *Sex in Education* among teachers and school administrators referred to Clarke's book to justify increased professional autonomy for teachers, many of whom were women. Through my analysis of the professional reception of *Sex in Education*, I demonstrate that the discussion of Clarke's book served as a site for describing the nature of professionalism. Notably, that characterization was not entirely hostile to women; indeed, some of the material, epistemic, and discursive features attributed to the professional (including a preference for statistical evidence over anecdotes, the use of neutral language rather than moral dogma, and the construction of a broad scope of authority for teachers) actually opened space for women to enter the professions and to claim their expertise and prestige.

Despite the volume of responses to *Sex in Education* published in the popular and professional press, the silences in its reception reveal how narrow the book's nineteenth-century reception actually was. Chapter four, "Silence as Reception," argues that silence is a rhetorically meaningful form of reception. By examining the silences and the instances of indirect reception among African American, Indigenous, and working-class women, all of whom could be seen to have a stake in Clarke's argument, I explore a range of functions of rhetorical silence, including intentional silences that enact resistance and agency and enforced silences that mark exclusion. Using the nineteenth-century reception of *Sex in Education* as an example, I ask what we can learn about the social, cultural, material, and educational factors that might affect who responds to a text and how they respond. This chapter also analyzes two instances of professional writers ostensibly speaking for working-class women, arguing that the professionals' social positions (one was a woman; one was a man) and political interests motivated their claims about the effect of continuous labor (that is, labor patterns that did not accommodate women's supposedly periodical nature) on working-class women. Identifying and looking closely at the various silences in the reception of *Sex in Education* also foregrounds the racism, classism, and hostility toward immigrants embedded in a text that has primarily been read as an example of nineteenth-century popular and medical misogyny.

Despite the furor around *Sex in Education*, Clarke's argument did not deter women from pursuing education, and discussion of the book faded by 1900. Beginning roughly one hundred years after its initial publication in 1873, however, as part of second-wave feminism's recovery of women's history, *Sex in Education* and several of its book-length responses were republished, and Clarke's effect on women's history was assessed and analyzed. In the fifth chapter, "The Receptive Repurposing of *Sex in Education*, 1973–2023," I look at the reception of Clarke's book in the late twentieth and early twenty-first centuries. The writers participating in this later round of reception treated *Sex in Education* differently than the immediate receivers did. Because women's right to education was no longer an open question and because Clarke's physiological arguments had been discredited, they did not engage with his claims directly. Instead, they treated the book as an artifact, as a shorthand representing medical and popular misogyny in the late-nineteenth-century US. This reception of *Sex in Education* demonstrates how reception changes over time and illuminates the fact that through reception, audiences affect texts, changing their meaning, value, and rhetorical function.

In my analysis of the academic and popular books, articles, and podcasts that discussed *Sex in Education* over one hundred years after the book's initial publication, I identify four ways that writers have characterized this book: as a synecdoche representing the historical misogynistic medical-social attitudes hindering women's individual and collective aspirations, as an accidental supporter of women's opportunities, as representative of erroneous ideas from the past that continue to threaten women today, and as a target for mockery. Together, these four uses of *Sex in Education* demonstrate that, even though the book was at one time perceived to be a powerful threat to women, through reception, audiences have exerted power over the book, adapting it to their (often feminist) purposes. Likewise, my own reception of *Sex in Education*, which I also explore in this chapter, illustrates the complex, embodied, situated processes involved in rhetoric's ability to "do something to audiences," while audiences also "have the power to do something to the rhetoric they encounter" (Kjeldsen and Andersen 311). My individual experience receiving *Sex in Education* participates in the prolific recent reception of Clarke's book; that body of commentary demonstrates the power of collective rhetorical action in the form of reception to remake a once-authoritative text in the service of audience members' own needs.

Chapters one through five demonstrate the potential for feminist rhetorical research focused on reception, using the response to *Sex in Education* across contexts as an example. In the conclusion, I bring together some of the pathways that feminist rhetorical reception studies might pursue that are suggested by my observations in those chapters and by my research processes for this book. Referring back to earlier chapters as examples, I describe some of the theoretical and methodological opportunities and issues that may emerge from increased attention to reception by feminist rhetoricians. Acknowledging that rhetorical scholarship is itself a specialized form of reception with significant influence over how other researchers and students perceive texts, I ask us to consider the ethical obligations and possibilities that accompany turning our attention to the prolific, common, and powerful rhetorical work performed through reception.

In the 150 years since Edward H. Clarke first published *Sex in Education*, perceptions of the book and its writer have evolved, from a book addressing the live question of whether or not women could (and should) pursue advanced education by a highly respected professional to a polemic screed written by a misogynist who used his (inaccurate) physiological expertise in a failed attempt to maintain the gendered status quo. In all that time, across all eighteen editions, the text itself hasn't changed. The words, the arguments, and the evidence were all presented in the edition published in 2023 just as they were in 1873 (though the book is available for Kindle today). Instead, it is the reception of *Sex in Education* that has changed, and that change reflects and participates in dramatic shifts in attitudes toward women, science, education, professionalism, and rhetoric. A feminist rhetorical analysis of its reception demonstrates not only how those social changes emerged but also foregrounds women's roles in that process. But perhaps even more important, feminist rhetorical reception studies helps us see how rhetoric works, how it shapes perceptions and motivates actions, by focusing our attention on what audiences *do* with texts. For a field that, at its core, not only studies but also enacts discursive activism in the service of social change, such a focus is crucial to our academic and our practical commitments.

1 A Physiological Education: Audience Constitution, Reception, and the Construction of Gender in *Sex in Education*

When Edward H. Clarke published *Sex in Education*, he entered into a longstanding public debate over women's education, a debate that had implications for women's occupational and political opportunities.¹ At issue was not just the extent of women's education, where they would be educated (co-educational or single-sex schools), and by what methods, but also their participation in the meaning-making activities of the professions and of the educated citizenry more broadly. Published in 1873, *Sex in Education* joined a wide-ranging public and scientific discussion about the past and future of humanity. Charles Darwin's *On the Origin of Species* had been published in 1859, followed by *The Descent of Man* in 1871. Social Darwinist Herbert Spencer had published his *Principles of Biology* over the years 1864 to 1867. The ideas in these books captured the public's imagination, tapping into and contributing to an emerging public faith in, or at least curiosity about, what science could reveal about the nature of humanity. Evolution, inheritance, and the concept of health at the level of the species (not just the individual), fundamental principles in these books, were also featured in *Sex in Education*. Clarke used the science of physiology to translate those species-level concerns into an argument about individual women's educational choices, decisions that he believed affected reproductive prospects and should therefore be guided by the theories underlying evolutionary science.

In this chapter, I examine Clarke's constitution of his audience as committed to scientific epistemology alongside of his medical-scientific construction of gender in order to explore some of the ways gender construction is embedded in and reinforced by audience constitution. Audience constitution is a contact point between the rhetor's inventive choices and the audi-

---

1. This chapter was first published as "A Physiological Education: Audience Constitution and the Construction of Gender in *Sex in Education*." *College English*, vol. 81, no. 6, 2019, pp. 485–507. Copyright 2019 by the National Council of Teachers of English. Reprinted with permission.

ence's receptive choices. Constitutive decisions, including how the rhetor positions readers, the values and priorities he or she attributes to them, and the "story" the readers are invited to join affect receptive decisions, such as who perceives themselves to be members of the audience for a text, how they interpret the text, and how they act in response to the text. In the case of *Sex in Education*, audience constitution, reception, and constructions of gender were tightly intertwined. Clarke's reliance on reproductive physiology to identify limits on women's education aligned with his invitations to readers to see themselves as inclined to make decisions based on scientific facts and theories. An analysis of the reception of *Sex in Education*, however, reveals that not all audience members accepted Clarke's audience constitution exactly as he intended it. Some even used their receptive rhetoric to re-constitute the audience for the debate over *Sex in Education* in ways that were less compatible with Clarke's argument.

In other words, even though the way that an audience is constituted by the rhetor to some degree determines how a text will be received, receivers do not always accept the identity and values embedded in particular audience constitutions. Some of these readers might respond to the text by attempting to re-constitute the audience in ways more favorable to their positions. Others might reject the constitution altogether and determine that they are not part of the intended audience. Even when readers do adopt the audience position as it is constituted by the text, receivers may adapt that constitution for their own ends. By looking at some of the texts written in response to *Sex in Education*, I demonstrate that both Clarke's construction of gender and his constitution of his audience were challenged by his contemporaries, an outcome that suggests the limitations of audience constitution as a strategy for shaping reception. My examination of the reception of *Sex in Education*'s gender construction also proves that our understanding of how a text constructs gender is incomplete without assessing the text's reception, without considering whether or how that construction was taken up, promoted, challenged, or subverted by its audience.

Feminist historiographers have identified the study of rhetorical gendering as a productive complement to existing scholarship that recovers women rhetors, that questions the gendered assumptions underlying the rhetorical tradition, and that expands what counts as worthy of rhetorical study. For example, Jessica Enoch calls for a "mode of historiography [that] interrogates the rhetorical work that goes into creating and disturbing the gendered distinctions, social categories, and asymmetrical power relationships that women and men encounter in their daily lives" ("Finding" 115). Sarah Hallenbeck asserts that the models of femininity that are operational in a particular rhetorical situation, which are often treated as context, or as sets of constraints and opportunities for women rhetors to negotiate, are worthy subjects of study themselves ("Toward a Posthuman" 18). Such research examines the rhetorical networks in which understandings of gender are developed and maintained.

Like rhetorical gendering, there is no escape from the rhetorical processes that constitute audiences; they are, as Maurice Charland puts it, "part of the discursive background of social life" (147). I use the terms *audience constitution* and *gender construction*, not only because they are the terms commonly used by scholars to discuss these rhetorical processes, but also because their connotations suggest the differences between them. Audience constitution is a different process from adapting one's writing to an audience's expectations; instead, it operates by interpellating audience members into a set of values and motives that the persuasive aspect of a rhetorical act can then address. *Constitution* conveys the sense of being called into being, of being "invoked" in Lisa Ede and Andrea Lunsford's sense: "the writer uses the semantic and syntactic resources of language to provide cues for the reader—cues which help to define the role or roles the writer wishes the reader to adopt in responding to the text" ("Audience Addressed" 160). *Construction*, on the other hand, suggests building or creating something, as in Enoch's work on spatial rhetorics, in which she "investigate[s] how the composition of space creates, maintains, or renovates gendered differences and understandings" ("Finding" 116). Both terms convey the idea of putting something together, but *constitution* suggests a whole made of many individual parts, like an audience in which certain aspects of members' identities are foregrounded, while *construction* suggests a figurative edifice, like the social, material, and ideological "building blocks" that make up gendered systems.

Although the constitution of audiences and the construction of gender are different rhetorical processes, they often complement each other. Audiences can be constituted as gendered (in the nineteenth century, for instance, the readers of a professional medical text were constituted as exclusively masculine). Audiences can also be constituted as people who accept a certain model of gender roles and relationships (for example, Clarke suggested that his readers were people who privileged women's reproductive potential over their educational aspirations). The construction of gender can be a part of how an audience is constituted (one audience invoked by *Sex in Education* was fathers concerned about their daughters' supposedly inherent physical frailty). It is also possible, however, that in the act of receiving a text, a reader can realize that she has been constituted in a way that is incompatible with the gender construction performed by the text (some women who read *Sex in Education* were constituted as part of its audience through their work as teachers but did not identify with the model of *woman* that Clarke offered). Although acts of constructing gender and constituting audiences are not necessarily aligned, they often do reinforce each other, and the alignments and disconnections become evident in how various readers receive a text, so the three rhetorical processes (audience constitution, gender construction, and reception) can be considered together productively.

In what follows, I examine the gender construction (how women and men were described) and the audience constitution (the cues or invitations in the text that suggest who the readers ought to be) at work in *Sex in Education*, paying particular attention to how the constitution of the audience reinforced the model of gender promoted in the text. Clarke's audience constitution set the stage for his book's reception, as it welcomed some reader positionalities and excluded others, and as it crafted a narrative of scientific investigation for audience members to read themselves into. To explore the connections between audience constitution and reception, I conclude by analyzing some of the published criticisms of *Sex in Education*, looking in particular at how those writers responded to both Clarke's gender construction and his audience constitution. In doing so, I demonstrate the value of examining audience constitution and reception as a means of gaining a clearer picture of how gendering is accomplished, reinforced, and at times resisted through rhetoric. First, however, I describe the biographical and rhetorical context in which Clarke wrote *Sex in Education*.

At the Intersection of the Cultures of Eloquence and Professionalism

Edward Hammond Clarke was born February 20, 1820, the youngest of four children of Reverend Pitt Clarke and Mary Jones (Stimson) Clarke. He entered Harvard College in 1836, when he was sixteen years old; while in college, he suffered from repeated rounds of ill health (a recurring respiratory condition as well as a condition that affected his eyes). He was prescribed rest and travel, so Clarke's educational progress was delayed, and he graduated in 1841.[2] He earned his medical degree from the University

---

2. Clarke's personal health entered the debate around *Sex in Education* when Thomas Wentworth Higginson used his memory of Clarke's college days to demonstrate that poor health in college was not limited to women. Higginson wrote, "In all colleges some will break down. The first scholar in my own college class lost his health in some way—I forget the source of trouble, it may have been only a disease of the eyes—and left college forever, though he obtained his degree. It may

of Pennsylvania Medical School in 1846 and afterwards established himself as a specialist in diseases of the ear. Clarke practiced in Boston, initially pursuing both his specialty and a general practice, but his general practice eventually grew so large that Clarke gave up the specialty. In 1855, he was appointed Professor of Materia Medica (what we might today call *pharmacology*—the body of knowledge about the properties of therapeutic substances) at Harvard Medical School, a position he held for seventeen years. According to his obituaries, Clarke was an effective teacher, "the admiration of his pupils," who "made a subject commonly thought among the least interesting of a medical course a great centre of attraction to the students of the medical school" (O.W.H.). After he resigned his faculty position, Clarke became a member of Harvard's Board of Overseers.

Among Clarke's friends and patients were American physician Oliver Wendell Holmes (who published a character sketch of Clarke upon his death), British physician Sir Henry Holland, philanthropist George Peabody, and scientist Louis Agassiz (W.O.W. 65). In addition to his medical practice and scholarship, Clarke participated in matters related to public health in Boston ("Edward Hammond Clarke"; Ware; O.W.H.). In eulogizing Clarke following his death from cancer in 1877, Rev. John Fothergill Waterhouse Ware spoke of the effect of Clarke's scientific inclinations on his faith. Unlike the men of science whose academic work caused them to doubt, Clarke's "religion was the religion of a Christian, supplemented by the religion of the man of science" (6). Ware explained that "Dr. Clarke was an inquirer. He must question everything" (7). Notices of Clarke's death described him as "at once inquiring, observant, reflective, and judicial" ("Edward Hammond Clarke" 437), as well as hard working and honest (Ware). Some recounted stories that highlighted his leadership as well as his patience in the face of the suffering that resulted from his poor health as a young adult (W.O.W. 63–64).

Several obituaries noted that although Clarke was widely sought as a practitioner, his greatest fame came from *Sex in Education*, which one eulogist described as "a trumpet-call to battle, [which] started a contest which is not yet over" (O.W.H.). This writer admitted that Clarke received both support and "attacks" for his arguments about co-education, and he claimed that Clarke "bore [the criticism] with perfect equanimity, feeling that he had honestly given the results of his experience, having only the good of the community in view" (O.W.H.). According to one obituary, shortly before he fell ill, Clarke "had begun to feel that he could do more good as an au-

---

not be improper to add, that it was my good friend, Dr. Clarke, himself" ("Physician and Pedagogue").

thor than as a practitioner. The marked attention which his treatises on *Sex in Education* and *The Building of a Brain* [the sequel to *Sex in Education*] received, could only have encouraged him to persevere in this direction" (W.O.W. 66). One obituary suggested that his early illnesses had left him too weak to produce the great work that many believed he was capable of: "The man was, in the estimate of all who knew him well, far greater than any work he has left behind him." The same writer praised Clarke's rhetorical abilities: "he was a man of wide culture, a charming companion, a ready speaker, and, as his clear and energetic style shows, a master of wholesome, vigorous, and simple English" ("Obituary Record").

Clarke's career spanned the transition between what Paul Stob, citing James Perrin Warren and Burton J. Bledstein, calls the nineteenth-century US's "shift from a 'culture of eloquence' to a 'culture of professionalism'" (2). The culture of eloquence, which was most prominent from the 1830s to 1850s—years in which Clarke attended college and medical school and established his practice—featured "a robust spirit of public engagement" (3) in which noble citizens sought to improve their communities and their nation, primarily through oratory. According to Stob, "for much of the first half of the nineteenth century, knowledge and eloquence were inexorably linked. Being able to articulate one's ideas compellingly became inseparable from what it meant to be learned, as effective speaking defined the properly cultivated mind" (4). A lecturer collaborated with the audience to solve common problems and to improve the collective moral standard. Eloquent intellectual practice was wide-ranging:

> [Speakers] did not have to live according to disciplinary boundaries, so long as they could articulate an insight eloquently and so long as audiences remained interested. The same lecturer might speak on literature, history, and philosophy before turning to biology, astronomy, and botany. If a speaker was able to inspire, entertain, and enlighten, he or she was in a perfect position to work with popular audiences on crafting a shared vision. (6)

The culture of eloquence privileged rhetors who could engage the public in intellectual and moral development; the lyceum, lecture hall, and popular periodical were the sites in which this rhetorical work took place.

In contrast, the culture of professionalism performed much of its intellectual and rhetorical work in laboratories, universities, and professional journals and meetings. Following the Civil War, Americans became increasingly convinced that science could solve many of society's problems. The public was enthralled by several of science's new theories, such as the laws of thermodynamics and Darwin's ideas about evolution, and it was impressed by the substantial changes to life brought about by technologies like the railroad and the telegraph (Stob 18). After mid-century, elite Americans, including Clarke, traveled to Germany to observe that country's research institutions; they returned with commitments to objectivity, the scientific method, and technical vocabularies (19). US universities, led by Harvard, reinvented themselves as research institutions (19).

According to Stob, the emergence of the culture of professionalism prompted four major changes from the previous culture of eloquence. First, intellectuals no longer saw public engagement as their primary responsibility; instead, their most important duty was to focus objectively on specific questions (20). Second, scholars specialized, often seeking academic credentials to deepen and validate their expertise. Professional specialization diverged from the culture of eloquence's wide-ranging interdisciplinarity (20). Third, the rise of the culture of professionalism was accompanied by "the privileging of specialized discourse—precise ways of talking shared by members of a professional enclave but more or less inaccessible to general audiences" (20). The emergence of technical vocabularies further distanced the professional and his or her expertise from the public, which led to the fourth major change associated with the rise of professionalism: the public was no longer imagined to be the audience for intellectual work. Instead, professionals envisioned other professionals as the recipients and judges of their work. According to Stob, "It was no longer necessary for scholars to speak in a way that could edify, educate, and entertain a wide swath of the community" (21). Instead of making collective popular intellectual progress, professionals would first develop the new knowledge, then transmit it to the public: "Scholars spoke not as concerned citizens contributing to communal deliberations but as experts who had truths to pass on to the masses" (21). No longer the active co-constructors of knowledge as in the culture of eloquence, the non-professional audience was now imagined to be passive in receiving expertise, deferent to the authority of the professional.

Clarke, educated at the time of the culture of eloquence but teaching and writing during the culture of professionalism, reflected both of these intellectual ideals in *Sex in Education*. The book was intended for a popular audience, but Clarke did not hesitate to use medical vocabulary or to insist on the authority of science and his own professional status. Aside from the controversial nature of its topic, some of the intensity of the reaction evoked by *Sex in Education* resulted from its uneasy attempt to reach a popular audience through interdisciplinary, and often emotional, arguments reminiscent of the culture of eloquence while also invoking the language, expertise, and authority of the professional. Clarke's position in the transition from a culture of eloquence to a culture of professionalism is reflected in the ways that he constructed gender and constituted his audience. Both rhetorical acts depended on Clarke's use of science and professionalism: how he claimed scientific epistemology in his argument, how he relied on scientific evidence to define woman's sphere, and how he expected his audience to accept his authority as a professional. In fact, the transition from a culture of eloquence to a culture of professionalism likely facilitated and sometimes required changes in how audiences were constituted and how genders were constructed. *Sex in Education* participated in this crucial nineteenth-century shift in rhetorical values, and the book's reception reflects the public's varying reactions to this change.

Speaking and Writing as a Professional to the Public

The roots of *Sex in Education* can be found in Clarke's earlier commentary on the movement to educate and accept women as fully qualified physicians. On December 16, 1869, Clarke published an article in the *Boston Medical and Surgical Journal* titled "Medical Education of Women." In it, he asserted what would become a central premise of *Sex in Education*, which he published four years later: "Whatever may be the final decision of this question [the status of women in society], it is evident that the light which physiology can throw upon it—the facts which physicians can best supply—will contribute largely to its correct solution" (345). Although Clarke advocated a fair test for the women pursuing medical degrees, he could not support medical co-education: "God forbid that I should ever see men and women aiding each other to display with the scalpel the secrets of the reproductive system; or with crucible and microscope investigating the constituents of the urine; or charmingly discussing together the labyrynthine [sic] ways of syphilis" (346). Clarke concluded by insisting that the women who wished to pursue a medical education must do so at separate educational institutions. Even though he claimed that the objective study of physiology would determine women's capabilities, Clarke was confident that physiology would support his beliefs about appropriate interactions between men and women.

Despite the warning signs evident in this article, the New England Woman's Club was heartened by the fact that Clarke had not condemned women's medical education outright and by his support of the "experiment" of women in medicine, so the group invited Clarke to appear before its members in December 1872. The club, founded in Boston in 1868 as one of the earliest women's organizations in the US, hosted lectures on a range of topics intended to enrich the knowledge of its members, who also engaged in a variety of social initiatives through the club. The New England

Woman's Club was particularly interested in higher education for women because its members understood women's education to be a necessary step in their pursuit of wider political, civic, and occupational opportunities. The subject was also timely. US women's access to collegiate education was relatively new, but it was growing rapidly (Zschoche 545). Indeed, women's petitions to enter Harvard University sparked a heated debate in the early 1870s, and Clarke would join many of his colleagues in opposing women's admission to the medical school, divinity school, and undergraduate college (Solomon 56).

Henry B. Blackwell published an account of Clarke's lecture to the club in the December 21, 1872 issue of the *Woman's Journal*.[3] According to Blackwell, Clarke began by "cheerfully conced[ing] that women can successfully pursue every department of study that men pursue, and can reach equal eminence of attainment in every department of intellectual culture" ("Sex in Education"). This promising beginning was quickly qualified by Clarke's argument that men and women should be educated through different methods. Because girls were being educated through "subjection to a rigid routine suited to boys alone, and to which the periodicity of functions in the feminine organization is utterly unsuited," women's health was deteriorating to the extent that it "endanger[ed] the future of the Race." According to Blackwell, Clarke then recounted several clinical cases as evidence for his claims. After reporting some of the discussion that followed Clarke's address, Blackwell's account ended with a description of the group's "impression": "the facts and suggestions, so far as they had been developed, were exceedingly important, but . . . they did not really militate against the wisdom and usefulness of the co-education of the sexes."

The rather subdued reactions of the New England Woman's Club did not last long, however. By the next week, derisive comments about Clarke had worked their way into the *Woman's Journal*. For example, a brief note on the death of Mary Somerville, the English mathematician, included this

---

3. Henry Browne Blackwell (1825–1909) was an ardent women's rights advocate and part of a family of activists, which included his sisters, pioneering physicians Elizabeth and Emily, as well as his sister-in-law Antoinette Brown Blackwell, the first woman ordained in a mainstream denomination in the US and a prolific public speaker. Blackwell himself married suffragist Lucy Stone. The *Woman's Journal*, which Blackwell edited alongside Stone, was the official organ of the National American Woman Suffrage Association, and several of its editors and contributors were also members of the New England Woman's Club, so the periodical regularly carried news from the club and articles on topics of interest to club members. Blackwell's account was also published in the Boston *Daily Advertiser* on December 21, 1872.

line: "We commend the healthy and vigorous old age of this most highly educated English lady to the special attention of Dr. E. H. Clarke" ("Notes and News"). By January 4, Lucy Stone and Henry Blackwell ("Progress Involuntary") had published opinion pieces challenging Clarke's arguments. By mid-January, letters to the editor questioning Clarke's conclusions began to appear (E.S.P.). From January to August 1873 at least one article or letter challenging Clarke appeared almost every month; in addition to those already named, contributors to the argument included abolitionist and women's rights activist Lydia Maria Child ("Physical Strength of Women"), suffragist Elizabeth Cady Stanton ("An Old Story"), and James H. Fairchild, president of Oberlin College ("Experience of Oberlin"). Witnessing the controversy his lecture had initiated in the *Woman's Journal* and elsewhere, and in response to queries he had received privately, Clarke decided that a fuller treatment of his ideas on co-education would benefit the public, so in October 1873, shortly after his retirement from Harvard (Bittel 123), he published *Sex in Education; or, A Fair Chance for the Girls*.

Sex in Education consists of five chapters:

> I. "Introductory," in which Clarke acknowledged that women had the right to do anything they wanted to do, but he also asserted that physiology would ultimately determine what women were physically capable of doing;

> II. "Chiefly Physiological," in which he summarized the medical and biological science that supported his claim that women's health would be damaged by pursuing education in the same ways that men did;

> III. "Chiefly Clinical," in which he recounted seven medical cases illustrating the physical and mental disorders that could arise when women did not arrange their education or work according to nature's periodic demands;

> IV. "Co-Education," in which Clarke outlined the social consequences of a decline in fertility resulting from the continuous education of the "best" women, asserted that women who succeeded intellectually might fail physiologically, and declared that young women between fourteen and twenty-five years old should not study more than four or five hours each day with an additional remission in effort every fourth week;

V. "The European Way," in which Clarke claimed that women in Europe and Canada were healthier than American women because, according to the letters from physicians and well-educated women that he cited, their educational systems better adhered to the demands of female physiology.

With the exception of a preface added to the second (1873) edition and a note added to the fifth edition (1873), the content of *Sex in Education* did not change across its eighteen editions; even the page numbers are consistent across editions.[4] Clarke may have opted not to revise his book because he published *The Building of a Brain* (1874) as an extension of his argument in *Sex in Education* instead; furthermore, around the time *The Building of a Brain* was published, Clarke's final illness set in, making it difficult for him to work. Thus, *Sex in Education* circulated in a consistent form into the early twentieth century.

Constituting the Audience of *Sex in Education*

In *Sex in Education*, Clarke asserted that human physiology (the branch of biology that studies the functions and processes of the body and its systems) was the appropriate epistemology for identifying the characteristics and abilities of the sexes. Clarke wrote *Sex in Education* in a social and scientific context that was very concerned with the nature of humanity, particularly the appropriate roles men and women were to play in human progress, and he grounded his theory in the most influential scientific research of his day about individual and collective human development. In addition to Charles Darwin's theory of biological evolution and Herbert Spencer's application of evolutionary theory to social Darwinism, Clarke knew of Alexander Bain's measurements finding women's brains to be smaller than men's, of Henry Maudsley's studies of the heritability of mental illness, and of Hermann von Helmholtz's work in thermodynamics supporting the principle of the conservation of energy, which Clarke used to argue that force exerted in intellectual work would not be available for reproductive functions (R. Rosenberg 6–7). In particular, Crista DeLuzio explains, Clarke followed Spencer (and the dominant medical theory of the time) in asserting that

---

4. In the preface to the second edition of *Sex in Education*, Clarke commented on the consistency between editions: "Excepting a few verbal alterations, and the correction of a few typographical errors, there is no difference between this edition and the first. The author would have been glad to add to this edition a section upon the relation of sex to women's work in life, after their technical education is completed, but has not had time to do so" (8).

reproductive processes exacted a high cost from women in the form of "vital nerve force" (67). Consequently, Clarke argued that women should study less intensively than men, taking regular time off from school to preserve energy for the development and function of the reproductive system. Although Clarke's opponents found much to criticize in his ideas, his thesis was well-grounded in contemporary biological and medical research.

Most scholarship on *Sex in Education* notes the importance of Clarke's ethos as a medical professional (see, for example, Douglass 65–66; Bateman 38). As a physician, Clarke's authority on matters of human anatomy and physiology aligned with the keystone of his argument: the question of women's rights and opportunities was best answered by the science of physiology. In his introductory chapter, Clarke distinguished physiology from other epistemologies that might seem relevant to the issue: "The problem of woman's sphere, to use the modern phrase, is not to be solved by applying to it abstract principles of right and wrong. Its solution must be obtained from physiology, not from ethics or metaphysics. The question must be submitted to [biologist Louis] Agassiz and [biologist Thomas Henry] Huxley, not to [philosopher Immanuel] Kant or [theologian John] Calvin, to Church or Pope" (12). According to this model, people did not have to decide which opportunities were appropriate for women; they merely had to act in accordance with physiological findings: "The *quæstio vexata* of woman's sphere will be decided by her organization" (12–13). As his own statements confirm, and in keeping with the emergence of the "culture of professionalism" (Stob), Clarke was moving the debate about women's social roles from the realm of rights and religion to the realm of science, from the question of what women ought to do to the question of what they were physiologically capable of doing (Douglass; Zschoche 548–49). Consequently, Clarke asked his readers to approach the issue of co-education as students of science, learning from Clarke's expertise, valuing "objectivity," and trusting the knowledge-making methods of physiology. In doing so, Clarke constituted his audience as science-minded and trusting of his representation of physiological facts.

In his foundational discussion of constitutive rhetorics, Charland, drawing on Kenneth Burke's description of identification and Louis Althusser's concept of interpellation, explains that rhetoric's conventional focus on persuasion overlooks a crucial rhetorical function that must precede, or at least coincide with, any act of persuasion: a text "calls its audience into being" (134). In other words, a text constitutes its audience by cueing its readers to adopt particular identities, motives, and interests and to operate from an ideology that is friendly to the persuasive purpose of the text (134; 137). Constitutive work is typically not limited to one text but is instead an ongoing process akin to socialization (138) that embeds readers in a narrative that offers them "a history, motives, and a *telos*" (140). Such a process, Charland asserts, is less an act of persuasion and more an act of "conversion that ultimately results in an act of recognition of the 'rightness' of a discourse and of one's identity with its reconfigured subject position" (142). Attempts to constitute audiences do not always succeed, however (141); in fact, the failure of readers to identify with the audience as it is constituted likely precludes any persuasive success. For the purposes of this analysis of the reception of *Sex in Education*, we might observe that audience constitution and the audience's uptake of the offered identity significantly affect a text's reception, in that the roles offered to and accepted by audience members limit some kinds of responses and encourage others.[5]

In constituting his audience as scientifically inclined, Clarke encouraged his readers to set aside unscientific sources of knowledge about women. He criticized what he saw as a trend outside of the scientific community, in education and in society more generally, toward treating women as if they were no different from men:

> The identity [that is, the identicalness] of boys and girls, of men and women, is practically asserted out of the school as much as in it, and it is theoretically proclaimed from the pulpit and the rostrum. Woman seems to be looking up to man and his development, as the goal and ideal of womanhood. The new gospel of female development glorifies what she possesses in common with him, and tramples under her feet, as a source of weakness and badge of inferiority, the mechanism and functions peculiar to herself. (129)

Having dismissed "the pulpit and the rostrum" as sources of information about women's abilities, Clarke encouraged readers not to listen to "The new gospel" but instead, through reference to technical matters like "the mechanism and functions" of the female reproductive system, reminded his readers to listen to scientists for advice about women's roles, reinforcing his constitution of his audience as those who privileged scientific knowledge over other forms of meaning-making.

Importantly, Clarke's audience constitution went beyond encouraging readers to value physiological facts to include inviting readers to take on the role of experimental scientists or at least of community members knowledgeable enough to participate in a debate grounded in physiology. Early in

---

5. Audience design takes the study of audience one step further, examining the ways in which texts position cohorts of audience members differently (as primary addressees, overhearers, and bystanders, for example), thereby prompting different kinds of responses (see Clark; Goffman; Thieme).

Sex in Education, Clarke stated that he hoped his audience would continue the research he outlined in his book: "If the publication of this brief memoir does nothing more than excite discussion and stimulate investigation with regard to a matter of such vital moment to the nation as the relation of sex to education, the author will be amply repaid for the time and labor of its preparation" (7). If readers took Clarke up on this invitation, they would extend his scientific approach to the woman question, not merely as readers of science, but as contributors to the physiological discourse about women's rights. Clarke's audience constitution, then, situated (at least some) readers in a narrative in which a scientific mindset prompts scientific investigation, which leads to the discussion of findings; these studies and discussions result, ultimately, in limitations on women's education. As Charland explains, constitutive rhetorics prompt particular material actions because audience members see themselves as playing out the narratives appropriate to the roles they are encouraged to adopt (143). Even if the culture of professionalism and the specialized nature of physiological knowledge put real scientific investigation out of reach for many readers, Clarke's constitution of his audience encouraged them to participate in the parts of the narrative that were accessible to them: adopting a scientific mindset, talking about women's physiology, and restricting women's education.

Modeling the attitude of an objective researcher studying co-education, Clarke claimed that he was willing to accept the conclusions of his research, whatever they might be:

> Without denying the self-evident proposition, that whatever a woman can do, she has a right to do, the question at once arises, What can she do? And this includes the further question, What can she best do? A girl can hold a plough, and ply a needle, after a fashion. If she can do both better than a man, she ought to be both farmer and seamstress; but if, on the whole, her husband can hold best the plough, and she ply best the needle, they should divide the labor. He should be master of the plough, and she mistress of the loom. (12)

Notable in this passage is the agentless phrase, "the question at once arises," which suggests that the question might arise in the reader's mind. Then, like Clarke, the scientifically inclined reader should investigate what women were capable of and abide by the answers. As a rhetorical strategy, relying on physiology not only allowed Clarke to assert his professional authority, but it also tapped into the public's growing faith in the solutions offered by science. Women's capabilities could be measured physiologically, and audience members who accepted Clarke's constitution of them as scientifically minded might prioritize those findings over any other claims women might make about the personal or social value of their education.

Finally, Clarke included his readers among the physiologically knowledgeable when he asserted that a woman's femininity (or lack of femininity, if she had studied too intensely) was discernable to all: "When arrested development of the reproductive system is nearly or quite complete, it produces a change in the character, and a loss of power, which it is easy to recognize, but difficult to describe" (92). A woman's presentation of femininity was available for public judgment, even by those who lacked the words to describe the characteristics of the "change in character" they could so easily identify. Importantly, however, Clarke noted that physicians possessed the specialized knowledge to identify the cause of women's apparent lack of femininity: "A closer inspection by competent experts would reveal the secret weakness which the labor of life that they are about to enter upon too late discloses" (108). By informing readers that physicians could make this diagnosis, Clarke simultaneously asserted the authority of medical professionals and constituted his audience as also privileged with a degree of specialized knowledge resulting from their reading of *Sex in Education*. Clarke's constitution of his audience as interested in science and as obedient to the social implications of scientific findings worked hand in hand with his construction of gender, which was also based in his understanding of reproductive physiology and development. Readers who were inclined to see themselves as aligned with scientific epistemology were primed to receive Clarke's text favorably and to accept his construction of men and women and the gendered model of education that he advocated.

Constructing Gender and Gendering Education in *Sex in Education*

In part because reproductive processes were poorly understood in the nineteenth-century United States, and in part because the subject was largely taboo, making it difficult for women to compare experiences, menstruation could effectively be invoked to justify limiting women's actions. As Joan Burstyn explains, "Since the chemical basis for sexual differentiation was unknown, doctors believed that how one behaved, dressed, worked, and played at puberty controlled the proper development of primary and secondary sex characteristics" ("Education and Sex" 79). Because the first of the "great changes" in a woman's life, menarche, coincided with her educational years, if and how girls and women attended school were appropriate topics for advice based in medical understandings of female reproductive physiology and therefore, in physicians' constructions of the female sex.

Clarke's construction of gender was bolstered by his constitution of his audience as favoring science. If readers accepted his constitution of them as scientifically inclined, they were also likely to be persuaded by the physiological facts and evidence that he used to support his construction of gender. By extension, they would also accept his arguments about proper educational methods for women and men. Clarke's physiological definitions of gender did not focus exclusively on femininity; he instead constructed femininity and masculinity reciprocally, highlighting the similarities and differences between female and male biology. For example, in the chapter "Chiefly Physiological," Clarke identified three primary bodily systems: the nutritive, the nervous, and the reproductive. According to Clarke, the first two systems are identical in men and women:

> They are so alike, that they require a similar training in each, and yield in each a similar result. The machinery of them is the same. No scalpel has disclosed any difference between a man's and a woman's liver. No microscope has revealed any structure, fibre [sic], or cell, in the brain of man or woman, that is not common to both. No analysis or dynamometer has discovered or measured any chemical action or nerve-force that stamps either of these systems as male or female. (32–33)

Importantly, it was the tools of medical science—the scalpel, microscope, and dynamometer (a device for measuring muscular force or power)—that identified the similarities between men and women. The common features of men's and women's nutritive and nervous systems led Clarke to conclude that men and women have the same capacity for mental achievement: "From these anatomical and physiological data alone, the inference is legitimate, that intellectual power, the correlation and measure of cerebral structure and metamorphosis is capable of equal development in both sexes" (33). Just as there were similarities in male and female bodies, Clarke identified common requirements for their education: first, both needed "a sufficient supply of appropriate nutriment"; second, their mental and physical effort should be arranged so that "repair shall exceed waste, and a margin be left for development"; and third, both needed "[s]ufficient sleep" (119).

Despite the similarities Clarke identified between men and women, he ultimately concluded that reproductive physiology produced deeply and inherently different sexes. One element of evolutionary theory in the nineteenth century was the idea that the "most evolved" humans manifested the greatest sexual differentiation. Combining that belief with common racist ideas about racial evolutionary hierarchies and anxiety about affluent white women's poor health, Clarke focused his arguments on white, middle-class women; not coincidentally, this group of women had just started attending college in significant numbers.

According to Clarke, the (white) female body was always at risk; if it, especially its reproductive functions, were not carefully attended to, a woman's health, fertility, femininity, sanity, and even life could be threatened. Women's reproductive organs were, according to Clarke, "among the marvels of creation" but required careful attention: "If neglected and mismanaged, they retaliate upon their possessor with weakness and disease, as well of the mind as of the body" (33). To maintain her health, a woman's education must be arranged to accommodate "the management of the catamenial function," particularly from ages fourteen to nineteen (120). Although both boys and girls experienced changes at puberty, according to Clarke, girls faced more substantial transformations in the development of their reproductive systems: "No such extraordinary task, calling for such rapid expenditure of force, building up such a delicate and extensive mechanism within the organism,—a house within a house, an engine within an engine,—is imposed upon the male physique at the same epoch" (37–38).[6] Because women's bodies, in Clarke's explanation, required such an extraordinary amount of force and nutrition to develop and maintain their reproductive functions, women must periodically limit the demands made by other organs, particularly the brain. In making this claim, Clarke followed contemporary medical thought about women's physiology. Describing late nineteenth-century medical arguments against women's college education, Burstyn points to texts by social Darwinist Spencer and psychiatrist Maudsley, who described the human body as a closed system with finite energy reserves; this belief led logically to the conclusion that if one exerted "too much" energy in one part of the body, other parts would suffer. This was especially true for girls, whose reproductive systems were believed to require considerable energy at puberty. The pursuit of intense education was thought to risk the healthy development of the female reproductive system ("Education and Sex" 85). The specter of "race suicide"—the fear that intelligent, white, middle-class women would be unable to bear children and so the country would be populated by the children of immigrants, of African Americans, and of the working class—was often the pinnacle of the men-

---

6. Clarke used the metaphor of the "engine" to describe female "organization" several times in *Sex in Education*. For a discussion of this metaphor and others used by Clarke, see Douglass (107–25).

strual argument against women's education.[7] Clarke was the most prominent promoter of these medical-scientific arguments linking reproductive potential to racist models of human evolution in the late nineteenth-century United States.

Relying on the physiological "fact" that women's brains competed with their reproductive systems for nutrition and force and on contemporary physiological theory, which maintained that ovulation accompanied menstruation, Clarke explained what the female reproductive system required to develop properly:

> Nature has reserved the catamenial week for the process of ovulation, and for the development and perfection of the reproductive system. Previously to the age of eighteen or twenty, opportunity must be periodically allowed for the accomplishment of this task. Both muscular and brain labor must be remitted enough to yield sufficient force for the work.... Force must be allowed to flow [to the reproductive organs] in an ample stream, and not diverted to the brain by the school, or to the arms by the factory, or to the feet by dancing. (41–42)

Following Helmholtz's work on thermodynamics, Clarke described the female reproductive system as in competition with the rest of the body for the resources it needed to function. When young women denied the reproductive system those resources by exerting themselves intellectually, the results for individual women might be weakness, pain, infertility, the inability to breastfeed, insanity, or death.

Consequently, healthy girls had less energy available for education than boys did: "It is . . . obvious that a girl upon whom Nature, for a limited period and for a definite purpose, imposes so great a physiological task, will not have as much power left for the tasks of the school, as the boy of whom Nature requires less at the corresponding epoch" (54–55). The ultimate result of this fundamental difference between men and women was summarized in Clarke's thesis: "Periodicity characterizes the female organization, and developes [sic] feminine force. Persistence characterizes the male organization, and develops masculine force. Education will draw the best out of each by adjusting its methods to the periodicity of one and the persistence of the other" (120–21). In defining gender according to physiological "laws,"

---

7. The effects of manual and domestic labor on reproductive functions were of much less concern to physicians, though some did address the effects of working-class women's labor on their reproductive health; see chapter four.

Clarke simultaneously gendered education, proposing a periodic system of schooling for young women and a persistent system for young men.

Clarke offered readers two principles of physiologically appropriate education for young women based on his construction of gender, which reflected his commitment to science as the appropriate epistemology for determining men's and women's abilities. First, "during the period of rapid development, that is, from fourteen to eighteen, a girl should not study as many hours a day as a boy" (154–55). Clarke suggested six hours of daily study for boys and four to five hours for girls (156–57). Second, "during every fourth week, there should be a remission, and sometimes an intermission, of both study and exercise" for girls (157). Schools that educated girls and young women should be organized to allow menstruating students to miss class without loss of rank and without requiring makeup work (158).

Once he had demonstrated that science dictated that members of each sex ought to be educated in accordance with the demands of their reproductive physiology, Clarke recruited his readers (constituted here as parents and others anxious about the health of young women, but not the young women themselves) into a shared concern, denoted by *we* and *our*, about the effects of study on women's physiological development:

> If we would give our girls a fair chance, and see them become and do their best by reaching after and attaining an ideal beauty and power . . . we must look after their complete development as women. Wherein they are men, they should be educated as men; wherein they are women, they should be educated as women. The physiological motto is, Educate a man for manhood, a woman for womanhood, both for humanity. In this lies the hope of the race. (19)

Unfortunately, from Clarke's perspective, the education system that young women were entering in greater and greater numbers in the later decades of the nineteenth century had been designed for young men and their ability to maintain continuous effort. To send young women to those schools, or even to follow the existing educational model at an all-girls school, risked "unsexing" the girls: "In the education of our girls, the attempt to hide or overcome nature by training them as boys has almost extinguished them as girls" (45). For Clarke, there was no need to go to these extremes: "Let the fact be accepted, that there is nothing to be ashamed of in a woman's organization, and let her whole education and life be guided by the divine requirements of her system" (45). According to Clarke's construction of women and his understanding of reproductive physiology, women's reproductive systems, which demanded an enormous amount of energy, should determine all aspects of women's lives, social roles, and intellectual capabilities.

To support his claims about the importance of establishing and maintaining healthy reproductive functions, Clarke presented seven patient cases describing the poor health, infertility, invalidism, insanity, and death that supposedly followed from young women's attempts to work and study continuously rather than adhering to the periodicity dictated by their "organization." The presentation of cases was a common genre in late nineteenth-century medical meetings and journals, where the audience was made up of other physicians and the purpose might be providing the details of an unusual case or sharing the procedures of an effective treatment. When presented to a popular audience, Clarke's cases functioned in part to allow his readers to imagine themselves as Clarke's medical colleagues, analyzing evidence of the consequences of continuous effort on the female body. If Clarke's readers had adopted his constitution of them as science-minded and if they had been persuaded by his argument that women's and men's bodies were fundamentally different, then they would have interpreted the cases he presented as proof of the damage caused by improper educational methods. Because his readers were not medical professionals, however, the cases also functioned as emotional appeals meant to frighten readers, especially potential students and their parents and teachers.[8]

For example, Miss A— "went to school regularly every week, and every day of the school year, just as boys do" (66). She engaged in "constant, sustained work, recitation and study for all days alike," was "a brilliant scholar," and experienced "a hemorrhage once a month that would make the stroke oar of the University crew falter" (67). Continuing his hyperbolic description of menstruation, Clarke wrote that Miss B— "worked her engine up to the highest pressure, just as much at flood-tide as at other times" (75). Women's bodies and their functions were thus described as risky and dangerous, like natural disasters. Women's bodies were also, according to Clarke, delicate machines that required perfect calibration to operate correctly. As noted above, Clarke referred to the female reproductive system as "the engine within an engine" (94) and as "the reproductive apparatus" (82). He described young women who attended college continuously as having to divide their resources; they were being "urged to meditate a lesson and drive a machine simultaneously" (95). Given the prominent theories about women's reproductive and nervous systems and the finite energy available to them, the educational methods in US colleges around midcentury seemed

---

8. In keeping with my claim that Clarke operated at the rhetorical intersection of the "culture of eloquence" and the "culture of professionalism," David Anderson Douglass describes *Sex in Education* as a "rhetorical hybrid" that combined discursive features of science writing with rhetorical devices more common in public rhetoric, such as emotional appeals (141–42).

entirely suited to produce the worst health outcomes for women. College students were expected to be present for every class meeting; furthermore, rather than taking tests at intervals throughout the term, students were graded on the daily performance of recitations delivered while standing (Burstyn "Education and Sex" 82). These continuous demands for intellectual and physical performance were incompatible with a physiological model of menstruation in which extra demands were placed on the female system periodically.[9]

Indeed, many activities associated with (a man's) college life could threaten a young woman's health, as Clarke illustrated in the case of Miss D—:

> She performed all her college duties regularly and steadily. She studied, recited, stood at the blackboard, walked, and went through her gymnastic exercises, from the beginning to the end of the term, just as boys do. Her account of her regimen there was so nearly that of a boy's regimen, that it would puzzle a physiologist to determine, from the account alone, whether the subject of it was male or female. (80)

Clarke's vision of gendered educational practices is evident in his implication that a physiologist ought to be able to recognize an education as male or female. After years of pursuing a "man's" education, Miss D— suffered "an arrest of the development of the reproductive apparatus" (82). She graduated, but, as Clarke concluded, she never "bec[a]me physically what she would have been had her education [been] physiologically guided" (82).

Importantly, teachers might be kept ignorant of their students' failing health by young women's efforts to disguise their conditions. Even in those cases, however, Clarke claimed that physicians could identify the symptoms and causes:

> Their teachers have known nothing of the amenorrhœa, menorrhagia, dysmenorrhœa, or leucorrhœa which the pupils have sedulously concealed and disregarded; and the cunning devices of dress have covered up all external evidences of defect; and so, on graduation day, they are pointed out by their instructors to admiring

---

9. Importantly to advocates of women's education, however, by the 1870s, many US colleges were giving up the expectation of daily performances (Burstyn, "Education and Sex" 82), moving toward exams and elective coursework, which meant that even if menstruation required times of reduced activity for women, the more flexible curriculum emerging at the time would allow women to adjust their levels of exertion accordingly.

> committees as rosy specimens of both physical and intellectual education. (108)

Young women, victims to diseases with imposing and frightening names, might have used "cunning devices" to deceive their instructors. The dishonest students thus led their teachers to promote education for young women, not realizing that they were inviting girls to a lifetime of disease. Although some physical results of continuous education were recognizable by all, some might be hidden, so that the supporters of co-education could never be certain of the health of the young women they held up as examples. Neither young women nor their teachers were to be trusted as reporters of women students' health—one might deceive and the other be deceived because of their shared commitment to women's education—but physicians could be counted on to identify the truth.

Relying on the nineteenth century's understanding of menstruation (and the fertility it represented) as indicative of femininity, Clarke warned his readers that pursuing education threatened young women's gender identity, as their ongoing studies might impede the growth and development of their reproductive organs:

> A woman, whether married or unmarried, whether called to the offices of maternity or relieved from them, who has been defrauded by her education or otherwise of such an essential part of her development, is not so much of a woman, intellectually and morally as well as physically, in consequence of this defect. Her nervous system and brain, her instincts and character, are on a lower plane, and incapable of their harmonious and best development, if she is possessed, on reaching adult age, of only a portion of a breast and an ovary, or none at all. (91)

Such a woman became at best unrecognizable, and at worst, a monstrosity:

> There are in individuals of this class less adipose and more muscular tissue than is commonly seen, a coarser skin, and, generally, a tougher and more angular makeup. There is a corresponding change in the intellectual and psychical condition,—a dropping out of maternal instincts, and an appearance of Amazonian coarseness and force. Such persons are analogous to the sexless class of termites. (92–93)

Clarke later wrote that a better analogy might be to eunuchs, and with few exceptions, "none of that class have made any impression on the world's life, that history has recorded" (93), so women who attended college with the intention of contributing to society would fail to achieve that goal, in addition to the physical consequences they would suffer. Clarke even coined the term *agene* ("without sex") to describe "a third division of the human race . . . formed by subtracting sex from woman" (93–94, n*).

Clarke admitted that women were perfectly capable of intellectual achievement (18–19). Consequently, a young woman might, like Miss A—, graduate "the first scholar, and an invalid" (68). Clarke was careful throughout the book, and particularly in recounting the case histories, to maintain that it was not education or work itself that harmed women, but *continuous* study or work; it was not pursuing "men's" activities that ruined women's health but pursuing those activities in ways that did not account for women's periodicity. He concluded one of his cases with this moral:

> And so Miss G— died, not because she had mastered the wasps of Aristophanes and the Mécanique Céleste, not because she had made the acquaintance of Kant and Kölliker, and ventured to explore the anatomy of flowers and the secrets of chemistry, but because, while pursuing these studies, while doing all this work, she steadily ignored her woman's make. Believing that woman can do what man can, for she held that faith, she strove with noble but ignorant bravery to compass man's intellectual attainment in a man's way, and died in the effort. If she had aimed at the same goal, disregarding masculine and following feminine methods, she would be alive now, a grand example of female culture, attainment, and power. (103–04)

In making the issue the manner in which women pursued education rather than education itself, Clarke presented himself not as an opponent of women but as a supporter who wanted to provide women with the physiological information that they needed to achieve their goals while maintaining their health. By extension, any poor health or supposed loss of femininity experienced by women who did not follow his advice was, quite possibly, their own fault. Women's position of being simultaneously controlled by and in control of their reproductive physiology reflected the late-nineteenth-century faith in the power of science to manage nature in order to improve quality of life even as (or because) that position reinforced a traditional model for women's social roles.

In constituting his audience as sharing the epistemology of science at the same time as he constructed gender based on physiology, Clarke predisposed his readers to be persuaded by his claims about the appropriate forms of education for men and women. Clarke's reliance on the public's trust in the effectiveness of science was also adopted by some of his opponents, though they tended to attribute women's poor health to causes other than identical co-education.[10] Clarke's privileging of science as the means to answer "the woman question" in large part set the terms for the debate that emerged as a result of competing receptions of *Sex in Education*.

RE-CONSTITUTION AND RE-CONSTRUCTION THROUGH RECEPTION

In her book about the history of US women in medicine, Mary Roth Walsh writes, "neither the number of printings nor their geographical distribution reflect the full impact of [*Sex in Education*]" (124). She later describes the public responses to the book as "less a discussion than an all-out battle" (128). This controversy was, of course, about more than Clarke's book; it was also, among many other things, about how that book constructed gender and constituted its audience. The numerous emphatic responses to the book were attempts to influence its reception, and by extension, the gender construction and audience constitution it promoted. As Jacqueline Bacon has demonstrated, each act of response is an opportunity for re-constituting, for an audience-member-turned-rhetor to resist the characterization of readers that was initially offered, to counter with an alternative construction, and to constitute all audience members in ways more conducive to his or her rhetorical agenda and personal well-being (77). Clarke's opponents reconstructed gender and reconstituted the audience for the debate over *Sex in Education*; in the process, they not only argued for greater opportunities for women but they also, through reinforcing or undermining Clarke's audience constitution, sought to control the reception of *Sex in Education*.

Because *Sex in Education* relied on medical vocabulary, concepts, and clinical examples but was intended by Clarke to reach a nonprofessional readership, some tension existed in his audience constitution. Not only was the book's content relatively technical, but its subject—women's reproductive physiology—was not something typically discussed publicly among nonprofessionals. Those who commented on *Sex in Education* seized the opportunity presented by this tension, shaping the reception of the book by suggesting who ought to read it. Some downplayed any perceived inappropriateness and recommended it to mothers and teachers, while others

---

10. Clarke's objection was not to men and women being educated in the same institutions, but rather to women being educated by the same methods as men were: continuously (in contrast to female periodicity) and at an intensity not compatible with female reproductive development. Such methods could be found at co-educational institutions as well as at women's schools modeled after men's schools.

pointed to accepted scientific meaning-making processes and argued that Clarke should have had his theory reviewed by his professional colleagues before addressing the public. Other critics opposed widespread readership because they found the book insulting to women.

Among those advocating a wide readership was the Methodist weekly *Zion's Herald*. In "Co-Education of the Sexes," one of several articles engaging the *Sex in Education* debate published in that magazine, the writer recommended that "The little volume, embodying the results of careful study, should be read in every family, by every guardian of a public school, and by every teacher" (November 27, 1873). *The Literary World* also endorsed the book as deserving a wide readership in November 1873, stating that it ought to be read by "every mother in the land" ("Minor Book Notices" 92). The March 1874 review in *The Eclectic Magazine* went even further, asserting that *Sex in Education* deserved the "attention of every mother and teacher, and all others who are engaged in the training of girls. Whoever ignores or remains ignorant of the considerations which it presents will incur the responsibility of sinning against light, and sinning, too, in a matter of the most vital importance to our branch of the race" ("Literary Notices" 374). In recommending *Sex in Education* to families, mothers, and teachers, these reviewers positioned the book as accessible to non-professional audiences. Although they often noted the specialized or delicate nature of Clarke's subject matter, their encouragement to mothers and teachers suggested that *Sex in Education* contained nothing that ought to embarrass modest women or that the importance of Clarke's message outweighed any qualms women might feel in reading about reproductive physiology. Rather than emphasizing readers' scientific interests, the audience constitution for *Sex in Education* offered by these writers foregrounded readers' responsibility, a responsibility that outweighed any discomfort they might have felt with Clarke's topic or his language.

In contrast to writers who called for a wide readership for *Sex in Education*, other commentators maintained that the book contained specialized information that was better suited for professional audiences. For example, in the introduction to their book responding to Clarke, husband-wife dean-physician collaborators George Comfort and Anna Manning Comfort[11] ar-

---

11. George Fisk Comfort (1833–1910) was involved in the founding of the Metropolitan Museum of Art in New York; he also served as the first dean of the College of Fine Arts at Syracuse University. Anna Manning Comfort (1854–1931) was a member of the first class to graduate from the New York Medical College for Women, where she later taught; Anna was also a strong proponent of woman suffrage. Both the names of George and Anna (who married in 1871) appear on the title page of *Woman's Education and Woman's Health*, but Frances E. Willard and

gued that Clarke should have sought approval of his physiological claims through peer review before imparting them to the public:

> It would have been more appropriate had Dr. Clarke presented his views to the members of his own fraternity, through medical journals, before giving them to the general public. The subject could there have been discussed by his professional colleagues with perfect freedom, and according to the laws of strictly scientific method. There is, besides, a certain degree of unfairness towards the general public, in giving out to them as fixed scientific truth what is at most a hypothesis of the writer. (xi)

In other words, using science to study the characteristics of the sexes was acceptable among educated professionals, but Clarke was wrong to act as if his readers were knowledgeable enough to interpret and evaluate the scientific claims that he presented to them. Nevertheless, Comfort and Comfort asserted that because Clarke had addressed the public, critics of *Sex in Education* must address the public as well (xi; see also Dall 90–91).

In fact, reinforcing the "scientific" nature of the audience constitution promoted by *Sex in Education* afforded some writers important opportunities to refute Clarke's gender construction. Clarke seemed to believe that the science he presented in *Sex in Education* was irrefutable; however, his contemporaries immediately recognized that he had drawn conclusions from only a handful of cases and had not pursued a systematic study of the relationship between continuous education and women's health. Because Clarke insisted that physiology should determine gendered educational methods, his opponents perceived the weakness of his evidence to be an especially opportune feature of the rhetorical situation, so they highlighted it by encouraging readers to approach *Sex in Education* with high scientific standards.

Some of the writers who challenged Clarke's scientific facts and theories, therefore, accepted Clarke's constitution of his audience as committed to scientific values, and accordingly took on the role of critical scientists. For example, Thomas Wentworth Higginson[12] asserted that Clarke lacked suf-

---

Mary A. Livermore's *A Woman of the Century: Fourteen Hundred-Seventy Biographical Sketches Accompanied by Portraits of Leading American Women in All Walks of Life* (1893) attributes the book only to Anna.

12. Thomas Wentworth Higginson (1823–1911) had been a classmate of Clarke's at Harvard. He was also a leader in the abolition, women's rights, and temperance movements. As a colonel in the Civil War, Higginson led the Union's first official regiment made up of formerly enslaved men.

ficient evidence: "It seems to me . . . that Dr. Clarke by no means comes up to the recognized standard of science either in the quantity or the quality of the facts on which he bases his argument" ("II" 44). Opponents who took up this line of criticism challenged Clarke's lack of statistical evidence, his failure to consider alternative causes for women's poor health (such as corsets and lack of physical exercise), and his failure to isolate the variables he claimed to be studying by not also examining the effects of continuous education on men's health or of continuous labor among working women (see, for example, many of the contributors to Brackett, *The Education of American Girls*; Duffey, *No Sex in Education*; and Howe, *Sex and Education*). Writers publishing in this line of criticism included physicians, especially women physicians, who relied on their own medical expertise to refute Clarke. This set of arguments enthusiastically accepted Clarke's constitution of the audience as science-minded but used that scientific perspective to challenge the construction of gender that he claimed the science of physiology authorized.

Although some writers reinforced Clarke's audience constitution when they offered nonprofessional readers counterarguments based in science and its epistemology, other critics feared that the public was not qualified to understand such specialized evidence properly. The writers observed that misunderstandings could result when particular professional discursive features, like the case study in medical journal articles, appeared before the public. These critics objected to the unusual nature of the cases on which Clarke's argument relied, arguing that presenting them as typical misrepresented women. For example, Anna C. Brackett[13] called *Sex in Education* "unfair," because "It quotes exceptional cases which would have their proper place in a medical journal as exceptional, but which will not be here so considered by an indiscriminating reader, and which could not be more ingeniously calculated to leave a false impression" ("Dr. Clark [sic] Reviewed"). Brackett objected to the image of women's health produced by presenting a handful of extreme cases to a public audience lacking the expertise to recognize them as exceptional. Other writers noted that as a physician who spent his days caring for the sick, Clarke was likely to have a distorted view of women's health (see, for example, Duffey 12; Mann 68).

Extending the claims that the audience constitution of *Sex in Education* unfairly suggested that the public was capable of assessing specialized knowledge, feminist writer and reformer Elizabeth Stuart Phelps suggested that Clarke might have blurred what she called "the precise defining line

---

13. Anna Callender Brackett (1836–1911) was an educator who served as principal of the St. Louis Normal School and advocated for women's higher education. In addition to her writing on education, Brackett also wrote on topics in philosophy.

between a work adapted to popular instruction and a medical treatise" because of the persuasive advantages it afforded him. She speculated on the rhetorical reasons Clarke might have had for crossing this line:

> He may have done so with the deliberate intention of a theorist who does not desire to be answered; he may have done so with the clear conscience of a zealot who desires only to do what presents itself to him as his duty. He has undoubtedly done so, at least, with motives which it were indelicate to call indelicate, whatever else might be said of them; but, all the same, he has put himself beyond this reach. From the medical lecture-room alone can he be answered. Only a physician can reply to "Sex in Education." (126–27)

In making this accusation, Phelps cast Clarke as a bully who used his expertise to intimidate and silence those who might challenge him. Such a characterization would prime readers to receive *Sex in Education* as an act of professional elitism, speaking over the heads of its non-professional audience, expecting readers simply to follow his advice.

Although she found Clarke's physiological argument untouchable by those outside the medical profession, Phelps believed other professionals possessed expertise relevant to the question of women's education. Physicians, she said, could speak only to the physical aspects of the issue, but there were additional considerations best addressed by those with other forms of expertise and experience: "The psychologist has yet his word to say. The theologian has a reason to be heard. The political economist might also add to experience knowledge. The woman who is physically and intellectually a living denial of every premise and of every conclusion which Dr. Clarke has advanced, has yet a right to an audience" (128; see also Greene 7–8; "Sex in Education" in *The World* of New York). In listing a variety of sources of knowledge that might have something worthwhile to contribute to the debate over co-education, Phelps declared that *Sex in Education* was not the final word on the matter and that physiology wasn't the only discourse with a relevant perspective. Phelps was joined by others who resisted Clarke's claim that medical science was the stance most capable of determining women's abilities. Mothers, educators, and social scientists all insisted that their experience and expertise led them to conclusions that differed from Clarke's. In claiming that other professions and epistemologies had knowledge relevant to this debate, these respondents challenged Clarke's constitution of his audience as submissive to medical science. This alternative audience constitution functioned to shape the reception of *Sex in Education* by offering readers positions from which to read that were friendlier to women's pursuit of education.

Finally, some reviewers questioned Clarke's intended audience by criticizing *Sex in Education* for its tone, which they found to be coarse and impertinent. These writers challenged the assumption that such an attitude could be appropriate or persuasive for modest readers. For example, writer, reformer, and woman suffrage advocate Julia Ward Howe defended the unmarried women whom she felt Clarke had mistreated, asking whether Clarke's tone was decent for any readers:

> We are left in doubt whether his book was written for men or for women, and we conclude that his method of statement is not good for either. Much of his remarking upon sex is justly offensive, and his statements concerning those single women of culture whom he terms *agenes* would scarcely be endured in any household in which these single saints bear the burthens of all the others, and lead lives divinely wedded to duty. (29–30)

Howe asserted that other statements in *Sex in Education* "would exclude the book, and the writer too, from some pure and polite circles" (30). Howe tried to limit the book's circulation and effect by claiming it wasn't fit to be read.

Other critics joined Howe in reminding readers that they had a right to expect to be addressed with politeness and respect. They asserted that Clarke had defied these expectations with an inappropriate tone, conveying "insult to woman," "ungentlemanly jeers," and a "vulgar attack upon the noble army of unmarried women" (Mann 52). This audience constitution—as worthy of gendered respect—invoked readers who perhaps did not identify as scientifically informed but who might privilege other values as members of "polite society." When Clarke presented his readers with the choice to limit women's education and protect their femininity or to allow women unlimited education and risk their femininity (and fertility), he left no room for the women who, according to writer and reformer Mrs. Horace [Mary Tyler Peabody] Mann, were "often in the respectable ranks of 'spinsterism,' as [Clarke] call[ed] it, out of self-respect, and because their ideal of the marriage state [was] far beyond that of the average woman" (52). Mann resisted Clarke's construction of gender—a construction that assumed women were not fully women unless they married and had children—by highlighting the societal benefits of the "maiden aunt" (56) and the poor health resulting from "unfortunate marriages" (54). These alternative constructions of *woman*, though still limited by contemporary standards, offered women positive identities beyond those presented by Clarke. In addition to re-constructing gender, Mann also re-constituted her audience as appreciative of unmarried women, as having "respect for those unmarried women whose independent lives bear the noble fruits of culture, benevolence, and devotion to human improvement" (58). Audience constitution is often not directly persuasive in the sense of consciously changing audience members' minds about a topic but rather depends on audiences recognizing themselves in or identifying themselves with the roles offered to them (Charland 142). When Mann suggested that everyone must know at least one example of an unmarried woman who behaved maternally or benevolently (56–57), she worked to broaden gender constructions by reconstituting her audience as people who had positive feelings toward the unmarried women in their lives. Such readers would have received Clarke's book skeptically.

In keeping with other opponents who questioned Clarke's authorial tone, the writer C. proposed that Clarke's "sneer" at childless women was a persuasive choice:

> The sneer is too studied to be accidental, and is to me the unpardonable sin of the book. Did the author willingly expose himself to justified attack on this point, for the express purpose of reaching the ear and heart of those superlatively weak women whom nothing can touch but a masculine sneer? Not quite believing in his own arguments, did he trust to satire to win him approval with that class of people for whom his book was written? Surely he is not so ignorant as not to know that the jeer will only weaken the argument with all thoughtful people. But was the book written for the thinking people, or for those whom ridicule, not reason, convinces? For those especially who fear masculine ridicule in all that relates to their external attractions; for those who can endure all loss save the loss of admiration; for those on whom an argument is wasted, while a sneer converts? (110–11)

C.'s response first questioned Clarke's intended audience, asserting that he could not have hoped to persuade "thoughtful people" by ridiculing childless women, though he might have won over "superlatively weak women." These women were not the audience one would expect for a book that claimed to be based in science. C. then suggested that Clarke resorted to his "sneer" to persuade where his argument was weak. Together, these two assessments of *Sex in Education* quite directly told readers how to receive the book; if they believed themselves to be thoughtful rather than vain and weak, readers could not be persuaded by Clarke's assertions (for more on Clarke's "sneer," see Phelps [137–38]; "The Education of Girls").

Although some writers were concerned with linguistic propriety, as C.'s commentary indicates, the debate over *Sex in Education* occasionally took less noble turns, with some writers mocking those who disagreed with them. This ridicule sought to shape the book's audience by characterizing some readers in undesirable ways, which warned readers to avoid sharing their fate by agreeing with them. For example, the *Galveston Daily News* mocked Mann because of her critique of *Sex in Education*: "Mrs. Mann, whose name aptly indicates the position she holds as to sex, complains of the 'disparaging tone toward woman' of Dr. Clarke's excellent book on 'Sex in Education,' and would like to have physiology remodeled so as to no longer afford undue advantages to the other sort of man" ("Personal"). Extending the common caricature of women's rights activists as "mannish," *The Christian Register* of Boston published this brief note: "We fear that the author of 'Sex in Education' will smile audibly when he hears that a bright lady said, 'All the Women's Rights women are down on Dr. Clarke's book, *to a man*'" ("Brevities"). The *Daily Whig* of Quincy, Illinois wrote that Clarke's proposal evoked "the fire of all the strong-minded, fanatical females in the land, reinforced by the virile efforts of their long-haired male co-adjutors, who are fain to believe that a woman is nothing if not a bass singer" ("Sex in Education"; see also "Social Life"). These personal, gendered attacks on those who criticized *Sex in Education* shaped the book's reception by constituting Clarke's opponents as gender deviants; in contrast, Clarke's supporters were implicitly constituted as reasonable and respectable in their gender performances.

On the other side of the debate, William B. Greene responded to the anxiety over American women's poor health, which was often supported through citations of observations made by visitors from Europe, by dismissing those visitors in a parenthetical aside: "[It frequently happens that the English observer, just landing on our shores, who is moreover a physiologist, is also an ass.]" (18). As might be expected in a debate as intense and voluminous as the discussion surrounding *Sex in Education*, some writers stooped to name-calling and stereotyping. Such rhetorical strategies might have been intended to silence potential opponents (the women who feared being characterized as "mannish") and to belittle anyone affiliated with the other side of the debate (the *Whig*'s effeminate men, Greene's useless traveling physiologists, and C's superlatively weak women). They also caricatured Clarke's supporters and opponents, steering readers toward and away from adopting particular audience stances and making the reception of *Sex in Education* appear much less nuanced than it actually was.

Although Clarke initially constituted the audience for *Sex in Education* by deciding to publish it for a non-professional readership that he cued to accept the values and motives of science, commentators also directed readers toward or away from audience positions in ways that supported their desired reception of *Sex in Education*. They guided readers to receive the book in a variety of ways: as advice for all caring mothers, as facts teachers and school administrators ignored at their students' peril, as too specialized for non-professional readers, as bypassing the intra-professional review of scientific findings, as an instance of rhetorical intimidation, and as offensive to childless women. Re-constituting an audience for a text inherently affects its reception, even as that re-constitution is itself a form of reception.

Articulating Reception, Constitution, and Gender Construction

As this analysis of *Sex in Education* and its reception demonstrates, investigating the rhetorical construction of gender alongside the rhetorical constitution of audiences has the potential to reveal many of the layers of how gender operates rhetorically. First, gender construction and audience constitution are interrelated; how a rhetor constructs gender is likely mirrored in how that rhetor constitutes an audience, and the audience constituted by a text likely accords with the model of gender promoted by that text. This reciprocity, however, is not always the case, as is evidenced by the critics of *Sex in Education* who accepted Clarke's invitation to approach the question of co-education scientifically but who rejected the limitations he placed on women's behavior. Looking at gender construction in conjunction with audience constitution can help us understand these rhetorical processes more thoroughly.

Additionally, considering audience constitution as a crucial launching point for rhetorical reception reveals the ways that constitutive rhetorics are not entirely in the hands of the initial rhetor. As the responses discussed above demonstrate, the way that an audience is constituted can be extended (as when recipients argued that readers should demand better science than *Sex in Education* offered) or challenged (as when recipients encouraged readers to prioritize sources of knowledge other than science) through reception. In altering the audience constitution initially proffered by *Sex in Education*, those receiving Clarke's book attempted to influence how others received it, and they participated in the rhetorical construction of gender that was at the heart of questions about co-education and women's rights more broadly.

Who perceives themselves as invited to or deterred from reading a text, what they will be primed to prioritize in their reading, and what forms reception can take—all matters affected by audience constitution—are fundamental to the patterns evident in a text's reception. One example of this dynamic relevant to both feminist rhetorical studies and reception studies comes from historian Sue Zschoche, who argues that the primary significance of *Sex in Education* was not its claim that women were not physically suited for advanced education, because that claim had been made for centuries; instead, it was its premise that biology should determine women's roles (548–49). I have argued above that one important way that that premise achieved its effect was by constituting the audience of *Sex in Education* as scientifically inclined. The assertion that biology was the epistemology best suited for deciding the woman question constrained the book's reception. Zschoche articulates the restrictions women's rights advocates faced in receiving *Sex in Education*:

> This then was the specter that haunted supporters of women's higher education: the proposition that biology alone defined true womanhood. The reformers' response to *Sex in Education* was therefore neither as straightforward nor as assured as their unwavering rejection of Clarke's conclusions might suggest. Clarke's biological reductionism did not destroy the reformers' faith in the importance of intellectual development, but it did rob them of a ready vocabulary by which to justify it. (550)

Zschoche later continues this line of thinking: "Clarke had placed the reformers in what appeared to be a hopeless bind: to answer him satisfactorily demanded that they do so on his terms, but to reply in the language of biology seemed to many of them a concession speech" because it would have meant discounting the social and moral values on which many of them based women's identity and value (560). Zschoche's analysis suggests that the epistemological premise on which *Sex in Education* is based—which, I maintain, was accompanied by a supporting audience constitution—limited the kinds of reception of Clarke's book that women's rights activists could offer. Pulling all of these threads together, we can see that Clarke's audience constitution, the reception of his book, and the gender constructions that emerged in the debate around *Sex in Education* were mutually reinforcing.

The idea that audience constitution strongly shapes reception should be important to scholars of feminist rhetoric, not only as it applies to issues of gender construction, but also as it affects how a range of calls for social change are taken up or disregarded. To be interpellated into a position as an audience member "is not," as Katja Thieme explains, "the same as providing arguments, evidence, and appeals" (42); in other words, constitutive rhetoric operates differently from and can even preclude persuasion as we typically think of that term. The role of constitutive rhetoric in recruiting audiences to accept and promote social change should be considered in analyses of (successful and unsuccessful) feminist activism and in our feminist analyses of rhetorical activity. Recognizing the role of reception in extending and resisting audience constitution (and the arguments and gender constructions that correlate with that constitution) is vital to the project of understanding how rhetoric works to promote or hinder more equitable conditions for everyone.

2 The Popular Reception of *Sex in Education* and the Role of Science in Public Discourse

In 1874, Julia Ward Howe[1] edited a collection of previously published criticisms of Edward H. Clarke's book titled *Sex and Education. A Reply to Dr. E. H. Clarke's "Sex in Education."* In her own contribution to that work, Howe asked what kind of book *Sex in Education* was:

> Is the book, then, a work of science, of literature, or of philosophy, or is it a simple practical treatise on the care of health? We should call it none of these. It has neither the impartiality of science, the form of literature, the breadth of philosophy, nor the friendliness of counsel. It is a work of the polemic type, presenting a persistent and passionate plea against the admission of women to a collegiate education in common with men. ("I" 13–14)

Howe's question about *Sex in Education* pointed to the various challenges the book posed to the reading public: what was its genre, its purpose, its audience? Bridging the styles of the professional and the eloquent (Stob), the scientific and the polemic, the technical and the popular, *Sex in Education* elicited responses that sought to make sense of the book and to assert the measures by which it should be judged. In chapter one, I discussed the ways that readers attempted to shape the reception of Clarke's book by reconstituting its audience as expecting high scientific standards or as eschewing a scientific standpoint in favor of other ways of articulating women's value and capabilities. In this chapter, I argue that the reception of *Sex in Education* served as a venue for debating the rhetorical role of science by asking who could claim to be scientific, by articulating standards for the research methods that would be persuasive to a non-professional audience, and by expressing concern that the public might be bullied or misled by ostensibly science-based arguments.

The first publication notice for *Sex in Education* that I've been able to locate appeared in the October 1, 1873 issue of *The Literary World; a Monthly*

---

1. Julia Ward Howe (1819–1910) was a writer, philanthropist, abolitionist, and suffragist, famed as the author of the Civil-War era "The Battle Hymn of the Republic." She served as editor of the *Woman's Journal* beginning in 1872.

Review of Current Literature: "Dr. E. H. Clarke, an eminent physician of this city [Boston], has written a book on Sex, with reference to educational processes. He takes strong ground against the movement in favor of a uniform system of education for boys and girls. J. R. Osgood & Co. will publish the book" ("Literary News"). With this notice, a deluge of public commentary about *Sex in Education* began. In this chapter, I examine the popular reception of *Sex in Education* from its initial publication in October 1873 through December 1874. In these first fifteen months, at least eight[2] editions of *Sex in Education* were published, and hundreds of notices, reviews, commentaries, and critiques of the book appeared in the popular press. I have located over 290 texts substantial and original enough to analyze for this chapter; there were hundreds more that included only brief mentions of *Sex in Education*, reprinted earlier articles, or operated primarily as advertisements for the book. *Sex in Education* was discussed across the country, starting in Clarke's hometown of Boston and extending to New York, Chicago, St. Louis, Louisiana, California, Oregon, and other locations.

Contemporaries of Clarke recognized and commented on the voluminous debate *Sex in Education* initiated. On January 3, 1874—fewer than three months after *Sex in Education* had been published—Frances D. Gage[3] began her column, titled "'Sex in Education' Once More," with an effort to assuage readers who might have grown tired of the debate: "Don't be frightened, DEAR JOURNAL, at my heading, for I am not going into a criticism of Dr. Clarke." That the debate had already become self-referential indicates the volume of responses generated. That Gage felt she needed to reassure readers that she didn't intend to write yet another full critique of Clarke suggests the ferocity of the debate. In June 1874, the *Boston Daily Advertiser* observed that commentary on *Sex in Education* was still going strong:

---

2. Tracking the pace at which new editions of *Sex in Education* were published is difficult because the early editions released in rapid succession were not identified by edition number; the second and fifth editions are identifiable only because they feature additional prefaces. In February 1874, the *Chicago Daily Tribune* announced the publication of the eighth edition, and in December 1874, Clarke's friend Oliver Wendell Holmes wrote that "about a dozen editions" had been printed.

3. Frances Dana Gage (1808–1884) wrote and spoke on women's rights, temperance, and abolition. She presided over the women's rights convention in Akron, Ohio in 1851 where Sojourner Truth spoke; Gage published her recollection of Truth's speech (featuring a stereotypical Southern African American dialect that did not reflect how Truth actually spoke and attributing several statements to Truth that deviated from what she likely said) as "Ain't I a Woman" in 1863. Despite the inauthenticity of Gage's characterization of the speech, her version has been widely circulated and studied (Royster, "'Ain't I a Woman'").

"Appearances indicate that the discussion begun by Dr. Clarke, instead of coming to an end, is only beginning to get its scope defined" ("Magazine Notes"). In September 1874, the *Chicago Daily Tribune* concluded its review of one of the book-length responses to *Sex in Education* by noting that it was almost impossible not to contribute to the published debate: "But we had no intention of adding to a discussion that has already become tiresomely long and repetitious. The subject, once touched, is inviting, and it is difficult to withhold either tongue or pen from toying with it" ("Sex in Education"). Indeed, *The Jewish Messenger* of New York stated in October 1874—one year after *Sex in Education* had first been published—that the book had "founded a library of pamphlets" ("Literature of the Day"; see also "Literary" in *Appletons*'; "New Publications" in Boston's *Daily Evening Traveller*).

The reception of *Sex in Education* reflects several features of its historical and rhetorical moment. First, the flourishing periodical press of the late nineteenth century created the conditions for responding to *Sex in Education* on a broad scale. The material systems for publishing and quickly distributing the book and its responses; the genre conventions for reviews, editorials, and letters to the editor; and the cultural expectations for topics of interest and controversy all made the initial debate around *Sex in Education* possible. Furthermore, Clarke's book tapped into existing public interest in science and in questions of middle-class white women's roles and capabilities. In keeping with Clarke's exclusive concern for the reproductive health of white women, the reception of *Sex in Education* also reflected the racial and class divides at the time. As far as I have been able to determine, the women and men who directly participated in the public reception of *Sex in Education* in 1873 and 1874 were all white and members of the middle and professional classes.[4] Finally, the reception of this book demonstrates that late-nineteenth-century readers were aware of the stakes of inserting science, which had already achieved a good deal of authority, into contested social issues like the higher education of women.

Reception can exceed the scope of the original text, not only shaping the meaning and effect of the text beyond the control of the writer, but also by using the text as a basis to discuss issues that are larger than the text's expressed purpose. The reception of *Sex in Education* demonstrates this tendency to exceed a text's original scope, as Clarke's argument about adapting educational methods to suit the supposed constraints of women's reproductive physiology served as a starting point for a discussion of the rhetorical role of science in public decision-making. This debate over rhe-

---

4. I discuss the silences in the reception of *Sex in Education,* including those of African American and working-class women, in chapter four.

torical values (What research methods would be persuasive? What ethos positions would be perceived as authoritative? Might references to science be used to mislead?) appeared in only the reception of *Sex in Education*, not in the book itself. The articulation of new values and expectations around the rhetorical uses of science affected the women's rights issues at the heart of *Sex in Education*, but it also participated in the much larger re-orienting of public conceptions of meaning-making and persuasion accompanying the professionalization of science in the late-nineteenth-century US. Of course, the reception of *Sex in Education* was not the only site of this rhetorical and epistemological work. It was a prominent one, however, and it was one in which women participated. Attending to the reception of one of the most infamous texts in the history of the nineteenth-century US women's rights movement affords a fuller picture of how women worked alongside of (and often in opposition to) men to shape how non-professional readers would understand not only *Sex in Education* but also the rhetorical role of science in public decision-making.

Public Scientific Rhetoric

Scientific rhetoric as it circulates and persuades among public audiences operates differently from intra-professional scientific rhetoric. Importantly, the public's purposes for engaging with science often include practical decision-making (Should my daughter go to college?), while scientists might prioritize learning about the natural world (What are the physiological mechanisms by which menstruation occurs?). Celeste Condit recommends accepting public uses of science on their own terms, rather than perceiving them as incomplete or inadequate renderings of "pure science," in part because the public has its own uses for science, which often do not align with the values or the timeline of scientific research: "the function of the public arena is not to produce or reproduce factual truths, but to come to shared determinations of how we should live together" (12). In other words, the public uses science rhetorically, to select courses of action collectively (222).

Condit's description of research into science's rhetorical functions in public discourse points to the necessity of attending to reception in such work:

> To explore public discourse requires . . . that we read across the entire score of the public orchestra (or, quite often, cacophony) to identify the range, dispersal, and clustering of various ideas, many of which might not appear to belong together in a rigid, unified philosophical system, but which nonetheless tend to "go together" as a matter of empirical fact in the public discourse of an era. (12)

As I will demonstrate, in the reception of *Sex in Education*, two movements that might seem unrelated—the women's rights movement and the emergence of scientific professionalism as an authority in public discourse—were in fact closely connected. Both pro- and anti-women's rights camps claimed to value science more than their opponents did. Additionally, some women called for better science and better rhetorical uses of science in the public sphere, often in the hopes that more accurate science and more responsible scientific rhetoric would support their claims for greater rights.

In his work tracing the history of "science talk" in popular culture, Daniel Patrick Thurs explains that the nineteenth century was a turning point in the emergence of science as a distinct entity. In the first half of the century, there was little in how people talked about science that distinguished it from other ways of making sense of the world, but by the last quarter of the century, terms like *scientific method* and *scientist* as well as comparisons between science and religion appeared frequently in public discourse to set science apart (11). The reception of *Sex in Education* in 1873 and 1874 would have been at the early end of this transformation. According to Thurs, writers perceived the 1870s and 1880s to be a "boom time for public interest in scientific works, frequently those involving evolutionary ideas" (62). Many periodicals ran science sections, and general-audience science publications, such as *Popular Science Monthly*, emerged (62). One topic covered in these periodicals was evolution, which was hotly debated in the 1870s and 1880s (69). In the context of this debate, Americans were coming to terms with what evolution might mean for various aspects of their individual and collective lives (74). Thurs names religion as one aspect of culture that faced reassessment in light of evolution; I would add the role of women in society as another. Clarke relied on evolutionary thought in his argument that white women who pursued identical co-education would not bear healthy children and so would hinder the "progress and development of the [white] race" (161). Importantly, at this time, the boundaries around science, what was meant by *science*, and what it was appropriate for science to do were being debated not only among those who considered themselves professional scientists (a group that was itself emerging alongside of a distinct notion of science), but also by members of the public. That debate, in which the reception of *Sex in Education* participated, constructed what science was, its values, and the rhetorical functions its invocation might serve.

Unlike the increasingly exclusive world of professional scientific discourse, the site of much of the public negotiation of science—the periodical press—was accessible to women. Sally Shuttleworth, Gowan Dawson, and Richard Noakes assert that nineteenth-century women had more access to scientific knowledge and rhetoric than contemporary scholars might assume:

"The sheer range of scientific ideas and debate available to the nineteenth-century woman reader has generally been wildly under-estimated" (58–59). The volume of popular writing about science meant that "Women writers, like the majority of men, would usually have gained their understanding of evolution, or other major scientific issues, not from primary texts, but from discussions in periodicals" (58).[5] Because people learned about science through periodicals, one effective means of shaping how the public understood scientific findings, theories, and applications was through contributing to the discussion of scientific topics in magazines and newspapers. When Clarke first lectured on co-education, and then published *Sex in Education*, men and women who advocated for advanced education for women immediately recognized that they needed to shape how the public received Clarke's ideas, as did opponents of higher education for women. The hundreds of reviews, letters, and commentaries on the *Sex in Education* controversy published in little over a year are evidence of the public's interest in how science might illuminate the issue of women's education and of the intense efforts on both sides to control how Clarke's argument was received.

In what follows, I analyze a variety of responses to *Sex in Education* published within fifteen months of the book's first edition, focusing on texts that expressed readers' beliefs about the role of science in public decision-making. The reception of *Sex in Education* illustrates how the public wrestled with the shifting rhetorical values accompanying the emergence of what Gregory Clark and S. Michael Halloran call the "new public morality of expertise" accompanying the increasing influence of the sciences and professions in the nineteenth century (3). The reception of *Sex in Education* was not just the site of an intense debate over women's education; it was also the site of deliberation about the role of science as a public rhetorical resource, a deliberation in which women actively participated, shaping rhetorical values in significant ways.

Physiology and the End of the Debate over Women's Higher Education

Many nineteenth-century commentators used their reception of *Sex in Education* as an opportunity to assert that the debate over girls' and women's education had finally been resolved, thanks to science. As a means of identifying facts and shaping arguments that was relatively new to many ordinary

---

5. Although Shuttleworth, Dawson, and Noakes write of nineteenth-century British society, the vibrant periodical press in the US makes it likely that their claims apply to US women as well.

Americans (compared to religion or philosophy, for example), physiology seemed to offer a way out of the well-established ruts of the pro- and anti-arguments. Moreover, science's association with objectivity and with observable facts appeared to provide a more solid basis for resolving the question of women's education (and, by extension, women's rights more broadly) than religion and philosophy, which provided answers complicated by faith, interpretation, and perspective. Furthermore, the near monopoly that men held over scientific expertise and research all but ensured that physiology would be found to support conventional notions of women's roles and physical and mental capabilities, making it an appealing rationale for those opposed to expanding women's opportunities. Consequently, despite science's promise of novelty and the transformation it was beginning to work in the lives and ideas of late-nineteenth-century Americans, science entered the women's rights debate as a conservative force.

Early reviews of *Sex in Education* supported Clarke's application of physiology to the question of women's rights. For example, in December 1873, the editor of *Appletons' Journal of Literature, Science and Art* recommended that "every one interested" in "the education of our girls" should read *Sex in Education*. He also argued strongly for the role of science in determining appropriate educational methods: "Whether boys and girls should be educated together is preëminently a physiological question . . . . The only authoritative decision must come from Science." After acknowledging that it might be possible to teach boys and girls the same things, the editor insisted, along with Clarke, that science dictated that different methods must be used: "Admit that men and women are equal, they are still not the same; and the nature of their differences Science, and not Ethics, is alone competent to decide. And if we do not abide by the decision of Science in the education of our girls, we shall ruin their health, and, with their health, that of future generations" ("Editor's Table" December 6, 1873, 730). Echoing Clarke's claim in *Sex in Education* that answers to questions about women's sphere "must be obtained from physiology, not from ethics or metaphysics" (12), the editor also reinforced Clarke's dire predictions about the consequences of continuous education for the health of individual women and of the "race" (see also "Literary Review" 484).

In insisting that science provided a definitive judgement on the advisability of higher education for women, reviewers made the question of women's education larger than an individual woman deciding whether or not to go to college; instead, it was a matter that affected the survival of the (white, middle-class) species. Positioning women's education in this way cued the reading public to think of Darwinian evolution and to view the issue on the species level; whereas ethics and personal rights might apply to individual decisions, evolutionary science delivered verdicts on a larger scale.

Several reviews went further, suggesting that Clarke had ended the debate over women's education because science was superior to any other rationale that could be applied to social problems. For example, the review appearing in *The Eclectic Magazine* stated that "In this little book . . . the long discussion about woman's education at last touches solid ground. Hitherto, the question has been discussed as if it were a moral or religious one, to be settled by ethical considerations." The real issue, this writer noted, was not whether women could excel academically, but rather how they should learn, "and this must be settled, has already been settled in fact, on physiological grounds alone" ("Literary Notices," March 1874). *Harper's New Monthly Magazine* also highlighted the value of bringing science into the conversation about women's education: "It is very much a physiological question, to which science, actual knowledge, must furnish the solution" ("Editor's Easy Chair" 444). *The Christian Watchman* characterized "the plain indisputable facts of physiology" as superior to an "abstract principle of right" as the basis for determining the correct method of educating girls and young women ("New Publications"; see also "Current Literature" 103; "The Education of American Girls" in *The Galaxy*; "Literary Review" in *The Congregationalist*; "Sex in Education" in *Old and New*). Situating physiology in opposition to political, moral, religious, ethical, and sentimental considerations, commentators received *Sex in Education* as providing a definitive assessment of the advisability of women's education, compared to the endlessly debatable arguments based in other epistemologies.

In addition to claiming the authority and prestige of science for the side of those opposed to women's education, characterizing *Sex in Education* as the source of new, ostensibly objective knowledge allowed opponents of women's extended education to replace earlier claims of women's intellectual inferiority with claims of their physiological incapacity (Jacobi, "Mental Action and Physical Health" 259). Women's record of success in higher education, including earning top honors over men in their classes, made doubt about women's intellectual abilities difficult to sustain. Clarke circumvented this obstacle by maintaining that the women who succeeded in college, even those who appeared healthy at graduation, might later succumb to reproductive ailments caused by their intense study (107–08).

The shift to resisting women's advanced education on physiological grounds, then, offered several rhetorical advantages to opponents of women's education. In its review of Anna C. Brackett's collection of responses to Clarke's book, *The World* of New York attributed exactly this argumentative shift to Clarke. The review credited Clarke with "having cleared the ground of a great deal of rubbish, and for removing the question of girls' education out of the region of empirical generalization to a physiological basis. The old question of inferiority of mind has given way before the suspicion of inferiority of body; and the advocates both for and against the higher education for women accept this as the true issue." In this case, the reviewer went on to acknowledge that the women who contributed to Brackett's collection possessed personal experience as women that might outweigh Clarke's ability to "theorize" and draw on his "observations and experience" as a physician ("Sex in Education"). Even though the question of women's education was to be determined by physiology, according to this reviewer, (men) physicians did not have a monopoly on physiological evidence.

In fact, one consequence of *Sex in Education* that Clarke likely did not anticipate, but that was mentioned in several commentaries, was an increased demand for the combined medical expertise and lived experience as women that was offered by women physicians. *Harper's New Monthly Magazine* suggested that women physicians were better positioned to speak on the health effects of education for women than Clarke was. This was particularly true of the resident physician at Vassar, who had denied some of Clarke's claims about students at that college:

> When an accomplished and scientific woman, whose treatment of this question shows that she knows, and who has had very large experience, directly opposes Dr. Clarke, and says that in her opinion, not as an advocate, but as a woman and a parent, there is no reason whatever of the kind he suggests why the girls during the time that he mentions should not study precisely as boys do, and that her experience fortifies the conclusions of her science, the doctor must lower his pennon and withdraw. ("Editor's Easy Chair" 444; see also Jackson 158; Comfort and Comfort 64; Dall, "Caroline H. Dall," 101–04; Phelps 130)

Taking this argument even further, Brackett, editor of *The Education of American Girls* (1874), a collection of responses to Clarke, used the occasion of her letter critiquing *Sex in Education* to call for funding to support women's medical education, so that women would have physicians to turn to who possessed first-hand knowledge of women's physiology:

> If the women of America have any money to spare, let them give it to form funds for the endowment of our women's medical schools, till their students shall have, in lectures, in hospital practice, in every respect, as thorough a medical education as the men . . . . We shall then have at least physicians who will understand their

patients and the needs and purposes of American women to a somewhat greater degree than the author of "Sex in Education." ("Dr. Clark [sic] Reviewed")

Although many advocates of *Sex in Education* praised its writer's professional expertise, Brackett suggested that scientific knowledge alone was not enough to determine women's physiological capabilities accurately. Brackett added lived experience as a woman as a necessary qualification for deciding the question of women's education. This undercut Clarke's authority by arguing that there were others with even more comprehensive expertise.

While calls for formally educated women physicians constituted one response to the assertion that physiology resolved the debate over women's education, another response asserted that all women would be well served by a more thorough knowledge of physiology so that they could better manage their own health. Although such a reform might not seem as revolutionary as the education of professional women physicians, widespread knowledge of physiology by women would also increase women's authority and autonomy in their day-to-day lives (C. Skinner, "'She Will Have Science'"). For instance, Caroline Dall[6] imagined a world in which women spoke publicly from their scientific knowledge: "I am not one of those who believe that girls require more care than boys through [puberty], if the laws of life are properly observed in both cases; and I think that when women and mothers come to utter words of the same scientific weight on this subject, their testimony will differ entirely from that of the leading physicians who now hold the public ear" ("The Other Side" 167). Assertions like these acknowledged the authority and expertise of the medical scientist while preserving some knowledge, unattainable by contemporary research methods, for women. This was a complicated position for women to take; it drew on the nineteenth-century belief that women possessed especially feminine knowledge and perspectives, but it was not compatible with the emerging model of "objective" science. Of course, Clarke and those like him were not objective when they interpreted physiology through the lens of their beliefs about women, but such bias was implicit, embedded in the culture in which they spoke, and so could pass for objectivity. In contrast, when women expressly claimed feminine knowledge, they risked excluding themselves from the powerful scientific discourses associated with objectivity. As long as the cul-

---

6. Caroline Wells Healey Dall (1822–1912) was a prominent writer and reformer, involved in the women's rights and abolitionist movements. She published several books, including *Woman's Right to Labor; or, Low Wages and Hard Work* (1860) and *The College, the Market, and the Court; or, Woman's Relation to Education, Labor and Law* (1867).

ture assumed women and men were inherently different from each other, and until women had full access to scientific information and professional education, insisting on the knowledge they possessed as women was one of the few available strategies for engaging with science in public rhetorical spaces.

The reception of *Sex in Education* reveals the extent to which members of the American public (especially those opposed to expanding women's roles) were eager to adopt physiology as a means of resolving the issue of women's education conclusively. Because the woman question existed at the intersection of biology and society (What, if any, limitations did women's bodies put on the social roles—college students, voters, professionals—that they might adopt?), the debate over women's rights was an ideal site for the insertion of science into public decision-making. Consequently, women's rights discourse was a crucial component of the rhetorical shift toward using science for collective deliberation. As the rest of this chapter will demonstrate, relying on science to discuss women's capabilities—the primary rhetorical innovation of *Sex in Education* (Vostral 29; Kenschaft 157; Zschoche 549) and its reception—involved the negotiation of new rhetorical values for deploying scientific evidence, argument, and authority in public discourse.

SCIENTIFIC FACTS AND SCIENTIFIC IMPRESSIONS

One of the most important contests over the meaning of *Sex in Education* occurred around the question of what Clarke's attitude toward women's education actually was. He had briefly admitted that young women's diet and dress contributed to their physical weakness (23); Clarke had also acknowledged that women had a right to pursue any opportunities, including educational opportunities, that did not overtax their physiology (12). A reader could, therefore, characterize *Sex in Education* as a text that did not attribute women's poor health exclusively to education and as one that did not intend to curtail women's access to education but instead promoted a model of education suited to women's physical needs. According to this interpretation, Clarke used physiological principles to help women achieve their full reproductive and intellectual potential. Some respondents, however, insisted that the weight of Clarke's evidence and his reference to physiology exclusively in the context of continuous education's deleterious effect on reproductive development (omitting the physiological implications of dress and diet, for instance) created the *impression* that education, not diet or dress, was the primary source of women's poor health. This tension between readers who focused on what Clarke said and those who emphasized their perceptions of what he implied suggests the public's uncertainty about the role of science in public discourse.

The initial public reception of *Sex in Education* reflected the contrasting interpretations of Clarke's book. For example, a frequently cited review originally appearing in the *Boston Daily Advertiser* took pains to specify Clarke's position, quoting from *Sex in Education* to highlight Clarke's actual words: "It is not education for women to which Dr. Clarke objects; he repeats emphatically that they have a right to the best education and the finest culture. He does not doubt their intellectual ability; but the essential thing in a good education is complete development, so that 'boys may become men, and girls women, and both have a fair chance to do and become their best.'" Later, the writer reiterated, "We repeat, that Dr. Clarke does not oppose the education of women; he only opposes the present method of education," that is, education modelled after men's continuous study rather than adapted to women's periodicity ("The Education of Girls"; see also McAdam).

Some reviewers insisted on Clarke's support of women's education to a degree that might seem quite remarkable to readers who are accustomed to the modern infamous reputation of *Sex in Education*. For example, the review in *The New Church Magazine* asserted that "So far from offering the slightest objection to the education of woman, no abler champion than Dr. Clarke has appeared in favor of the highest and best education of that sex" ("Current Literature" 105). A correspondent to *Zion's Herald* also tried to clear up perceived misconceptions about *Sex in Education*, maintaining that Clarke intended to help women achieve their goals:

> Observe, that the Dr. is not arguing . . . that women may not, under equally favorable circumstances, make equal mental attainments with men, but that they must make them in their own way. He is not arguing that, when a woman's physical development is once complete, and her health once established, she may not endure at least nearly as much mental strain as her brother . . . . When will our critics do the author of this little book simple justice? . . . Strange that so many of the very class intended to be benefited by this discussion, so far from appreciating the same, seem rather disposed only to ridicule and persistently misrepresent it? [sic] ("Editorial Paragraphs" February 26, 1874).

In emphasizing the claim that Clarke believed in women's intellectual abilities and merely sought the best methods for attaining academic success, commentators like those cited above insisted on a literal reading of *Sex in Education*, one that interpreted Clarke's use of physiology as a means of benefiting women, rather than a justification for restriction.

Although many reviewers, especially those inclined to agree with Clarke's conclusions, took his declarations of support for women's education at face value, others doubted his sincerity. For example, Rena Michaels[7] described *Sex in Education* as "Sensational in the extreme, ofttimes appealing to the emotional nature to conceal its biased and unsound reasoning, dogmatically asserting a theory and principles which find no place or authority in medical science" (350; see also Duffey 64). Despite, or perhaps because, *Sex in Education* did not adhere to the epistemological and rhetorical principles that Michaels identified with science, she argued that the book misled the public: "[I]t succeeded in deceiving the public mind, and received marked and favorable attention from many critics. None of these reviewers attempted to follow Dr. Clarke in his peculiar line of discussion; they either did, or did not, believe in a thorough education for woman, and accordingly either accepted or rejected his premises and conclusions" (350). When she said that reviewers had not pursued Clarke's "peculiar line of discussion," Michaels highlighted a possible difficulty in adapting science for the public: readers were often not capable of or interested in tracing the details of the research or reasoning presented. Michaels's assessment of the responses to *Sex in Education* suggested that science, instead of being referenced as a means of exploring the facts of a situation, was deployed in support of writers' pre-established opinions.

Other critics of *Sex in Education* argued that readers could easily infer from the book that women could not safely pursue extended education, despite some reviewers' emphasis on Clarke's stated interest in discovering the best form of education for women. These critics frequently referred to the *impression* readers would receive from *Sex in Education*. For example, Brackett distinguished between what Clarke said in *Sex in Education* and what she believed readers were likely to infer from it: "However much the author may assert that he does not say this or that, no one can deny that the popular impression received from the book will be that excessive brain-work is, after all, the one thing most dangerous to our girls" ("Dr. Clark [sic] Reviewed"; see also Duffey 102). Also concerned about the *impression* created by *Sex in Education*, a writer identified as C. wrote, "[Clarke] leaves the

---

7. Rena Michaels earned a BS (1874), MS (1879), and PhD (1880) from Syracuse University, where she was a founding member of the Alpha Phi sorority. Although biographical information on Michaels is incomplete (and she is inconsistently identified as Rena A. Michaels and Rena S. Michaels across texts), it seems likely that she served as a professor of modern languages at Upper Iowa University, Albion College, and DePauw University before becoming the dean of women at Northwestern University in 1886. In addition to writing on the topic of women's rights, Michaels (later Atchinson) lectured for the Women's Christian Temperance Union.

impression, and he means to leave the impression, that the regimen of the schools, if not the sole cause, is the prime and direct cause of the ill-health of American women" (119–20). In her essay, "Girls and Women in England and America," collected in Brackett's *The Education of American Girls*, Mary E. Beedy[8] acknowledged that American women were thin, nervous, anxious, and weak, but asserted that several causes contributed to their poor health; unfortunately, "any one of [them] . . . may be clearly made to appear responsible for almost the whole; and such, in some degree, is the temporary effect of the very clever feint of Dr. Clarke—nothing else can it be called" (214). Beedy went on to reinforce what she perceived to be the illusory nature of Clarke's claims: "The book gives us the impression. . . . It makes us believe . . . and it makes us fear" that Clarke would undercut the prevalent methods of educating women (214). Beedy's characterization of Clarke's argument as a "feint [that] has created a sensation" (215) places it far from the concrete evidence and facts supposed to be the terrain of science. Together, these and other advocates of women's education worried that *Sex in Education* would be received, despite Clarke's own statements to the contrary, as arguing that education was the primary cause of women's poor health (see also K.N.D.; D.).

The editor of *The Unitarian Review and Religious Magazine* also questioned the impression conveyed by *Sex in Education*:

> [A]lthough [Clarke] expressly states that a wrong method of education is only one among many causes of the ill health of women, yet the whole impression of the book is that too much study is the crying evil, and that it is desirable to check women's aspirations after high intellectual culture—a position which we regard [as] so unwarranted by any kind of proof, and so opposed to the best interests of human advancement, that we are sorry for any seeming support that is given to it by connecting with it facts and arguments which properly considered only prove that, in the pursuit of such culture, heed must be paid to the conditions of our physical organization. ("Editor's Note-Book"; see also Dall 95)

The tensions among what Clarke said, the impression allegedly created by *Sex in Education*, and what could be justified by scientific evidence were foregrounded by this writer's observations that the book's "impression" was

---

8. Mary E. Beedy (1835–1910) founded the Girls' Higher School in Chicago with Rebecca S. Rice. Beedy also gave lectures on women's education and supported the settlement house work of Jane Addams.

"unwarranted by . . . proof" and that "facts and arguments" only "seem[ed to] support" it.

Advocates of Clarke's position noticed the liberal interpretations articulated by his opponents and insisted on a reading that hewed closer to Clarke's words. For example, after noting that "the press has lately teemed" with objections to Clarke's argument, *The Eclectic Magazine*'s review concluded by finding fault with those criticisms:

> [W]hen they are not simply meaningless attacks, they are based on misapprehensions or misinterpretations, or failure to appreciate the comprehensiveness of the principle laid down. There has been absolutely no serious challenge either of the facts or the conclusions. Nor, as to the former, would a challenge be possible; Dr. Clarke's entire treatise simply gives new meaning and application to a law of sex which is universally known, and which has been nearly as universally ignored. ("Literary Notices," March 1874)

Where Clarke's opponents saw an impression communicated by *Sex in Education* that advanced education should ultimately be out of reach for most women, this writer saw "misapprehensions or misinterpretations" among those who perceived Clarke to be hostile to women's education. For this writer, instead of intangible impressions, the "facts or the conclusions"—the concrete evidence and statements offered in *Sex in Education*—pointed to a scientific "law of sex."

The tension in *Sex in Education*'s reception between those who insisted that Clarke should be taken at his word and those who argued that Clarke implied much more than he said points to uncertainty over the role of science in public discourse. Did evocations of science merely present facts and findings in service of better-informed decision-making, or were references to science themselves rhetorical, serving persuasive ends in their impressions that went beyond what was stated? One response to this question came from physician Mary Putnam Jacobi, who, like Michaels, doubted the sincerity of the public's interest in using science to identify the truth.[9] Instead, she

---

9. Mary Putnam Jacobi (1842–1906) was among the earliest women to practice medicine in the US, earning her medical degree in 1864. She later taught at the Women's Medical College of the New York Infirmary for Women and Children; in 1872, she became the first woman admitted to the New York Academy of Medicine. Over her career, she wrote prolifically for both public and professional audiences. Here, I focus on her contribution to the public reception of Clarke's book, which was often characterized as authoritative, owing to her professional expertise. Jacobi also participated in the professional reception of *Sex in Education*, and I analyze her role in that discussion in chapter three.

thought most people were interested in using science to support their pre-existing social theories:

> The singular avidity with which the press and the public have seized upon the theme discussed in Dr. Clarke's book on *Sex in Education*, is a proof that this appeals to many interests besides those of scientific truth. The public cares very little about science, except in so far as its conclusions can be made to intervene in [sic] behalf of some moral, religious, or social controversy. ("Mental Action and Physical Health" 258)

Although much of her response to Clarke refuted his argument by pointing to his weak evidence, false logic, lack of consideration of possible alternate causes of women's poor health, and incomplete understanding of human physiology, Jacobi began her essay with an extended analysis of the role of science in public discourse. For example, she compared the frenzy over *Sex in Education* to the public's response to other scientific theories:

> In the present case, a delicate physiological problem has become as popular as theories on epigenesis, spontaneous generation, or Darwinian evolution, and for an analogous reason. As the latter are expected to decide in the doctrines of natural or revealed religion, so the former is supposed to have a casting vote in regard to the agitating claims for the extension of new powers to women.... In both polemics, arguments are not accepted because they are demonstrated, but enlisted because they are useful; ranged with others recruited from the most distant quarters, with nothing in common but the regiment into which they are all thrust, to be hurled against a common enemy. (258–59)

In this passage, Jacobi offered an insightful analysis of the rhetorical use of science for persuasive, rather than the purely truth-seeking, ends in the late nineteenth century.

Turning to science offered rhetors important persuasive resources, according to Jacobi. Through science, "the old conclusions [about women's appropriate roles] may be urged with even greater force than before, because apparently based exclusively upon . . . cool and impartial investigation" (260). In contrast, Jacobi suggested, physiology might provide "food for the imagination," which might cause a writer, such as Clarke, to be swept up in its possibilities: "Would it be disrespectful to Dr. Clarke's far better informed judgment and technical knowledge to suggest, that he himself does not seem to be perfectly free from the influence of the glamour that invests the study of physiological peculiarities in women, wherever these can be made to tell upon any social or moral relations?" (261). Clarke himself, Jacobi suggested, drew on the sensational science of women's reproductive physiology to support his pre-existing beliefs about women's social roles. In her public reception of *Sex in Education*, Jacobi undermined the threat that the book's references to physiology posed to women's rights' efforts by casting doubt on Clarke's objectivity. She also called on readers, in their own reception of Clarke, to question their attraction to arguments about social issues that purported to be based in scientific theories or findings.

Like Jacobi, Dall recognized the rhetorical advantages Clarke gained in relying on science. In particular, Dall anticipated the difficulty women would have in responding to *Sex in Education* because they could not match Clarke's expertise:

> Every woman who takes up her pen to reject [*Sex in Education*'s] conclusions knows very well that it will penetrate hundreds of households where her protest cannot follow; and Dr. Clarke must be patient with the number and weight of our remonstrances, since he knows very well that upon the major part of the community our words will fall with no authority, our experiences invite no confidence. We must gain the public ear by constant iteration, and by our "importunity" prevail. ("V." 89)

Dall's response acknowledged the rhetorical advantages Clarke gained in relying on science and on his status as a physician in his argument. If the quantity of criticisms of *Sex in Education* seemed extreme, she asserted, it was because most women could not refer to science as Clarke did and so their perspectives would be heard only through repetition (see also Greene 20–21).

Despite her doubts that women could match Clarke's scientific authority, Dall went on to assert that women needed to speak up in opposition to *Sex in Education*. Dall cited Thomas Wentworth Higginson, who criticized Clarke, as evidence. Despite his support of women's education, Dall noted, Higginson also "said that [*Sex in Education*] is not *coarse!*" This reaction (in T. W. H., "Sex in Education") from an otherwise supportive man to a book that Dall believed caused women "personal humiliation and dismay" proved to Dall that women could not rely on even well-intentioned men to defend them: "Surely never was a sentence written that more eloquently betrayed the need women have to speak for themselves!" (91). Like many women who wrote in opposition to Clarke, Dall called for the education of women as physicians as one solution to the rhetorical and social dilemma women faced as science grew in value as a rhetorical resource for public discourse (90). The debate over *Sex in Education* drew attention to the need for women to access the expertise needed to critically evaluate references to science in public contexts, as well as to learn to deploy the persuasive resources of both the facts and the impressions of science for themselves.

CLAIMING A SCIENTIFIC STANCE IN THE WOMEN'S RIGHTS DEBATE

Because *Sex in Education* claimed that physiology should determine the limits on women's rights and roles, the book's reception featured a fair amount of jockeying among pro- and anti-women's rights advocates for the title of "most scientific." Those opposed to increased rights for women characterized women who desired more opportunities as at best ignorant and at worst defiant of women's physiological limitations. For instance, an editorial in *Appletons'*, responding to a review of Clarke's book in *The* [Boston] *Commonwealth*, asserted that science was needed to restore the proper understanding of the roles of men and women:

> The reason why Dr. Clarke's book is necessary, and likely to render much good service, is that the old-fashioned theory of differences between the two sexes has been assailed. We find all around us now the claim of *likeness*, and it is because a certain popular spirit would force women into wrong positions, that it becomes necessary for Dr. Clarke and others to establish, on purely scientific grounds, the *unlikeness* of the sexes . . . . [I]t is the province of science to reëstablish the truth as regards [woman's] place in social life. ("Editor's Table," December 27, 1873, 827)

Although science might have been a new epistemology, for this writer it confirmed old beliefs about men and women. Those who opposed expanding women's rights and opportunities, therefore, had science on their side.

Contrasting the "physiological data" in support of arguments to limit women's sphere to the "abstract assumptions" of those in favor of increased rights, the review of *Sex in Education* in *Popular Science Monthly* characterized reformers as uninformed and dangerous:

> One would think that there is sufficient physiological knowledge current in the community to prevent an educational system that does not recognize and conform to the radical differences of sex; but, under pressure of a so-called reform, which starts from abstract assumptions rather than physiological data, the strong tendency is to put students of both sexes upon the same footing, regardless of all consequences. ("Literary Notices" 377)

The review concluded by noting that Clarke's chapter, "Chiefly Clinical," was "full of startling facts, given in detail, that should arrest the attention of some of our headlong reformers" ("Literary Notices" 378). Comments like these suggested that *Sex in Education* provided facts that could correct the rash and unscientific positions of women's rights advocates.

From this perspective, scientific evidence buttressed arguments for limiting women's rights and opportunities. Furthermore, as the article "The Replies to Dr. Clarke" observed, the emergence of a scientific approach to women's rights necessitated conversation in language and on topics that might cause some discomfort:

> We simply wish to give our readers some idea of the present position of a controversy which has certainly had no parallel in ancient or modern times, and which furnishes a most curious illustration of the change which is coming over our manners under the influence of what we may call the scientific mode of dealing with social problems. The discussion in which Dr. Clarke and his assailants are engaged is a discussion over the physical constitution of the female sex, and it deals with topics of so delicate a nature that they have hitherto never been touched on in literature except in medical books, and never orally except in the confidence of professional consultation or in medical lecture-rooms. The introduction of these topics into popular literature, and indeed into general conversation, is, however, something which has been impending for some years past. We have ourselves ventured to predict more than once that the question of woman's rights would never be settled without debates of extraordinary indecency. (408)

The writer explained that reformers had emphasized the similarity between men's and women's physiology, while ignoring the differences, putting conservatives in the awkward position of knowing that men and women were physiologically different, but unable to speak bluntly in public about those differences and their effects. Once co-education and other reforms were seriously under consideration, however, the conservatives had to "meet this . . . by a physiological argument of the utmost plainness":

> We would rather not handle [women's physiology] in the newspapers or in the family circle . . . . But if you insist upon it, and upon treating our reticence as a sign of acquiescence in the serious changes you propose in our laws and manners, we certainly shall not be restrained by considerations of decency, and give you fair

notice that we shall "invade your privacy" in a manner you will not like. We shall not sacrifice society to our squeamishness. (408)

The threat embedded in this passage referred to some opponents who faulted Clarke for violating women's modesty in writing publicly about female reproductive physiology (see, for example, Howe 7). In addition to the physical intimidation conveyed, the writer also suggested that the full knowledge of science would be applied to put women back in their place.

What's significant about "The Replies to Dr. Clarke" is the story that it told about how this subset of science entered public discourse: women's rights activists proposed reforms that defied physiological facts, and so conservatives had no choice but to introduce the facts of female reproductive physiology to the public, initiating a full discussion of the issue. Without a full and public conversation about women's reproductive physiology (a conversation that many respectable women might shy away from), the demands of women's rights activists would not be granted: "[W]hether this argument, as used on the conservative side, be conclusive or not, it is quite certain that the new régime which the friends of woman's rights propose to us, cannot and ought not to be adopted until the argument has been thoroughly weighed" (408). In this version of events, the women's rights agenda had called forth the physiological arguments against women's extended education and other sought-after rights. One implication of this narrative is that women's rights advocates had brought arguments like Clarke's upon themselves, after years of provoking conservatives. Another implication is that the women's rights movement was crucial to the rhetorical shift toward using science to deliberate public matters.

Once those opposed to increased rights and opportunities for women had asserted that science supported their position, they could characterize women's rights advocates as unscientific. Writing in December 1873, E.H. Sears[10] dismissed complaints that Clarke had employed a derisive tone and accused anyone who perceived such a tone of unscientific bias: "[Clarke's] method is purely scientific; and the 'sneers' in the book, or the disparagement of women as teachers, we think must escape the eyes of all but those who are determined to make this a partizan [sic] question instead of a question of pure science." Other commentators insisted that ordinary readers—including many of those who favored increased educational opportunities for women—lacked the knowledge to evaluate *Sex in Education* effectively. For example, a writer in *The Literary World* began by stating that "Dr. E.

---

10. This writer is possibly Edmund Hamilton Sears, a Unitarian minister and writer who composed the lyrics for the Christmas song "It Came Upon a Midnight Clear."

W. [sic] Clarke's 'Sex in Education' has called out much bitter and ill-considered comment from those to whom his opinions are not welcome. These critics seem to forget that his book is one of those that cannot be fairly judged except by a person possessed of thorough technical knowledge of the subject of which it treats." For anyone lacking thorough knowledge of physiology to judge *Sex in Education*, this writer continued, "is a burlesque of criticism" ("Literary News," January 1, 1874; see also "Current Notes"). This reviewer was happy to report that a book would soon be published (Brackett's collection) that would rise above "a warfare of mere abuse" by arguing with facts, suggesting that this writer was not opposed to well informed criticisms of Clarke.

Just as *The Literary World* praised writers who grounded their arguments in facts, the *North American Review* encouraged respondents to Clarke's book to consider the physician's standpoint carefully. Although this review challenged some aspects of Clarke's argument, the writer agreed "most heartily" (144) with Clarke's objection to identical co-education and had this advice for supporters of women's education:

> [Clarke's] words demand respectful consideration, especially from those friends of female education whose ardor at having identical coeducation attacked would seem rather to indicate anxiety to maintain a conspicuous theory than an earnest desire to establish the best possible plan in [sic] behalf of women. We are friends of the cause of women's education, but we consider it of the utmost importance that the testimony of physicians, as well as of teachers, should be taken with regard to the best methods to be adopted. ("Art. V" 146)

Warning potential critics of Clarke's work that they might seem more committed to having their way than to achieving what would be best for women, this reviewer encouraged women's rights advocates to take professional opinions, from teachers and physicians, into account.

In contrast to the argument that supporters of increased opportunities for women defied physiological facts, supporters of women's rights insisted that reform-minded women had long sought better and more widespread physiological information. Higginson, co-editor of the pro-suffrage *Woman's Journal*, was one of several who made such an argument. In his review of *Sex in Education*, Higginson explained that the advocates of women's rights who had written for the *Woman's Journal* wanted physiological facts: "Instead of shrinking from these facts, we are constantly begging for them" (see also C.'s call for statistical data demonstrating the effect of education on women's health: 118, 120, 125). Contrary to those who suggested that promoters of women's education acted in ignorance, if not in defiance, of physiological facts, Higginson characterized the women's rights movement as highly supportive of widespread knowledge about physiology. In fact, Higginson claimed, the women's rights movement "has been constantly under criticism . . . for encouraging too minute a study of physiology in schools, and for thus making young girls too well acquainted with those special laws of their own being, about which they were once studiously kept in ignorance" ("Sex in Education"). Likewise, in its early review of *Sex in Education*, *The Daily Graphic* of New York credited women's rights advocates with calling for physiological education for girls and young women before Clarke had: "The physical training he lays so much stress upon has been urged with more discrimination and equal force by the reformers he condemns, but has always been resisted by the devotees of fashion and the Madame Grundys" ("Literary Resume").[11] Responses like these challenged the idea that women's rights advocates sought to defy physiological knowledge; instead, they demonstrated that women's rights advocates' interest in physiology was longstanding.

Also writing for the *Woman's Journal*, Gage, like Higginson, insisted that proponents of women's rights had nothing to fear from physiology. Instead, they had been misunderstood and limited by people, like Clarke, who sought to add restrictions beyond those actually imposed by physiology. She asked parenthetical questions to build a more nuanced model of gender difference than she found in *Sex in Education*. First, she clarified the position of women's rights activists: "The author frankly admits the equality of the sexes, but not the identity. (Has any one ever asserted the identity?)." A few paragraphs later, she used parentheticals to apply Clarke's claims about girls to boys: "Two things at the same time cannot be done by girls, he thinks. (Can they by boys?) They are expected to learn a lesson and to keep their own strength and force. (Are not boys called upon for the same?)" ("Sex in Education"). In asking these questions, Gage followed a line of argument common in critiques of Clarke: he had applied a standard to girls that he had not applied to boys. This evaluation of *Sex in Education* insisted on a more comprehensive line of reasoning than Clarke had offered; in doing so, she suggested that a full examination of the physiology involved in education (for both women and men) would reveal facts that would support the expansion of women's education. By implication, women's rights advocates were "more scientific" in seeking thoroughgoing evidence about the

---

11. In Thomas Morton's play *Speed the Plough* (1798), one of the characters constantly worries about what Mrs. Grundy, who never appears onstage, might think. In common usage, "Madame Grundy" came to refer to someone who judged others' morality and respectability.

relationship between education and health than those who sought to limit women's education by reference to partial (incomplete and biased) research.

In the popular reception of *Sex in Education*, it is evident that co-education and other women's rights issues were entwined with the public's still-emerging understanding of what science was and what it offered the public, materially and rhetorically. Importantly, both pro- and anti-women's rights writers claimed to value physiology and attempted to position themselves as "more scientific" than their opponents. In doing so, the women's rights debate participated in reshaping rhetorical values to reflect (and extend) the public's interest in science as a source of evidence and authority in collective decision-making. In particular, the fact that both sides in the popular reception of *Sex in Education* could reasonably claim a scientific stance and portray opponents as unscientific suggests that the characteristics of a scientific ethos in public discourse were unsettled. Did one demonstrate a scientific stance by accepting expert opinion or by seeking knowledge for oneself? By identifying continuity between science and "commonsense" knowledge, or by challenging reasoning that seemed to be one-sided? The features of a scientific rhetorical stance for public debates—particularly whether that stance was accessible to women and friendly to reform causes or not—would affect whose voices could be heard and what could be said in a context where the audience increasingly turned to science for answers.

Articulating the Features of Public Scientific Rhetoric

Perhaps because participants in the debate over *Sex in Education* recognized that science was so persuasive to public audiences, one feature of the reception of Clarke's book was an effort to articulate the characteristics—methodological and rhetorical—that the public should expect from references to science. By December 1874, a little over a year after the initial publication of *Sex in Education*, *The Eclectic Magazine* felt confident enough to argue that the book's scientific claims and evidence were irrefutable: "Dr. Clarke's main thesis may now be said to be established on the irrefragible [sic] proofs of theoretical physiology and practical experience" ("Literary Notices" 763). Of course, many advocates of women's education would have disputed that assertion, and they used their reception of *Sex in Education* to establish the rhetorical values that they believed the nineteenth-century public should demand from uses of science in the service of persuasion, especially when that science was intended to justify limitations on women's activities.

For example, the reception of *Sex in Education* frequently featured challenges to the evidence on which Clarke had based his argument. Although most of Clarke's readers—especially his public audience—lacked Clarke's expertise and his access to a "physician's notebook" (26) from which to draw evidence, readers could, Clarke's opponents suggested, assess the quality of the evidence that Clarke had presented. Writers encouraged the public to read scientific evidence critically, with high standards for its applicability to the issues at hand. Most frequently disputed was the case of Miss A—, whom Clarke claimed had entered a women's college in New York (widely believed to be Vassar) at the age of fifteen, when she was healthy. However, after years of continuous education, she suffered hemorrhages, fainting spells, dyspepsia, neuralgia, and ultimately infertility (65–72). Critics knowledgeable about Vassar's policies immediately faulted Clarke for citing this case in support of his thesis, because Vassar did not admit students as young as Miss A— was reported to have been, because the workload at the college was intentionally designed not to overwhelm young women, and because the resident physician kept a watchful eye over the students.[12] Reviewing Dall's letter criticizing these aspects of Clarke's argument (published first in the Boston newspaper *The Commonwealth*, then included in Brackett's collection), *The Daily Graphic* of New York claimed that her letter "thus convicts Dr. Clarke of citing cases in support of his theory which have no existence. It is well known that physicians who write in defense of any pet theory too often yield to the temptation to invent cases of extreme appositeness, and in more than one medical treatise published in [New York City] nine-tenths of the cases quoted are simply fictions" ("The End of Dr. Clarke"). Far from respecting Clarke's professional experience and authority, this writer accused all physicians of a tendency to exploit the public's respect for their status by offering false cases to support their favorite notions.

Responding to the publication of *Sex in Education*, Higginson also criticized the evidence Clarke had presented. On November 8, 1873, Higginson wrote that Clarke's "premises are inadequate, and his conclusions insufficient." Higginson said that he had "opened this book honestly, hoping to find an array of facts that should be impressive, not merely by their quality but by their quantity." However, the seven clinical cases Clarke presented, from which Higginson subtracted two because the women involved were

---

12. Because secondary and college education was not standardized in the nineteenth-century US as it is today, the girls attending "colleges," "academies," or "seminaries" were often in their teens; some even graduated before the age of eighteen. This meant that a young woman's "college years" might coincide with her adolescence, justifying Clarke's concerns about the stresses of education interfering with reproductive development.

not students (one was an actress and the other a clerk), disappointed him: "This does not seem to me what would be called, in any other branch of science, a satisfactory basis of facts" ("Sex in Education"). In this argument, Higginson participated in the articulation of the rhetorical values that the public should expect from references to science by claiming to approach *Sex in Education* with an open mind (a position his readers might hope to emulate) but then expressing his disappointment with the quality and quantity of Clarke's evidence. In the process, responses like these, which questioned Clarke's scientific rigor, suggested to readers what they ought to expect from science deployed in the service of public decision-making. According to Higginson's model, the public should be presented with ample, convincing evidence, and readers should examine that evidence critically, looking for logic and consistency in the writer's argument.

In *No Sex in Education*, Eliza B. Duffey's[13] book-length response to *Sex in Education*, Duffey, like Higginson, used her criticism of Clarke as an opportunity to describe the rhetorical values the public should expect from appeals to science. For instance, she encouraged readers to seek logic rather than sentimentality when she questioned a trope Clarke invoked. After noting that he had compared women to vines and men to oaks (following Washington Irving[14]), she asked, "If Dr. Clarke wishes for a perfect simile, why did he not compare the sexes to a male and female tree of the same species? Why? Because the facts would not accord with his theories; for do they not show that the female tree has more vigor and vitality than the male?—just what he is trying to disprove" (119). Duffey demonstrated that Clarke had selected a sentimental comparison rather than a true scientific comparison between the sexes, highlighting the biases that, she suggested, undermined his objectivity.

Duffey also identified unanswered questions in *Sex in Education*, pointing to the importance of isolating variables in scientific studies so that the researcher can be certain that results are attributable to the variable in question. In other words, the simple correlation of two events (a woman's educa-

---

13. Eliza Bisbee Duffey (1838–1898) was a painter, writer, and editor who often wrote about women's issues, including education and health. Before publishing *No Sex in Education*, Duffey wrote *What Women Should Know: A Woman's Book about Women* (1873), a book that discussed female puberty, love, marriage, pregnancy, infant care, and the responsibilities of motherhood.

14. In "The Wife" (1832), Washington Irving characterized the relationship between husband and wife as that between an oak tree and a vine, with the vine depending on the oak until the oak is struck by lightning; then the vine holds the oak together (30). In Irving's story, the wife supports her husband through a financial loss.

tion and her illness) does not prove that one (education) caused the other (illness). In *Sex in Education*, Clarke asserted that continuous education was the primary variable that caused poor health in women. One of Duffey's objections to Clarke's argument was that he had not accounted for variables other than education that might have affected women's health. For example, after observing that Clarke had not included information on how one of his clinical cases dressed, how much she exercised, or how much she slept, Duffey suggested that readers should not be persuaded without this information: "Very possibly the doctor knew nothing about these points himself, yet they are all most important ones; and until the reader is enlightened on them it seems unreasonable to ask him to accept the doctor's conclusions" (77; see also 83, 87, 89). In this passage, Duffey's critique of Clarke's argument was also an assertion of the discursive features a reader should expect before accepting an argument that claimed to be scientific. Importantly, she articulated for her public audience a crucial feature of scientific epistemology and insisted that non-professional readers should not be persuaded by texts that did not meet that standard, no matter how educated, experienced, and authoritative the writer might seem (see also Badger). According to Duffey, Clarke's (or any scientist's) ethos alone should not be sufficient reason for the public to accept his claims.

Lillie Devereux Blake[15] objected to *Sex in Education*'s argument on grounds similar to Duffey's. Blake claimed that Clarke did not draw logical conclusions from the evidence he provided: "His analysis of the physical resemblances and differences between man and woman is careful and able; with his statements, so far, no one can disagree[;] it is only a pity that he failed to draw the logical deductions from his own premises" (6). She proceeded to demand a more systematic study of the health effects of education:

> He tells us . . . that he is having careful inquiries made as to the health of certain [women] graduates of the Michigan University and Antioch College. Will he please, as a mere matter of fairness, select an equal number of young ladies of equal social position, who have had little or no education, and follow out their future careers also, and then tell us whether he finds any advantages in health among the votaries of fashion over those of study?
>
> Or, again, will he take an equal number of male students of similar scholastic standing with their female companions, and tell us how many of them are suffering from excessive nervousness, dyspepsia, and general loss of vitality[?] To judge from some of the

---

15. Lillie Devereux Blake (1833–1913) was a prolific fiction writer who was a leader in the suffrage movement in New York state and nationally.

hollow cheeked, pale, and miserable specimens of manhood one sees among every graduating class at our large colleges, it is high time that our boys as well as our girls had a "flexible system of study." (7)

In addition to questioning the logical connection between Clarke's observation of the similarities and differences between women and men and his exclusive focus on sick women in his book, Blake offered readers alternatives to Clarke's presentation of selected cases. In suggesting other forms his research could have taken—comparison to women who did not pursue extended education or to college men—Blake primed her readers to expect more valid comparisons in scientific studies.

One of the most forceful and comprehensive challenges to Clarke's reasoning appeared in George F. Comfort and Anna Manning Comfort's *Woman's Education and Woman's Health: Chiefly in Reply to "Sex in Education"* (1874). Comfort and Comfort charged Clarke with a number of errors in scientific and logical thinking, devoting an entire chapter in their book to "Wrong Reasoning." Their list of his errors included *a priori* reasoning, hasty generalizations based on insufficient evidence, ignoring the opinions of other experts, asserting the universality of physiology while admitting that not all women suffer as a result of defying its supposed laws, introducing irrelevant issues, contradicting his own argument, not taking into account all the likely causes of women's poor health, making false comparisons, and confusing correlation and causation (23–45; see also the similar list in Duffey 18; Jackson 153). In accumulating this extensive list of flaws in reasoning—errors that are, of course, not exclusively symptoms of poor scientific thinking, but errors that an ideal scientist would not succumb to—Comfort and Comfort taught other readers to expect logical reasoning from science-based rhetoric.

Continuing this line of criticism, in their next chapter, Comfort and Comfort faulted Clarke for a "lack of scientific precision" and for "tak[ing] positions which are greatly at variance with the latest well-established physiological principles" (46). For example, they observed that Clarke mischaracterized the development of female reproductive organs in stating that they "developed during the four or five years succeeding the commencement of . . . the catamenial function" instead of "during the few months, or at most a year or so preceding that event" (49). Such a difference in the physiological facts underlying Clarke's argument would change his advice for girls' schooling entirely. Comfort and Comfort pointed to several additional physiological errors they found in *Sex in Education*, including mischaracterizations of ovulation and menstruation and of the relationship between menstruation and "nervous power" (50–58). They argued that "the inexact language and the incorrect physiological statements of Dr. Clarke will greatly mislead the general reader. The erroneous impression thus produced will greatly favor his argument" (53–54). Comfort and Comfort identified inaccuracies and imprecisions in Clarke's argument that might yield rhetorical advantages when addressed to an uninformed audience. Comfort and Comfort corrected Clarke so that readers would see the flaws in his argument and reject his conclusions.

Not all of the commentary articulating rhetorical values for science in public discourse was hostile to Clarke. A writer for *The Boston Daily Globe*, for instance, defended Clarke's tone as appropriate for a physician and a scientist, even as he acknowledged that not all writers should be so direct:

> [Clarke], as a physician, has the right to be blunt, and he exercises this right to his readers as he would to his patients; but we, not having the right, can only refer our readers to his book, if they wish to learn indispensable truths in language which is indispensably close to facts. Plain speaking, in such a matter as this, is the peculiar privilege of scientific thinking; and what might be coarse in our statements is modest in the statements of Dr. Clarke. ("New Publications")

In this passage, the writer for the *Globe* asserted that the public should accept stylistic features in science-informed writing that they might not accept in other public discourse. Rather than being repulsed by any seeming vulgarity in Clarke's language, readers should perceive his language as "close to facts," as truer than polite language would have been. This writer maintained that "[p]lain speaking" was a right associated with "scientific thinking"—not with scientists themselves, but with the intellectual work of science. Finally, this writer suggested that decorum in language was relative, so *Sex in Education* should not be judged by the standards of ordinary usage. In fact, this writer admitted that efforts to convert Clarke's argument into modest language had failed: "We have tried various forms of rhetorical circumlocution, and have abandoned them in despair. We cannot say what he says . . . . He plants himself on physiological facts which are too modest to discuss, but which we hope that fathers and mothers of girls will duly weigh and appreciate." Science, it seems, offered knowledge that could not be discussed publicly according to the norms and values of most language use, but that all parents should access for the health of their daughters. Because *Sex in Education* framed the question of women's appropriate education as a matter dictated by their reproductive physiology, the discussion of Clarke's book necessarily involved terms and topics not usually considered polite.

In this sense, *Sex in Education* and its published reception introduced the public to specialized vocabulary and concepts that might not only be unfamiliar, but also uncomfortable, making the women's rights discussion a site for testing the public's tolerance for such technical discourse. Some writers, such as the author published in the *Globe*, insisted that Clarke's language was entirely appropriate, describing a rhetorical feature readers might expect from science writing, even when addressed to a non-professional audience.

The reception of *Sex in Education* featured respondents, particularly those opposed to Clarke's conclusions, articulating the rhetorical values that they believed readers should expect from invocations of science in public discussions. If the public were to use science to inform their collective decision-making, readers needed to know how to interpret findings and assess research methods. For audience members, like Clarke's opponents, who had not been served well by traditional patterns of authority and power, the emergence of science into public discourse presented an opportunity to identify new rhetorical resources that might support their efforts to claim new rights. The professional experience and expertise that Clarke relied on in *Sex in Education* was inaccessible to nearly all of the women who would be affected by his arguments about education and physiology. In contrast, arguments that highlighted the flaws in his reasoning, his limited sample size, and his failure to isolate education as the variable that caused women's poor health were manifestations of critical thinking that were available to non-professional readers, including women. It is, then, perhaps not surprising that most of the receptive rhetoric criticizing Clarke's science and articulating an alternative model of what readers should expect from science in the public sphere was produced by those who supported increased rights and opportunities for women.

THE INTERSECTION OF THE WOMAN QUESTION AND SCIENCE

As I noted in chapter one, in the preface to the first edition of *Sex in Education*, Clarke expressed his wish that his book would "excite discussion and stimulate investigation" (7); the voluminous published reception of *Sex in Education* demonstrates that Clarke succeeded in achieving this aim. Reception, however, often exceeds the scope of the original text, and contemporary commentators noted that the discussion surrounding *Sex in Education* had led to conclusions beyond those likely intended by Clarke. For example, *The Christian Union* recounted the major threads in the reception of *Sex in Education*, and then stated that Clarke himself might not have foreseen the consequences of the debate he had initiated:

> The sharpest critics concede the value of the work on scientific grounds, but insist that the Doctor's inferences from the facts he cites are far from justified, while the champions of the old ideas respecting "woman's sphere" appear to think he has conclusively shown the folly and the danger of sending girls to college to pursue the same course of study with boys . . . . We suspect that the thorough discussion evoked by Dr. Clarke's book will lead the public to a very different conclusion from that which he anticipated, serving to clear the way for the admission of girls to our colleges. ("Sex in Education"; see also Duffey 119)

The fact that this writer could suggest that Clarke himself might have misjudged the effect of *Sex in Education* points to the powerful role of reception as a rhetorical phenomenon affecting the meaning of all texts, but perhaps especially this text, for which so much—the overall argument, the evidence, the implications—was debated.

Although today we tend to see *Sex in Education* as a misogynistic text that used poor science to limit women's educational opportunities, audience members at the time it was published saw it in a variety of ways: as a text that used poor science to limit women's educational opportunities, as a text that used science productively to clarify the intractable social dilemma of women's education, as a text intent on preventing women's invalidism and infertility and thereby averting "race suicide," and as a text that might inadvertently improve women's access to education. The meaning of *Sex in Education* was not set with its publication; its interpretations and uses were negotiated through acts of reception.

The reviews and commentary appearing in the fifteen months after *Sex in Education* was first published demonstrate the tensions around the role of scientific discourse in public decision-making. As Condit observes, the public uses science for its own purposes, which are not necessarily those of professional scientists (12). If this is the case, then the public also has to work out its own scientific standards. Because science in the public sphere is not focused on discovery, but is instead deployed to decide social matters, public standards for science are inherently rhetorical standards. Although *science* as variously deployed by Clarke and his respondents was still a somewhat nebulous discourse and certainly did not consistently adhere to the principles of science as we understand it today, the debate over *Sex in Education* depended on, and in some cases sought to further, an epistemology that valued methodical observation, an objective relationship to the subject under study, the identification of facts and causal relationships, and a system of general laws predicting natural phenomena. The ability to claim to speak from a scientific standpoint (and to deride opponents as unscientific) constituted a significant rhetorical advantage. Even as respondents to *Sex in Education* sought to appear scientific and to shape the methodological and rhetorical features of public-facing science, some warned that science and the impressions it might make on readers offered persuasive powers possibly more significant than the facts, findings, and theories conventionally associated with the ideals of science.

Tracking the reception of *Sex in Education* reveals the role of science-based public discourse in the debate over women's rights. For some of Clarke's readers, science offered a way to resolve the woman question where religion, philosophy, and politics had failed. Because women's education was crucial to other rights and opportunities sought by women (including political rights and professional careers), scientific assessments of women's capacity for study permeated the nineteenth-century women's rights movement.

Of course, science had previously been used in the nineteenth century to justify limiting women's opportunities: women's smaller brains, their "overactive" nervous systems, and other supposedly objective biomedical observations were deployed to assert that women were not capable of extended education, careers, or public engagement. What the reception of *Sex in Education* highlights, however, is that the debate over women's rights intersected with the debate over the nature of science. These debates interconnected in the physiological definition of *woman* and her capabilities. Disproving the scientific findings that seemed to establish women's limitations required insisting on particular features of science: an objective stance; a methodology that could demonstrate causation, not just correlation; and meaningful sample sizes. Although it would no doubt be going too far to say that the public's expectations for science and scientists owe themselves to the women's rights debates spurred by *Sex in Education*, I believe it is plausible to say that the reception of *Sex in Education* participated in the development of science as an epistemology and a rhetorical resource for public decision-making. In other words, the women's rights movement did not just depend on and react to science-based assertions about women; the development of public-facing science as we know it today was also shaped by the women's rights movement.

Significantly, women—scientists and doctors as well as women who were not members of the scientific professions—actively participated in the articulation of rhetorical values for science in public decision-making that occurred through the reception of *Sex in Education*. Historical women are often cast as the victims of (masculine) science, and there is little doubt that women's traditional knowledge, skills, and autonomy were frequently dismissed by scientific professionals. Analysis of the reception of *Sex in Edu-*

cation, however, demonstrates that women were also active promoters of science-informed decision-making, and they participated in negotiating the rhetorical values that science should adhere to in public discourse. Women were not naïve in their acceptance of science as a rhetorical resource in collective decision-making, however. Even as some women called for more and better science to support public decision-making, others worried about the implications of greater reliance on science as a rhetorical resource.

As this study of the immediate public reception of *Sex in Education* demonstrates, feminist rhetorical reception studies offers important insights into rhetorical and social developments. For instance, we can see how intensely contested the book's claims were, an aspect of rhetorical history that would be elided through an exclusive focus on *Sex in Education* itself. We can see that the degree to which *Sex in Education* persuaded its audience—the archetypal purpose of rhetoric—was strongly influenced by factors out of Clarke's control, suggesting a less individualistic and rhetor-centered model for rhetorical action. We can also see the rhetorical processes that occurred alongside of the attempts at persuasion: the efforts to claim that one's position was more scientific than the opposition's, the demands for rigorous research methods, and the discussion of science as a rhetorical resource for public debates. These processes were pursued by men and women, complicating narratives that cast women as the victims of nineteenth-century science.

Notably for scholars of women's rhetoric, studying the reception of *Sex in Education* reveals the intersections between women's rights discourse and the emergence of science as a rhetorical resource for public debate. The reception of *Sex in Education* also demonstrates women's involvement in interpreting Clarke's argument for others, in articulating the values that would come to characterize science as a public rhetorical resource, and in advocating for the authority of alternative sets of expertise and experience (such as those of teachers and mothers) in public decision-making. In sum, this chapter has shown that feminist rhetorical reception studies is necessary for identifying a fuller range of rhetorical activity by women, for understanding how rhetoric works in society in a sense much broader than persuasion or achieving the rhetor's purpose, and for tracking rhetorical processes (like the invocation of science) that affect constructions of gender and, therefore, the rights and opportunities available to all of us.

3 The Construction of Professionalism in the Reception of *Sex in Education*

In September 1874, the medical journal *Cincinnati Lancet and Observer* noted that Edward H. Clarke's *Sex in Education* had "attracted a great deal of attention and criticism both from the [medical] profession and those engaged in education" ("Reviews and Notices" 569). Indeed, given Clarke's reliance on his knowledge of female reproductive physiology and the implications of his claims for pedagogy and systems of education, it is easy to understand physicians' and teachers' interest in Clarke's work. These two fields may also have been especially interested in *Sex in Education* because they attracted the greatest numbers of women practitioners of any nineteenth-century professions (Morantz-Sanchez, *Sympathy* 50). The professional discussion around *Sex in Education*, however, went well beyond a debate over Clarke's argument. Instead of limiting themselves to confirming or refuting Clarke's claims, teachers and physicians used the controversy around the book as an opportunity to articulate the values and characteristics of science-informed professionalism in education and medicine, often calling on their colleagues to pursue actions that they believed would enhance the standing and authority of their respective fields.

According to historian Corinne Lathrop Gilb, efforts to organize state and national professional societies reached a high point in the 1870s (28), just as *Sex in Education* was being debated.[1] It is important to note that professionalization did not evolve uniformly; consequently, "country doctors" practiced at the same time as early scientific physicians and teenaged girls who committed to teaching only as a short-term job worked at the same time as college-educated women who saw teaching as a career. Reflecting the still-emergent nature of professionalism at the time, the reception of *Sex*

---

1. In *The Culture of Professionalism*, Burton J. Bledstein traces the foundation of numerous professional societies and credentialling processes (including higher education) in the nineteenth-century US. He reports significant increases in the number of professional schools in the last quarter of the century, and he identifies ten medical specialty societies founded between 1864 and 1888 (84–85). Bledstein discusses the founding of the institutions in the context of the science-informed, meritocratic "culture of professionalism" that justified the professional's status and authority.

in Education in medicine and education served as a site for articulating professional priorities, authority, and epistemology for these fields.

Historians and sociologists of science have long noted that the emerging professions defined themselves as masculine. For example, Tracey Lynn Adams finds gender, race, and professionalism near the turn of the century to be intertwined: "gender relations and ideas about gender came to infuse the very definition of professions. Male-dominated professions were defined *by* middle-class white men, *for* middle-class white men" (4). The characteristics that typically defined the professions were associated with masculinity in the nineteenth-century US: autonomy (as individual practitioners and as a profession free of public oversight), specialized (often monopolized) knowledge, and extended education resulting in certification, as well as social power and authority (Morantz-Sanchez, *Sympathy* 355–56). Not coincidentally, at the same time as the professions were defining themselves along masculine lines, the professions (especially medicine) were also defining what it meant to be men and women.

The distinction between sex (the biological and physiological characteristics of males and females) and gender (the socially constructed roles of men and women) that would become common by the late twentieth century was not part of medicine's discourse, which largely assumed that women's and men's social roles were natural expressions of their anatomy and physiology. This is not to say, however, that all physicians perceived sex and the related social roles to be immutable; in fact, their mutability was believed to be dangerous, so it was used to reinforce gender expectations. Clarke himself asserted that if reproductive development were interrupted (as a woman's might be through intense study), the result would be physical and social expressions that merged masculinity and femininity as they were understood in the nineteenth-century US:

> When this sort of arrest of development occurs in a man, it takes the element of masculineness out of him, and replaces it with adipose effeminacy. When it occurs in a woman, it not only substitutes in her case a wiry and perhaps thin bearded masculineness for distinctive feminine traits and power, making her an epicene [one of indeterminate sex], but it entails a variety of prolonged weaknesses, that dwarf her rightful power in almost every direction. (44)

Although Clarke did not distinguish between gender and sex, he did see gender/sex as mutable, and he viewed variation from conventional masculinity and femininity as harmful, both physically and socially.

In fact, Clarke's belief that gendered behavior could influence one's sexual characteristics comes close to recent theorizations that unsettle the notion that biological sex precedes gendered social constructs. Kristan Poirot observes that sex is rhetorical just as gender is (14). She explains how the rhetoricity of sex was key to nineteenth-century American women's activism: "it is difficult, if not impossible, to separate the cult of true womanhood from biological notions of sexual difference.... The emphasis on purity, submissiveness, and domesticity was directly tied to the anatomy of reproduction, for example, grounding gendered womanhood in biologically sexed distinctions" (33).[2] In a similar vein, Mara Viveros Vigoya identifies the role that the biological sciences have played in asserting that there are two sexes and that gender socialization follows from sex designation. In contrast, she argues, "Gender constructs sex, a process that is masked by a sex/gender opposition based on the nature/culture opposition, which sciences like biology have contributed to producing and reproducing" (859). Nineteenth-century US physicians participated in this phenomenon, frequently using their biological expertise to weigh in on social questions around women's rights and capabilities. In fact, the rise of science and professionalism in the nineteenth-century US offered an alternative to (and for some, an extension of) the religious explanation for supposedly inherent masculine and feminine roles: nature, in the form of human biology, dictated that females act like women and that males act like men (Rowold xvi).

The work of physiologically describing human females/women and learning how to treat perceived female pathologies medically and surgically coincided with medicine's efforts to professionalize.[3] Although the description of professionalization as a process of excluding women (as well as members of minoritized racial groups and the working class) through aligning *professionalism* with *elite white masculinity* is helpful in understanding the ways the professions accumulated and protected their power in the late nineteenth and early twentieth centuries, such an explanation needs to account for the fact that professions like medicine were determining women's "nature" and capabilities at the same time that they were articulating the features of their own profession in alignment with masculinity. As this chapter demonstrates, these rhetorical processes did not always smoothly coincide to exclude women from the professions.

Furthermore, the explanation that professionalization primarily involved adopting supposedly masculine characteristics assumes that professionalization was a force affecting only men (Brumberg and Tomes 275–76). In

---

2. Poirot goes on to discuss "the ways biology, roles, and capacities were linked differently when articulated in terms of the [B]lack body" (33), reflecting the ways that race intersects with notions of sex and gender.

3. For this history, see Morantz-Sanchez (*Conduct* 88–137).

fact, as Joan Jacobs Brumberg and Nancy Tomes observe, scholarship that categorizes nineteenth-century women as either domestic "ladies" or as working-class "mill girls" overlooks the substantial number of middle-class women who pursued careers in feminized service professions like teaching, nursing, social work, and librarianship due to economic necessity or as protection against future financial hardship (279). Brumberg and Tomes go on to assert that the need to prepare young women to support themselves was frequently invoked to justify extending women's education, resulting in a substantial increase in women's literacy and education levels, ultimately changing the qualifications employers could expect of job candidates (279). In the context of the *Sex in Education* debate, we can see these trends toward increased educational and career attainment for women coinciding with anxiety about the consequences of education and professional careers for women, with women teachers and physicians participating in and subject to the processes of defining *woman* and *professional*.

Clarke's reliance on his own scientific-professionalism to condemn extended education for women makes the reception of *Sex in Education* a particularly useful site for exploring the interrelations between the constructions of professionalism and gender in the late-nineteenth-century US. Even in a conventionally masculine field like medicine, the professional values that emerged in the reception of *Sex in Education* often suggested the potential for greater access to education and to the professions for women. The analysis in this chapter reveals that the development of the professions involved not simply a process of reifying existing masculine characteristics and expunging feminine characteristics from the ideal of the professional. It also involved continuing to insist on the masculinity of the professional despite material, epistemic, and discursive changes that had the potential to make the professions more welcoming to women.

Professionalism is constructed rhetorically, just as gender is. Adams identifies the overtly persuasive work involved in the emergence of the professions: "professionalization can be seen as the process through which a group of practitioners strives to define their occupation as a profession—that is, how they go about convincing the public, the state, and other professions that their occupation is deserving of professional status and privileges" (6). In analyzing the reception of *Sex in Education* as a collective of rhetorical acts through which medicine and education demarcated professional boundaries, described ideal professional characteristics, and accrued professional status and authority, I respond to Sarah Hallenbeck and Michelle Smith's call for studies of "work-related rhetorics" that "would consider the rhetorical positioning of work itself" (200). The complex issues addressed in the professional reception of *Sex in Education*—including research standards, rhetorical values, professional autonomy, and the compatibility of *woman* with expertise and professional practice—demonstrate that studies of reception can be used to track how the professions developed. In the case of *Sex in Education*, the book's reception did far more to articulate professional values and expectations than the book itself did—famous as it was.

In this chapter, I first examine how medical leaders—journal editors and contributors as well as prominent physicians—received *Sex in Education* in its journals; I also discuss Mary Putnam Jacobi's prize-winning thesis *The Question of Rest for Women During Menstruation*. Medicine used the occasion of *Sex in Education* as an opportunity to articulate emerging values for research, primarily through critiques of Clarke's methods; these new research standards ultimately undermined the conventional model of femininity that Clarke's argument both relied on and reinforced. In other words, in striving to be more professional, medicine prioritized values, particularly objectivity, universal (rather than local) knowledge, and an unadorned writing style, that produced scholarship demonstrating that women were capable of extended education and professional work.

Then I consider how leaders in education—including college presidents and directors, journal editors, and educational reformers—responded to Clarke's work in professional venues. I include in this discussion Clarke's sequel to *Sex in Education*, titled *The Building of a Brain* (1874), which was based on his 1874 invited address to the National Educational Association meeting in Detroit. Educators referred to *Sex in Education* to justify their concerns about working conditions and practitioner autonomy, to call for professional unity around the "science" of education, and to highlight the importance of college education for women who wanted to become teachers. In other words, educators invoked Clarke alongside their calls for improved professional autonomy and credentials for primary and secondary school teachers, most of whom were women. I conclude this chapter by considering what the professional conversations around *Sex in Education* reveal about the rhetorical processes of professionalization and of gendering women as students and as professionals.

MEDICINE'S RECEPTION OF *SEX IN EDUCATION*

Around the time Clarke published *Sex in Education* in 1873, the profession of medicine was, as historian of medicine Charles E. Rosenberg characterizes it, "very much between two worlds, one of traditional medical practice and one of the twentieth century with its new ideas, institutions, and modes of therapeutics" (22). Rosenberg explains that, in 1879,

> The average medical man still practiced much as he had in past generations. He saw patients in their homes or in his office and submitted bills to his "families" at leisurely intervals. He treated children and adults, delivered babies, lanced boils, and set broken bones. But the bulk of his therapeutics consisted, as it had for centuries, of the administration of drugs and the dissemination of reassuring words. (22)

At the same time, however, elite urban physicians were developing a different approach to medical education and practice, one that "emphasized the practice of medicine in an institutional setting, specialism, systematic clinical observation, and publication" (24). Medicine's concept of disease had not yet incorporated a robust understanding of bacteriology: "Many physicians ... still found it natural to believe that one disease could transform itself into another and that undesirable environmental conditions could—of themselves—breed sickness" (28). For many physicians and patients alike, experience with a family or a particular region's climate was more valuable than scientific expertise. Instead of identifying and treating a specific and universal cause for a particular illness, physicians often relied on their judgment, decision-making skills, relationships with their patients, and moral authority to prevent and treat illness (Morantz-Sanchez, *Conduct* 97–98).

According to Rosenberg, the content of medical journals in the late 1870s reflected the minimal impact of laboratory science on the field's thought:

> Even the most intellectually exacting of the clinical journals found little space in their pages for articles on the laboratory sciences. . . . The great majority of the journal literature still consisted of case reports (albeit increasingly in the specialties), essays of clinical reflection and speculation, and transcriptions of clinical lectures at the nation's leading hospitals and medical schools. (29–30)

Clarke's approach in *Sex in Education*, with its review of physiological principles and report of seven clinical cases, aligned with medical scholarship of the time as Rosenberg describes it. Moreover, the substantial attention the book received in professional venues, despite the fact that Clarke had addressed *Sex in Education* not to his colleagues but to a popular audience, reflected the still-permeable boundary between professional and nonprofessional at the time.

Several medical journals published approving reviews of *Sex in Education*. Many of them confirmed Clarke's description of female physiology and of women's social roles, which they saw as natural extensions of their physiology. For example, one review that expressed satisfaction with Clarke's use of science to support his claims about the risks of co-education appeared in December 1873 in the *Cincinnati Lancet and Observer*. The main argument of *Sex in Education* was, the review asserted, "abundantly fortified by physiological, clinical, and general illustrations and arguments" (J.B.H. 767). Other positive reviews suggested that Clarke's introduction of physiology into the public discussion had created an opportunity for physicians to assert themselves in the women's rights debate. For example, a review of *Sex in Education* published in December 1873 in the *Philadelphia Medical Times* by S.W.M.[4] claimed that American "prudishness" around reproduction "has interfered with the frank admission of the relations of sex to business or professional life, and even to education." This reluctance to mention women's reproductive potential had, the reviewer stated, skewed public discussions of women's capabilities: "Hence it is that all sorts of absurd discussions upon these matters go on daily in our [popular] periodicals, with so little allusion to the sexual difference and its consequences that one might well suppose we were merely arguing upon the relative capacities of two tribes of males" (156–57). S.W.M. credited Clarke for insisting that the public always remember "that girls menstruate, and that, as the real purpose of women is to have healthy babies healthfully, . . . whatever interferes with these ends is wrong in principle" (157). This reviewer appreciated Clarke's direct talk about female reproductive physiology because it corrected the public discussion, which had so far lacked that component. Shifting the "woman question" to physiology and tying a woman's capabilities entirely to her reproductive potential authorized the physician to take on an authoritative role in public discussions of women's education and occupation.[5]

Although some commentary on *Sex in Education* praised its science and its argument, several writers either challenged the rigor of Clarke's evidence or cited observations that contradicted Clarke's claims. As I demonstrated in chapter two, the public debate immediately following the publication of *Sex in Education* also involved questions about the quality of its science.

---

4. Silas Weir Mitchell, promoter of the "Rest Cure," practiced medicine in Philadelphia, so it is possible that he is the "S.W.M." who wrote this review.

5. Practitioners of "irregular" medical approaches were more likely to question Clarke's conclusions than so-called "allopathic" physicians were. This difference in perspective might reflect a difference in professional standpoint; practitioners of homeopathy, for instance, tended to be more accepting of women as physicians (C. Skinner, *Women Physicians* 141). For an example of a homeopathic response to Clarke's claims, see K.N.D.'s review of *Sex in Education* (1874). Hydrotherapist Russell Trall (1875) challenged Clarke's science, as did the writer for the *Medical Eclectic* (eclectic medicine was a branch of medicine that practiced noninvasive, botanical treatments) who wrote "Liberal Learning and Long Life" (1875).

In the context of intra-professional conversations, however, questions about what kinds of evidence counted as persuasive were also questions about the nature of the medical profession: would the field require objective data that controlled for variables other than the issue under study, or would it rely primarily on the experiential authority of its practitioners? Some of the more scientifically inclined physicians used their reception of *Sex in Education* to propose that medical decisions should be based on statistical data sets rather than on more idiosyncratic forms of evidence.

Such a position was articulated by the *Medical News* in 1882 in response to a circular, based on Dr. Adaline S. Whitney's paper "Physical Education for Women," published by the Association of Collegiate Alumnæ (ACA), the precursor to the American Association of University Women (AAUW). The circular reported on the physical education programs offered by colleges that enrolled women and criticized institutions that lacked such programs.[6] The *Medical News* approved of the ACA's project, calling it "a capital work," and appreciated its contribution to the debate over women's education: "It has been asserted again and again that girls cannot pursue a thorough college course, and yet enter womanhood physically fitted for the burdens of life, especially those of the mother and the housekeeper. Dr. Clarke, Dr. Goodell, and many another have pointed to 'Vassar Victims,' as examples of what ruin such an education will work" ("The Physical Education of Female College Students" 437). This writer believed that in order to decide the question, however, "It is of the greatest importance for us as a people to know definitely the facts in the case—not the isolated uncoördinated facts as to this girl or that, or even this college or that, but *all* the facts, from as large an area of country, and as large a number of colleges, and as large a number of women as possible" (437). Importantly, in addition to implicitly dismissing Clarke's evidence drawn from seven clinical cases ("the isolated . . . facts as to this girl or that"), the *Medical News* advocated a national view of medicine (in calling for data from a large area of the country), manifesting the profession's move away from medical practice based on the maladies believed to be associated with particular locations. The knowledge that this writer dismissed was experiential, not experimental. In contrast, a national (or even universal) view of medicine explained disease not as resulting from local conditions or climates, but from common causes across locations: the bacterium that caused cholera in New Orleans was the same bacterium that caused cholera in a small town in Ohio; a nutritional deficiency in one city would result in the same symptoms as the same deficiency in another city.

---

6. This study eventually led to a survey (which I discuss below) investigating the health of women college graduates. For more on the ACA's early research agenda, see chapter VIII of Talbot and Rosenberry.

Although the *Medical News* advocated what it called "broad truth" in explaining medical conditions, it acknowledged that the profession had not yet accumulated enough of that kind of knowledge: "Truth, broad truth is what we should seek. Individual experience is apt to be very erroneous; only large numbers eliminate errors. But until facts based on such numbers are forthcoming, each of us must use his own or his neighbor's personal experience as the best, and indeed the only guide" (438). In admiring the ACA's study, the *Medical News* supported the medical profession's shift toward statistical evidence and away from local expertise, but it also suggested that physicians had to rely on local expertise until it could be replaced by the new epistemology. However, in praising the ACA's survey method and in positioning it as a corrective to Clarke's account of "Vassar Victims," the *Medical News* also endorsed the study's assertion that women could succeed in college and maintain their health if physical education were part of the curriculum. In these receptive acts, the *Medical News* advocated statistical research, an objective research stance, and a universal approach to medicine, which cumulatively suggested support for greater opportunities for women.

In addition to finding fault with the science on which *Sex in Education* was based, some reviewers criticized Clarke for what they perceived to be an unprofessional writing style. For example, R.B., reviewing *Sex in Education* in 1874 for *The Clinic* of Cincinnati, Ohio, asserted that "A work which treats of so important a subject as 'Sex in Education' . . . should be executed with candor and with scientific accuracy and fairness" (9); in other words, physicians should adopt a professional style, especially when addressing vital topics. R.B. maintained that Clarke had not met this standard:

> [W]e must question the . . . propriety of the manner in which he has seen fit to convey [his statements] to the public. . . . Moreover, he has adopted a pertness and flippancy of style, and exhibits feats of acrobatic verbiage, out of place, as we conceive, in the discussion of such a subject. Much of the real force of his argument is concealed in its harlequin's dress. If the truth be as alleged by Dr. Clarke[,] its importance is so transcendent that any tricks of rhetoric, only excite the indignation of the reader. (9)

Rhetoric has long been associated with seduction; R.B.'s distinction between Clarke's argument and his "rhetoric" and the linkage between Clarke's rhetoric and the "harlequin's dress" fit into that tradition. In asserting that medical writing should be free of "tricks of rhetoric," R.B. articulated a rhetorical value for the medical profession. Later in the review, R.B. identified some of Clarke's "embellished" phrases, including "the periodical tides of her organisation," the "sluices of the system," the "neuralgic friction of an imperfectly developed reproductive apparatus," "the engine within an engine," and "an abnormal method of work may and does open the floodgates of the system, and by letting the blood out, lets all sorts of evil in" (9). Because what R.B. described as Clarke's "pertness and flippancy of style" involved language choices that mechanized reproductive processes, exaggerated the lived experience of menstruation, and characterized women as victims of their physiology, in advocating "candor[,] . . . scientific accuracy[,] and fairness" in medical writing, R.B. (intentionally or not) called for a writing style that, in addition to reinforcing medicine's professional status, also had the potential to foster discussions that did not automatically pathologize women.

R.B. went on to assert that "The pathological examples which Dr. Clarke brings forward, to prove his postulate and to enforce his warnings, seem to us singularly inappropriate. He ascribes to educational methods what may be the product of congenital defect, vice of constitution, bad hygiene, or evil habits" (10). R.B. complained that "Dr. Clarke does not stop to eliminate any of these causes of diseases in the cases which he presents for illustration; and his clinical reports strongly suggest that some or all of these causes were influential in producing the sad results which he has chronicled" (10). The alternative causes of ill health that Clarke had not ruled out were not necessarily related to female reproductive physiology; if they were proven to cause women's disease, instead of continuous education, then Clarke's call to restrict women's and girls' education would be invalid. In observing that Clarke had not controlled for all the other variables that could have affected his patients' health, R.B. demanded a different standard of evidence: the physician's instincts were not sufficient; a more rigorous process of ruling out causes was required.

R.B. even pointed to laboratory experiments to support a claim at odds with Clarke's:

> In the *normal state*, girls have a greater power of physical endurance and . . . have less [sic] demands made upon the central nervous system by the evolution of the sexual organs than boys. This statement is susceptible of proof. . . . In his recent ingenious work on "Animal Mechanics," Prof. Houghton states (p. 3) that he has "found by direct experiment, that the muscles of women are capable of longer continued work than those of men, although inferior to them in force exerted for a short time." (9–10)

In contrast to Clarke's observational evidence, R.B. cited "mathematical demonstration" and "direct experiment" to support the claim that menstruation did not pose an undue burden on women (10). In challenging

Clarke, R.B. suggested not only alternative answers to the question of men's and women's "power of physical endurance" (9) but also alternative research methods for learning about the capabilities of women. R.B.'s review of *Sex in Education* thus incorporated an articulation of professional epistemological and discursive values for medicine, including controlling for the variables under discussion, preferring conclusions drawn from laboratory research over those drawn from observation, and a professional, straightforward writing style.

Despite an extensive critique of how Clarke derived and presented his conclusions, R.B. still agreed with Clarke that "the co-education of the sexes does not and cannot produce good results" (9), suggesting that even as R.B. advocated a more rigorous science for medicine, the writer still perceived the incompatibility of women and co-education to be so obvious that it was true even if Clarke's evidence did not prove it. R.B's stance demonstrates the complexity of the interconnections between gender and professionalization. Although medicine's movements into laboratories and hospitals and away from the home and toward objectivity and away from personal experience were, by some measures, movements toward masculinity and the exclusion of women from the profession (Adams 4; Morantz-Sanchez, *Sympathy* 355–56), some of the shifts underway in medicine in fact had the potential to crack open conventional constructions of gender, possibly opening opportunities to women (Morantz-Sanchez, *Sympathy* 31–32; C. Skinner, *Women Physicians* 16). Despite that potential, nineteenth-century gender constructs were persistent, leading physicians like R.B. to "know" what was good for women even as emerging professional values challenged that knowledge.

The tensions between constructions of gender and of medical professionalism were especially pronounced in the work of women physicians.[7] The most substantial medical-scientific rebuttal of *Sex in Education* was

---

7. Although many women physicians, including Susanna Way Dodds, Anna Manning Comfort, and Mary Putnam Jacobi, roundly criticized *Sex in Education*, a notable exception was Marie Zakrzewska, who stated that she held "substantially the same views" as Clarke and announced that she and the other "women physicians of the New England Hospital for Women and Children, are very grateful to Dr. Clarke for having taken the first step toward this very important and necessary part of education." Clarke and Zakrzewska crossed paths throughout their careers. It seems that Zakrzewska assisted Clarke when he traveled to Europe to extend his medical education (Zakrzewska was head midwife at the Charité in Berlin at the time); they shared a commitment to "rational therapeutics," or scientific medicine; Clarke referred patients to Zakrzewska when she moved to Boston as a physician; and he served on the consulting staff of the New England Hospital, founded by Zakrzewska, beginning the same year he published *Sex in Education* (Tuchman 173–74).

The Question of Rest for Women During Menstruation, a study published by Mary Putnam Jacobi (Professor of Materia Medica at the Woman's Medical College in New York) in 1877. *The Question of Rest* had its origins in Harvard's annual Boylston Prize competition for the best medical essay. In 1876, the prize committee called for essays that responded to the question, "Do women require mental and bodily rest during menstruation; and to what extent?" (qtd. in Bittel 126). According to Carla Bittel, the committee, which was made up of prestigious physicians, wanted to invite further medical research on the topic because members had doubts about the medical-scientific quality of Clarke's work (126). In particular, "they welcomed other studies that were done 'dispassionately' and with 'statistics' to support their assertions" (126–27). Jacobi submitted (anonymously, to disguise her gender) just such a study, one that also happened to disprove Clarke's conclusions, and *The Question of Rest* was selected as the winning essay.[8]

Jacobi relied on multiple forms of evidence in *The Question of Rest*: she surveyed 268 women (27), whom she described as entering her study "at hazard" (58) and who responded anonymously (27); she tested three theories of menstruation by analyzing previous scholarship (Section III); and she collected biometric measures (including pulse, temperature, and arterial tension) to identify patterns in physiology throughout the menstrual cycle. Jacobi's recognition by the Boylston Prize Committee suggests that her ambitious research methodology was perceived to be more "scientific" than Clarke's reports of seven cases, his description of one theory of female reproductive development, and his reports on how Europeans managed women's education. The contrast between Clarke's and Jacobi's approaches to their topic—supporting a predetermined stance with anecdotal and moral evidence on one hand and proposing and testing a hypothesis on the other hand—reflected different orientations to the role of medical researcher. Importantly, Jacobi's approach, endorsed by the Boylston Prize Committee, also suggested that long-held beliefs could be subject to proof. Even women's social roles and physical capabilities could be tested and measured.[9]

---

8. When Jacobi published *The Question of Rest* in 1877, she caused a bit of intraprofessional consternation because she "neglected to include the required disclaimer . . . , that the [Boylston] committee did not 'approv[e] the doctrines contained in any of the dissertations'" (Bittel 128). Consequently, it appeared that the committee (and by extension, Harvard, where Clarke had been a longstanding member of the medical faculty) supported her denunciation of Clarke's work. Although the Boylston Committee awarded its prize to Jacobi, Harvard did not admit women to its medical school until 1945.

9. For more on how Jacobi challenged existing scientific writing conventions by including women's own words in her reporting on her survey results, see Wells (146–92).

From the statistics generated by her survey, Jacobi concluded that "As regards rest—the most important question for our purpose—we have seen that the above data do not suffice to inform us of its influence. We can only assert negatively, that in a large proportion of cases it has been quite superfluous" (62–63). Based on her study of three competing theories of menstruation, Jacobi argued that the menstrual cycle is gradual and continuous, not abruptly "periodical" as Clarke had claimed (130). She concluded that "*reproduction in the human female is not intermittent, but incessant, not periodical, but rhythmic, not dependent on the volitions of animal life, but as involuntary and inevitable as are all the phenomena of nutritive life*" (165). This finding directly refuted the model of menstruation that Clarke used as the basis for his advice to young women, their parents, their teachers, and their doctors. As a multi-layered instance of the reception of *Sex in Education* (including the call for essays on the topic, *The Question of Rest* itself, and the committee's decision to award the Boylston Prize to Jacobi), the research, writing, and publication of *The Question of Rest* demonstrates that the professional reception of Clarke's book involved competing notions of what constituted "good" medical research and writing, notions that were entangled with questions of women's capabilities as students and as medical professionals themselves.

THE DURABILITY OF CONVENTIONAL MEDICAL IDEAS ABOUT WOMEN

Despite Jacobi's research rebutting Clarke's arguments and the widespread professional criticism of *Sex in Education*, high-profile physicians still promoted the idea that women required rest during menstruation and that education could threaten their health and the health of future generations. It is not surprising that physicians did not immediately change their views of women's biological capabilities, just as they did not instantly adopt the scientific approach to medicine that would later dominate the field. Especially in a context of increased immigration, decreasing fertility rates among white middle-class women,[10] and a Darwinist (and often social Darwinist) outlook, physicians like Clarke understood their professional duty to

10. Louise Michele Newman observes that late nineteenth-century Americans were correct in their belief that the birth rate, especially among well-educated middle-class women, was lower than in the past. Their perception that fertility had begun to decline around 1860, however, was incorrect, as families had been gradually shrinking since at least 1790 (*Men's Ideas* 106). Despite the existence of census data depicting a long-term decline in birthrates, Americans did not express concern until the late nineteenth century, in the context of increases in immigra-

include ensuring the continued survival and "progress" of the white middle class that most prominent medical men represented.

Clarke's argument was remarkably long-lived in medical publications. For example, in 1880, textbook authors Thomas Addis Emmet (*The Principles and Practice of Gynæcology*) and William Goodell (*Lessons in Gynecology*) cited Clarke approvingly and taught medical students and practitioners that women required rest during menstruation. And as late as 1904, an editorial in the *Medical Record* asked, "Is a collegiate training harmful to women?" The response to this question cited Clarke, evincing no awareness of the challenges to his research. Instead, the editorial presented Clarke's argument as professional consensus: "The majority of medical men are of the opinion . . . that co-education is harmful to women—and hold the view that women are not fitted physically for the strain put upon them by strenuous professional or business careers" ("Collegiate Training of Women" 17). Despite acknowledging the rumor that *Sex in Education* had been written in part to support Harvard's decision not to admit women, the writer seemed unbothered by this possible unscientific motive and went on to reinforce conventional notions of women's roles. The editorial concluded by asserting that "The ordinary woman's true place is her home, and by far her most important duty to the race and to the State is the bearing and bringing up of children. Her educational training should at least not unfit her for the proper performance of this essential service" (18). Despite the questions raised about Clarke's objectivity and the validity of relying on a handful of cases to support his claims as well as the research findings produced by Jacobi and others who refuted Clarke, many in the medical profession still adhered to traditional views of women and of physicians as professionals.

The ease with which at least some physicians seemed to have ignored the challenges to Clarke's arguments and research methods suggests the intersecting resiliency of the concept of *woman* as a perpetual patient and of the physician as one whose authority was drawn from experience and morality rather than from scientific expertise. The way that medicine easily fell back on ideas about *woman* that were not supported by the evidence emerging from the new scientific model of medicine is a wrinkle in the accepted description of the process of professionalization as a process of excluding women through connecting masculinity and science with professionalism. As this analysis of the reception of *Sex in Education* makes clear, at least some of the features associated with the emerging concept of professionalism, such as objectivity, quantitative research, and an unadorned or neutral

---

tion (and the observation that immigrant families had more children than "native-born American" families did) and in women's pursuit of college education (107).

writing style, actually created space for women in the professions. Although these and other features of medical professionalism have rightly been criticized for their hostility to women as both patients and practitioners, it seems at least as important that medicine insisted on a conventional construction of *woman* despite research findings, produced by emergent professional values, that supported increased opportunities for women.

The medical profession's reception of *Sex in Education* illustrates conflicting perspectives on gender and professionalization. On one hand, physicians roundly criticized Clarke's research method and advocated methods that they perceived to be more "scientific"; on the other hand, some physicians continued to assert traditional notions of women's capabilities, even, in some cases, after acknowledging the flaws in Clarke's research. This inconsistency is perhaps evidence of the uneven nature of medical professionalization, but it also highlights an intersecting factor—the resilience of conventional gender ideology. Attending to the reception of *Sex in Education*, including how long medical writers continued to cite it favorably, highlights the fact that medicine's process of professionalization was not only tied up in, but also sprang from, affected, and was hindered by, some physicians' adherence to a limited view of women.

BRIDGING MEDICINE AND EDUCATION: *THE BUILDING OF A BRAIN*

Professional reviews of *Sex in Education* immediately recognized that Clarke's arguments called for changes not only in how individual girls approached schooling (which might be the province of a physician advising a patient), but also in how schools themselves structured their time and their expectations for girls (a scope for medical work that involved advising not individuals, but institutions). Consequently, medical journals and conferences featured physicians referring to *Sex in Education* as they advised and criticized teachers and administrators who had not yet adapted to a physiological model of education (see, for example, Parvin; Payne). Schools were widely criticized in the nineteenth century for poor ventilation, insufficient lighting, and furniture that contributed to bad posture (see Enoch, *Domestic Occupations* 46–52 for an overview of such complaints). Physicians, then, were not alone in claiming that schools were bad for children's health. *Sex in Education*, however, prompted physicians to pay particular attention to not just the material features of schools but also their pedagogical practices. This focus directly addressed teachers' area of expertise in a way that criticisms of schools' physical features (which might result from poor funding or decisions by the community) did not.

Education, with its largely feminine cohort of practitioners who often did not expect to make a lifelong career of teaching, did not match the model of professionalism emerging in medicine, the sciences, and engineering. It is important to remember, however, that in the 1870s and 1880s, medicine itself was not yet a coherent and prestigious profession. Consequently, when physicians advised teachers and school administrators, that advice was part of medicine's effort to assert itself, to establish its authority, and to determine the scope of its own professionalism (Petrina). Unsurprisingly, most of the advice physicians gave to teachers constructed education as subordinate to and dependent on medicine; the predominance of men in medicine and of women in primary and secondary education no doubt played a role in medicine's attitude toward education.

The most extensive intervention by medicine into education in the *Sex in Education* debate and the clearest evidence of the permeability of the fields' professional boundaries was Clarke's sequel to *Sex in Education*, titled *The Building of a Brain*, published in 1874 (with three more editions by 1880). In April 1874, the Executive Committee of the National Education Association (NEA) invited Clarke to speak on the "Education of Girls" at its upcoming meeting in Detroit. Although Clarke said that when he published *Sex in Education*, "it was [his] intention not to publish any thing more upon that subject, but to leave it for educators to discuss" (*Building* 8), he accepted the invitation.

Rather than simply repeating material from *Sex in Education*, Clarke took the invitation from the NEA[11] as an opportunity to write a new book. Given that many in his audience were concerned with primary and secondary education, Clarke's speech understandably focused on the education of students who were younger and at a more preliminary educational level than the college students and working women referenced in *Sex in Education*. Because Clarke's rhetorical situation required him to adapt the arguments presented in *Sex in Education* to a new audience (who was certainly familiar with Clarke's first book) and a slightly different topic, *The Building of a Brain* constituted Clarke's own response to *Sex in Education*. In this way, Clarke's address to the NEA, and the extended version of his speech

---

11. The NEA had just recently been founded in 1870 upon the merging of the National Teachers Association, the National Association of School Superintendents, and the American Normal School Association.

appearing in *The Building of a Brain*,[12] participated in the reception of *Sex in Education*.

In his address to the NEA (as represented in *The Building of a Brain*), Clarke described his conception of education's duties, grounded firmly in an evolutionary outlook on humanity:

> Two problems are presented to our educators. The duties are, first, to secure the perpetuation of the race in America; and, secondly, to provide also for the survival of the fittest here. The problems are, first, to develop the individual to the highest degree; and, secondly, to obtain this development without interfering with the perpetuation of the best. In other words, humanity demands, and our education must give, both the highest development of the individual, and the perpetuation of individuals thus developed, or, as it is commonly expressed, the perpetuation of the fittest. (15)

Interestingly, and likely reflecting his professional commitments as a physician, Clarke's understanding of the work of education was more biological than intellectual, emotional, or interpersonal. He made no mention of teaching or learning; in place of those terms, Clarke foregrounded "the highest development of the individual," but only insofar as individual development did not hinder "the perpetuation of the fittest."

Education at the time, however, was not designed to promote "the perpetuation of the race," according to Clarke, because it focused on mental development at the expense of other bodily organs and systems. Clarke identified "a physiological error that has already been grafted into our system of education, and which exerts its most pernicious influence in our common and high schools; viz., the error of exclusively developing one part of the organization at the expense of and by ignoring the rest" (16). In characterizing education as responsible for the survival of (white) humanity, Clarke gave it scope over not just the students' minds, but also their bodies. This conceptualization of a teacher's responsibility constructed a broad purview for the profession of education, but it simultaneously maintained that teachers ought to heed the advice of physicians. In other words, Clarke constructed education as a profession with a great deal of responsibility and authority, yet one that was also dependent on the medical profession.

Clarke identified a specific field for education's work: "The building of a brain: this is to-day's social problem; and teachers are largely charged with

---

12. In addition to an expanded version of Clarke's NEA address, *The Building of a Brain* includes a chapter reporting statements from people and organizations who supported Clarke's position on girls' education and another chapter sharing observations of English schooling by "a careful observer" (145).

its solution" (21). Clarke defined education broadly, suggesting the field might claim a wide scope for its work: "In this essay let us remember that education is used not in the narrow sense of book-learning, or of school-training, but in its proper philosophical and physiological signification,—of all that training, alike of the brain and of the body, which yields the just and harmonious development of every organ" (26).[13] Education could not do this work alone, Clarke asserted: "physiology can render infinite service to education,—a service that the latter cannot afford to refuse" (29). Clarke's particular definition of education as brain development, rather than learning, grounded education in physiology and justified his concern with women's reproductive development: "the brain grows by taking part in and supervising the growth and function of every organ. If a single organ is wanting, or a single function not performed, just so much less brain development results" (35). If teachers wanted to succeed as educators, then, they needed to take into account their students' entire bodies, especially the relationship between the brain and the other organs.

Importantly for those interested in girls' and women's education, the reciprocity between the brain and the other organs meant that women could not reach their highest intellectual potential if they did not also develop "normal" reproductive functions: "In both [sexes], the normal development of an organ aids the normal growth of the brain, and the abnormal growth of an organ reflects its error back upon the brain" (50). Worse, young women who suffered because their reproductive systems had not been allowed to develop "normally" due to inappropriate educational methods would have less "nerve-force" to devote to learning:

---

13. This definition of education matches the definition Clarke provided in the preface to the fifth edition of *Sex in Education*, which he seems to have written to defend himself against criticisms that assumed Clarke wrote with a narrower focus on academics in mind:

> The attention of the reader is called to the definition of "education" on the twentieth page. It is there stated, that, throughout this essay, education is not used in the limited sense of mental or intellectual training alone, but as comprehending the whole manner of life, physical and psychical, during the educational period; that is . . . as comprehending instruction, discipline, manners, and habits. This, of course, includes home-life and social life, as well as school-life; balls and parties, as well as books and recitations; walking and riding, as much as studying and sewing . . . . These remarks may be unnecessary. They are made because some who have noticed this essay have spoken of it as if it treated only of the school, and seem to have forgotten the just and comprehensive signification in which education is used throughout this memoir. (9–10)

> It should not be forgotten . . . that the pain (dysmenorrhœa) by which Nature so often and so severely punishes a neglect of this function [menstruation] uses up, that is, spends, an amount of nerve-force in exact proportion to the pain endured; and that this nerve-force represents power withdrawn from the brain. If proper methods of education are devised which will not develop pain, there will be greater nerve-force at command for brain-work in adult life. (60)

Education, therefore, needed to allow time for the growth and development of the female reproductive system, which Clarke understood to be elaborate, intricate, and vital to the success of "the race." Education, in Clarke's description, was responsible not only for learning, but also for the nation's fertility: "Brains of highest worth must be built by an educational process that leaves men potential fathers, and women potential mothers" (64). Interestingly, in characterizing education as dependent on physiology (as provided by physicians), Clarke simultaneously envisioned a broad scope for professional educators' influence, across intellectual and physical development, encompassing not only the school years but also students' future reproductive potential. In some ways, the wide range of responsibility and authority Clarke imagined for teachers mirrored the capacious span of work that many physicians imagined for themselves. Clarke's choice to construct the professional work of education so broadly is especially notable given the increasing numbers of women making up the field, at least at the primary and secondary levels. Conventional narratives of "feminized" occupations tell stories of limited authority accessible to practitioners; in contrast, Clarke proposed a wide and important sphere of authority for teachers. However, the teacher's reliance on the physiologist and the physician for advice regarding the biological aspects of education was perhaps a reflection of Clarke's sense of the superiority both of medicine over education and of men over women.

In the rather unusual case of self-reception occurring in *The Building of a Brain*, Clarke built on the premise presented in *Sex in Education*—that physiology rather than philosophy should determine women's rights—to describe the teaching profession as expansive, yet dependent on medicine. The tendency for physicians to be men and teachers (especially of girls and young women, especially in primary schools, high schools, academies, and female seminaries) to be women doubtlessly influenced Clarke's vision of the relationship between the fields. At the same time, however, the gender dynamics evident in this act of reception are not entirely clear-cut. Clarke did not exclude women (of any age) from the labor or profession of education, even as he prescribed limited hours for girls and women as students (five; six if music were included [60–61]), who would presumably need an extended education to prepare them for their careers. In fact, the scope Clarke envisioned for a teacher's authority was actually quite broad for any professional, let alone a woman teacher. Even in the limited case of Clarke's reception of his own work, the entanglement of gender with professionalism and of medicine with education as co-emerging fields of authority is evident.

EDUCATION'S RECEPTION OF *SEX IN EDUCATION*

Education did not professionalize as rapidly as medicine did. As David Tyack and Elisabeth Hansot report, most teachers in the nineteenth century belonged to local women's teaching organizations, not to the more elite NEA that Clarke addressed (*Learning Together* 136). As late as the Progressive Era, "teachers . . . were self-consciously attempting to become professional, and to acquire all of the attributes and privileges that, to them, professionalism entailed" (Brown 47). As JoAnne Brown notes, as a profession, education did not compare favorably with medicine: "As aspiring professionals, educators stood in pathetic contrast to physicians and engineers, their accomplishments, methods, and institutions ridiculed and attacked wherever medicine and engineering were celebrated" (47). The fact that many teachers were women was used to justify education's lower status, and teachers lacked the autonomy and expertise conventionally associated with other professions: "Teaching at the turn of the century had none of the conventional attributes of a profession. Women's commitment to teaching as a career was low, if measured by their longevity in their jobs; teachers could claim as their own no specialized knowledge or training; salaries were low; and control of teachers' conduct was strict and resided outside the occupational community" (49). In the context of the reception of *Sex in Education*, responses to Clarke's book by educational leaders were no doubt shaped by readers' perceptions of education's claims to authority and expertise relative to medicine's.

Brumberg and Tomes warn us, however, that the model of the professionalization process based on the "masculine" professions is of limited use for understanding "feminized" fields: "the anomalous position of the so-called 'semiprofessions' simply cannot be explained in terms of the professional attributes women have individually or collectively failed to acquire. Rather the structuring of women's participation in the professional workforce must be seen as a complex process in which gender distinctions are an organizing principle" (287). For instance, Brumberg and Tomes suggest, many of the feminized "helping professions" such as teaching, nursing, and social work involve interacting closely with people; the inherent complexity of such interactions is incompatible with some features of idealized professionalism (such as focusing on abstract principles, performing objective research, and controlling one's working conditions). At the same time, the existence of these feminized, often subordinate, professions allowed the more prestigious, masculinized professions to develop exactly the features identified as "professional" because the existence of "a vast workforce of helpers, regarded as intellectually inferior but altruistically superior" freed those practitioners of "the 'dirtiest' aspects of professional service" (287–88). In other words, the "highest" professions achieved their professional status in part because of the existence of what are sometimes termed the "semiprofessions."

Education's response to *Sex in Education* was complicated by several factors, in addition to the field's tenuous claim to professionalism. First, secondary schools and colleges often depended on tuition from women for financial stability. Furthermore, the Morrill Land Grant Acts motivated many colleges to admit female students because of the belief that, as citizens, women had the right to attend public institutions.[14] In part because of limited opportunities for women, education programs in universities and stand-alone normal schools were among the highest-enrolled higher-education programs in the country. Indeed, according to Geraldine J. Clifford, women planning to teach were crucial to the expansion of higher education: "For decades, women . . . made the education field the largest program of study in American higher education, subsidizing its geographic and curricular sprawl" (xiii). Claims that women should limit their educations would put these institutions in financial and political jeopardy. Second, women made up a large proportion of education's practitioners, so they were implicated in arguments about women's ability to pursue extended education, which were also arguments about women's ability to prepare for and to pursue careers as teachers. The more girls attended school, the greater the demand for women, who were believed to provide a safe and feminine atmosphere for girl students, as teachers (Tyack and Hansot, *Learning To-*

---

14. According to the 1903 *Report of the Commissioner of Education*, "An added impulse was given to the movement for coeducation in colleges by the passage of the land-grant act of 1862 and the general recognition of woman's claim to participate in this bounty . . . . In the West the opening of colleges and universities to women went on without much comment or agitation, but conservative sentiment in the East was somewhat excited over the question" (liv–lv). Indeed, representatives of Midwestern and Western institutions often led the defense of collegiate co-education.

gether 49). The greater the demand for women teachers, the stronger the movement to open colleges to women became (R. Rosenberg xv). At the same time, men in education decried women teachers for "feminizing" the field, due to their short tenure (when they resigned, as required, upon marriage), their low salaries relative to men, and their supposed inability to provide appropriate discipline and training for boys and young men (Tyack and Hansot, *Learning Together* 160; 163; 145). Education's reception of *Sex in Education* reflected these intersecting pressures on the professionalization and gendering of teaching and learning.

Commentary on *Sex in Education* in education periodicals was initially positive and welcomed physicians' advice to teachers. For example, an editorial in *Massachusetts Teacher* titled "Problems and Their Solution" (1874) elaborated on the value of *Sex in Education* for teachers. The editor acknowledged that the book might make some parents anxious that their daughters were working too hard in school and that Clarke's argument was incompatible with existing educational models. The editor encouraged the readers of *Massachusetts Teacher* to give Clarke a fair hearing, however, noting that Clarke could have kept his ideas to himself for professional gain: "If the case be as Dr. Clarke has represented it to be, would not a selfish view of the matter prompt physicians to withhold the facts, that the continuance of a vicious system might create and perpetuate a profitable patronage? But, as philanthropists, we all have a common motive to seek the truth, and bring all our educational methods into harmony with it" (4–5). The inclusion of the teacher-readers of this editorial in the "we" who, alongside Clarke, sought the truth for the good of humanity, put teachers on par with the professional physician who had sacrificed potential profit for public good.

"Problems and Their Solution" went on to further characterize the relationship between the professions of medicine and education: "Does not the proper settlement of some of these questions require a conference between able representatives of the medical and teaching professions? Hitherto, there has been little else than antagonism of views between teachers and doctors; because one class has regarded the other in the light of opponents. Is there not a more excellent way?" (5). This suggestion, contrary to Clarke's vision of education as dependent on medical expertise, posited a more equal "conference between able representatives" of both fields. Just as in the medical responses to *Sex in Education*, the reception of Clarke's work in education served as an opportunity to envision professional status for the field.

Further articulating a model of professionalism for education, this editorial concluded by calling on readers to unite as a profession to resolve questions like the role of sex in education:

Such a condition of educational matters should awaken educators to unusual earnestness, and incline them to united conference, for the purpose of reaching agreement on points of such vital importance that without harmony of action upon them the work of our schools must be to a large degree desultory . . . . The presidents and professors in our colleges should unite with the teachers of the public schools in a common effort to reach the wisest conclusions in regard to all these questions at issue. (5–6)

Professions are typically understood to "stress the application of special knowledge requiring long training, the exercise of discretion, and a commitment to some kind of standard to which the pursuit of self-interest is subordinated" (Gilb 27). In "Problems and Their Solution," a review of *Sex in Education* served as a site in which to promote these professional features within education.

Some educational commentators referred to *Sex in Education* to justify their concerns about conditions in the field. For example, Edine T. Howard asked her audience at the American Institute of Instruction in 1878, "Are examinations, either of teachers or pupils, as at present conducted, productive of good or evil?" (41). After quoting *Sex in Education* at length, Howard observed that the age that Clarke identified as requiring the most "physiological cell change and growth" in girls (Clarke 54)—fourteen to eighteen—"is the very time when [a girl] is expected to enter the Normal college to prepare for the teacher's duties, and when her powers are taxed to the very utmost to meet the requirements of her examination" (Howard 43). Some school districts required what Howard perceived to be excessive evidence of their teachers' professional preparation, all of which Howard feared would damage their health: "If the preliminary work for a teacher's first examination has already deranged her whole mental and nervous organization, what becomes of her fitness to enter upon what may be a life-work, or where is she to get the strength to pursue the study necessary for a second or even a third [examination], as I understand is the case in some school-districts?" (45). Howard believed that Clarke's thesis supported her argument that the preparation and qualification process for women teachers, much of which was dictated by school districts, not by institutions established and controlled by the teaching profession itself, demanded too much from young women, physically and mentally.

If the teachers' own testing did not exhaust them, the pressure of preparing their students to succeed in their public examinations surely would: "And how will it be possible for her to bear the wear and tear of the constant examinations to which the classes put under her charge will be subjected,—examinations on whose success her own reputation in the profession depends?" (45). Complaining about "show schools" that privileged public performance and that might "use up a set of teachers in three years" (45), Howard relied on Clarke to argue that the existing model of educational professionalism was harmful to young women. Locating the authority to determine which students had succeeded with the audience at the public examinations rather than with the classroom teacher was physically and emotionally exhausting for the teacher, Howard argued. Notably, her argument also highlighted how education as a profession lacked the authority to evaluate its own work and practitioners, because the examinations opened the teacher herself up to public judgement rather than the judgement of her colleagues in education. In place of a series of school- or district-level examinations of teachers and students, Howard proposed a system that located the prerogative to certify teachers with the normal schools (46–47) and the authority to measure student progress with teachers themselves (48–49). Both forms of assessment would position education closer to other professions, which valued their collective and individual autonomy to self-assess. Howard closed her paper with an assertion of teachers' professional value: "Put our school work upon a more rational basis, and let American teachers be treated . . . not like mere pieces of machinery, to be replaced when worn out, but as integral parts of the body politic, whose welfare is closely allied to that of the whole community" (49). In this case, the arguments presented in *Sex in Education* served as a rationale for better working conditions for individual teachers and as an opportunity to highlight the damage caused by education's incomplete professionalization.

Other educational leaders were less persuaded by Clarke's book; however, they nonetheless used the controversy around *Sex in Education* as an opportunity to call for greater professionalization in education. Lucinda H. Stone[15] contributed "Effects of Mental Growth" to Anna C. Brackett's collection *The Education of American Girls* (1874). First, Stone acknowledged Clarke's influence as a professional: "I am glad that the recent alarm of Dr. Clarke, certainly the most rousing of our time, has been sounded. Rung out from his high tower of professional eminence and authority, it must and does attract attention" (177). Then, Stone referred to her own experience as a teacher to counter Clarke's claims:

---

15. Lucinda H. Stone (1814–1900) taught for several years at academies, seminaries, and college preparatory schools for women; she directed the female department of Kalamazoo College for roughly twenty years. She spent her later years organizing women's clubs and successfully advocating for the admission of women to the University of Michigan, where she earned an honorary doctorate in 1891.

> The existence of the terrible evils [Clarke] depicts is not to be doubted; and she would be less than a true woman who did not protest, by precept, preaching, and example, against the follies and sins of school or social life that induce such evils: but that it was eating of the fruit of the tree of knowledge—"persistent brain-work" even—that furnished Dr. Clarke's cases, "chiefly clinical," an experience of teaching extending over forty years would forbid me to believe. (190)

Stone used her observations as a teacher to suggest causes other than continuous education that might have caused girls' and women's poor health, including uncomfortable shoes (182), "soul-loneliness" (191), and climbing long flights of stairs in heavy skirts (196). She also quoted several experienced teachers and administrators who provided evidence that women had succeeded intellectually and physically in high school and college.

In addition to challenging Clarke's conclusions, Stone also called for education to seek greater professionalization:

> The science of education is, to-day, where the science of geology was fifty years ago. We are just beginning to think of it as a science. Men and women are waking up to its demands.... Each child in the great crowd that gathers in our schools, is in some respects like a particular musical instrument, designed by God, in its complicated mechanism, to perform its particular part, to yield its own particular tone in the diapason of life; and I shudder when I think how rudely it is often played upon by untaught teachers—teachers who have drifted to their work, or resorted to it as a temporary occupation, for its profits, but who have never thought of studying its principles, as physicians, lawyers, [and] artists, study the principles of their professions. (191–92)

Stone used the *Sex in Education* controversy as an opportunity to call for teachers to professionalize, to conscientiously learn educational theories and to commit to the work as a career. Importantly, Stone's argument operated on two levels. First, in resisting Clarke's proposed restrictions on women's education, Stone protected women's access to the advanced education needed for a teaching career. Second, in calling for the professionalization and permanence of that career, Stone posited a working life for women that was incompatible with a "periodic" approach to work. In other words, the professionalization of education would contradict Clarke's claims about the restrictions on women's activities imposed by their reproductive physiology, because these two features of professionalism, extended education and a long-term commitment to the work of the field, would not be possible for a woman who took an "intermission" each month.

Even several years after *Sex in Education* was published, the book was still referenced in discussions of how and why education ought to professionalize. For example, in 1886, education reformer John Dewey was prompted by the debate around *Sex in Education* to call for education to professionalize following the lead of the sciences. In "Health and Sex in Higher Education," published in *Popular Science Monthly*, Dewey reviewed the recently published findings from a survey of women graduates conducted by the ACA. According to the history of the AAUW written by Marion Talbot and Lois Kimball Mathews Rosenberry, the organization perceived a study of college women's health to be so crucial to its interests that this was the association's first research project:

> It is of especial significance that the first subject which the newly formed Association of Collegiate Alumnæ made an object of study was health and its corollary, physical education. The obstacles which the young women who composed the first group of members of the A.C.A. had met in their insistence upon a college education had been many, but none was more serious than the opinion prevalent well-nigh universally, that young women could not, except at a price physically not worth while, undergo the intellectual strain which their brothers seemed to find no strain at all. In some circles this view was confirmed by the opinion of Dr. E. H. Clarke, a distinguished Boston physician, who declared, in a book called "Sex in Education," that "identical education of the two sexes is a crime before God and humanity that physiology protests against and that experience weeps over." (116)

To investigate the actual state of women graduates' health, a committee of the ACA prepared a set of questions, had them vetted by physicians and teachers, and sent them to the ACA's 1290 members, receiving 705 responses (118). The resulting data were published in pamphlet form and circulated among "the leading educational and medical journals of the day" (119).

In the introduction to his article, Dewey immediately commented on the value of the ACA's data, asserting that its epistemic worth was greater than the experiences and observations of either physicians or teachers:

> For the first time the discussion is taken from the *a priori* realm of theory on the one hand, and the hap-hazard estimate of physician and college instructor on the other. The returns have the value of all good statistics: they not only enable us to come to some

conclusion upon the main point discussed, but they are so full and varied that they suggest and mark the way toward the discussion of a large number of other hardly less important questions. The figures, in short, call up as many problems as they settle, thus fulfilling the first requisite of fruitful research. (606)

At this point, thirteen years after the initial publication of *Sex in Education*, Dewey was able to articulate a set of professional rhetorical and epistemological values: good evidence is based on neither untested theory nor individual experience, and it addresses the primary research question while also suggesting topics for future research. For years after it began, the debate over co-education initiated by *Sex in Education* continued to serve as a site in which to name the characteristics of useful research.

In particular, Dewey argued, education needed to adopt a more systematic approach to research. After discussing the implications of the ACA's survey results, he called for "The unbiased study by educational experts of the fruits actually borne by experience," which he claimed would be "invaluable, and the generalizations based upon such data will show the lines upon which reform must work itself out" (613). Dewey went on to outline three categories—health, life since graduation, and specific data for future movements (613–14)—that this rigorous study of the effects of education on women could fall into. Dewey concluded with a forceful appeal to educators to professionalize:

> Education must follow the example of the special sciences. *It must organize.* There is organization, and to spare, in the schools themselves; what we want is organized recognition of the problems of education; organized study for the discovery of methods of solution; organized application of these methods in the details of school-life. Co-operation in research and application is the key to the problem. (614)

One feature of a profession is its members' collective work on the field's major questions; Dewey used the publication of the results of the ACA's survey, itself a response to *Sex in Education*, as an occasion to appeal to other educators to unify their work to address the field's major questions, and specifically, to follow the professional research model developed by the sciences.

Clarke's work was referred to in discussions of educational professionalism into the twentieth century. For example, M. Carey Thomas, president of Bryn Mawr College, cited Clarke in some of her early twentieth-century speeches. She viewed the question of women's higher education from the perspective of a teacher's professional qualifications. In "Should the Higher

Education of Women Differ from That of Men?," a paper delivered at the 1900 meeting of the Association of Colleges and Preparatory Schools of the Middle States and Maryland, Thomas counted "Dr. Edward H. Clarke, Dr. S. Weir Mitchell, and other doctors whose specialties lead them to pass their professional lives among invalid women" as among the "ghosts" who "rise from long since fought-out battlefields" (8). She refuted several of the objections that had been raised by these "ghosts" before concluding that because one-third of women college graduates would become "professional teachers, probably for life," women should "have the broadest possible education," one that was "the same as men's" (10). The prospect of a professional career for women justified an education that was not only equal to, but identical with, men's college education (2; 4). Achieving such an advanced and lengthy education would be nearly impossible for women following Clarke's advice. That Thomas would call for women who planned to be teachers to seek extended education in 1900 was a sign not only that the debate over women's co-education had shifted in the quarter century since Clarke first published *Sex in Education*, but also that expectations for teachers had changed, both in terms of their preparation (a college degree) and their commitment to a life-long career. Both expectations aligned teaching more closely with conventional professionalism than had been the case earlier in the century.

Seven years later, when Thomas addressed the Quarter-Centennial Meeting of the ACA, she acknowledged the real effects of claims like those made by Clarke: "The passionate desire of women of my generation for higher education was accompanied thruout [sic] its course by the awful doubt, felt by women themselves as well as by men, as to whether women as a sex were physically and mentally fit for it" ("Present Tendencies" 64). Women had not only survived college, Thomas said, but had also become better prepared "for their great profession of teaching" (72). In fact, as she explained, college-educated women were raising the standard for teaching: "College women have proved to be such admirably efficient teachers that they are driving other women out of the field" (72). Compared to many mid-nineteenth-century teachers, who had little education and only a short-term commitment to the work, Thomas described an emerging class of professional teachers who were highly educated and "efficient" in their work and who were replacing less-qualified women.

Taking a more pessimistic view of women as teachers, Clark University president and pioneering psychologist G. Stanley Hall, in his famous *Adolescence* (1904), expressed beliefs about women's mental tendencies that called into question not only their ability to succeed as professionals but also the effect they might have on men in the professions and on the professions themselves. In his discussion of "Adolescent Girls and Their Education," Hall admitted that *Sex in Education* was "not very scholarly" and was not scientifically disinterested, because it "was suspected of being unofficially inspired by the unwillingness of Harvard College to receive [women]" (569); yet after summarizing Clarke's and several other physicians' work warning of the physical risks inherent in women's education, Hall found a "consensus of professional opinion" against extended education for women and girls (583). He also presented evidence that college-educated women had lower marriage and fertility rates than women who had not attended college.

In addition to the personal health risks Hall cited through reference to medical professionals' texts, he also identified the danger that he believed that feminization posed for the profession of education. He wrote that increasing numbers of women teachers in secondary schools fostered a "subtle demoralization on the male teachers who remain" (623). Beyond the supposed harm to the morale of the men on the faculty, women teachers could cause the men they worked with to become effeminate: "It is hard, too, for male principals of schools with only female teachers not to suffer some deterioration in the moral tone of their virility and to lose in the power to cope successfully with men" (623). According to Hall, the risk to men teachers' masculinity and professionalism arose not only from being surrounded by women teachers, but even from teaching girls: "the incessant compromises the best male teachers of mixed classes must make with their pedagogic convictions in both teaching and discipline make the profession less attractive to manly men of large caliber and of sound fiber" (623). In Hall's characterization, co-education, and the qualified women teachers who emerged from women's higher education, undercut the professional autonomy and the (related) masculinity of men in education.

Hall concluded his chapter on "Adolescent Girls and Their Education" with a lengthy description of "the ideals that should be striven toward in the intermediate and collegiate education of adolescent girls with the proper presupposition of motherhood" (636). After detailing the subjects that should be covered in a girl's education, he warned readers that "Specialization has its place, but it always hurts a woman's soul more than a man's, should always come later, and if there is special capacity it should be trained elsewhere" than the intermediate or collegiate institution (645). Here, Hall went beyond the claims of Clarke and others who asserted that extended, intensive education could harm women physically to assert that women's *souls* would be "hurt" by specialized study, the hallmark of the professional (Higham 4). Clearly, in Hall's view professionalization was not for women.[16]

Educational leaders who responded to *Sex in Education* used their reception of Clarke's work as an opportunity to advocate for greater professionalism in education. Some, like Hall, understood women's participation in education to undermine the field's professionalism, but others used their reception of *Sex in Education* to assert that women could succeed in such work. Notably, even the writers who expressed concern about women's health as they prepared for and pursued careers as teachers cited *Sex in Education* to support commentary on what the profession of education ought to look like. Clarke's book operated not simply as advice for how girls and young women should organize their studies in order to ensure optimal reproductive development; it also prompted educational leaders to launch quantitative studies of women college graduates, to call for organization and unity of purpose, and to imagine a career of autonomy and prestige. In other words, in responding to *Sex in Education*, educational leaders articulated a model of professionalism for education, including ways of gathering and making knowledge; of regulating practitioners' behavior within the profession; of perceiving teaching as a life-long work worthy of extended study and practice; and of establishing a shared vision for the purposes, questions, and practices of the field that could be pursued collaboratively. Just as in medicine, the reception of *Sex in Education* in education tended toward discussions of what professionalism could look like. That a book that was hostile to women's pursuit of extended education and careers was used to advocate for greater professionalization (and the status benefits accompanying professionalization) in a field that was simultaneously shifting toward higher proportions of women practitioners is astonishing; this aspect of the reception of *Sex in Education* demonstrates the unsettled nature of and the interconnections among professionalism, gender, and education in the US in the late nineteenth century.

The Reception of *Sex in Education* as a Site for Constructing Professionalism

My analysis of the commentary on *Sex in Education* by leaders in medicine and education reveals that the debate over Clarke's book was not just about

---

16. Yet Hall himself was criticized by Thomas for inadequate science. In "Present Tendencies in Women's College Education," she faulted Hall for the "sickening sentimentality and horrible over-sexuality [that] seemed to me to breathe . . . from every pseudo-scientific page" of *Adolescence* (65).

women's education. It was also about the rhetorical and epistemic features of the professions of medicine and education: what kinds of expertise and experience would be valued, what forms of research and argument would be perceived as valid, and what authority professionals could claim within and beyond the bounds of their fields. This discourse also had implications for women's place in the professions. As physicians and educators used the debate over *Sex in Education* to define professional behaviors, discourses, and epistemologies, they also proposed models of professionalism with the potential to include women and to elevate women's authority and autonomy.

The reception of *Sex in Education* by medicine and education is noteworthy precisely because of the profession-defining work it performed. Medicine and education could have debated the thesis of *Sex in Education* on its own terms: physicians could have published studies of female reproductive development, and teachers could have discussed pedagogical approaches that allowed students to pursue a flexible, independent course of study. Some in the professions did just that, following the expected scientific-professional course of turning to research to confirm or refute the claims made by another researcher. Many others, though, did not follow that discursive model in their reception of *Sex in Education*. These responses, published by leading physicians and educators, took up issues related to professionalism: epistemology, research methods, professional boundaries, the nature of medicine and education as professions, authority, autonomy, and the regulation of members. Writers like Thomas and Hall cited Clarke as part of their discussions of women's potential place in the professions. In other words, the reception of *Sex in Education* by readers in the professions most closely associated with its content participated in the rhetorical construction of these professions and of the idea of professionalism more broadly. These constructions were tightly interwoven with the constructions of gender that were simultaneously being developed by these same professions.

The varied uses to which *Sex in Education* was put by its readers demonstrates the importance of studies of reception in our efforts to learn about the rhetorical construction of concepts like professionalism and gender. On the surface, Clarke's book had little to do with constructions of professionalism, but this analysis of its reception reveals that *Sex in Education* served as an important site for exploring who could become a professional and what professional status might look like, for prompting the ongoing redefinition of *professionalism* and *gender*. The interlocking rhetorical constructions of these two concepts that occurred through responses to *Sex in Education* suggest that the late-nineteenth-century development of the professions was not simply a move *toward* masculine characteristics that excluded women; instead, it was also a process of *retaining* masculinity in the face of material, epistemic, and discursive changes that could have made the professions more hospitable to women.

Professionalism. Patricia Hill Collins observes that, despite the ways that science and scientists have participated in excluding and discriminating against women, people of color, and the economically disadvantaged, science has also provided some tools to resist discriminatory institutions and practices: "With its commitment to objectivity, rationality, and the search for reliable truths that transcend belief, opinion, or 'stories,' scientific knowledge continues to offer a powerful weapon for confronting bureaucratic structures of domination" (279). The responses to *Sex in Education* that called for statistical evidence of the effects of education on women's health, rather than practitioners' anecdotes and moral dogma, opened a space for an understanding of women less bound by conventional beliefs about their capabilities. Corresponding rhetorical values, such as unadorned language and prioritizing research questions (rather than moral judgements) could likewise yield studies that discussed women neutrally, without the historical associations often attached to women.[17]

At the time *Sex in Education* was published, US medicine was striving to establish itself as a profession; the promotion of science as the epistemology of medicine was a key part of the drive toward the profession we recognize today. However, in the late nineteenth century, many physicians were reluctant to adopt the new epistemology, fearing that it would undermine "the physician's intuition and clinical good sense," converting medical practice from an art dependent on expertise and judgment to a mechanized science (Morantz-Sanchez, *Sympathy* 237). Coinciding with this perceived threat to the physician's authority and autonomy, scientific findings and rhetorical values seemed to open at least a crack for the admission of women to the profession, risking further dilution of the physician's traditional masculine authority. Jacobi's performance of scientific research methods and discourse produced the finding that women did not require rest during menstruation to make the implicit case (which she made explicitly elsewhere; see "Shall Women Practice Medicine?") that women were capable of professional ca-

---

17. Jordynn Jack notes that discourses of objectivity and gender neutrality have "required women scientists to adopt dominant assumptions and habits that worked against the interests of women scientists, as a group, even when they worked in favor of some women scientists, as individuals" (*Science* 128). Objectivity and expertise also run counter to values, such as the importance of subjectivity, interconnection, caring, and experiential knowledge, held by many feminists. My focus here is less on the consequences of women's adoption of discourses of objectivity and more on representations of *woman* and *professionalism* that constructed the professions as accessible to women (or not).

reers. Other physicians' criticisms of Clarke's reliance on a handful of selected cases, their objections to Clarke's hyperbolic descriptions of women's reproductive functions, and their praise of statistical studies like those by Jacobi and the ACA, which supported the claim that women were not physically harmed by college education, suggest that medicine's move toward professionalization was not inexorably a project of excluding women. In other words, it was not the turn toward science itself that made medicine inaccessible to women; rather, medicine insisted on masculinity in spite of some of its own research findings and epistemological commitments.

In professions, like primary and secondary school teaching, where women constituted large numbers of practitioners, adopting professional characteristics gave women opportunities to claim authority and expertise not traditionally associated with femininity. The reception of *Sex in Education* suggested that education might encompass much more than classroom activities, potentially attributing to teachers, many of whom were women, the authority to advise across homes, schools, and communities. Obviously, the tension between the masculinity assumed by most models of professionalism and the increasing proportion of teachers who were women played a part in the way education emerged as a different kind of labor than medicine. Yet as Clifford observes, women teachers' achievements were substantial. Through their work, individual women gained independence, and they opened doors for themselves and their students to enter other professions (ix). Writing of the Progressive Era, Victoria-Maria MacDonald likewise identifies teachers' professional accomplishments despite a context that appeared to minimize their authority and expertise: "during this period in which teachers became de-skilled and women's access to top administration became limited, paradoxically female spaces and social organizations arose conducive to long service and career advancement at the lower echelons of the bureaucracy" (428). Furthermore, MacDonald argues, teaching apprenticeship programs and normal schools were opportunities for "the creation of a woman's culture in the profession" of teaching (438). Even rules requiring women to resign their teaching positions upon marriage allowed some women, particularly those uninterested in marrying men, to create the lives they wanted (452). Collectively, these observations suggest that the conventional model of professionalism that we have come to recognize is not the only way that professionalism can be understood, and that identifying professionalism in the ways we do reinforces the idea that professionalism is "masculine" and that it inherently excludes women.[18]

---

18. See Brumberg and Tomes for a longer discussion of the methodological implications of assuming professionalization was a process of masculinization.

Gender. Despite the opening that emergent scientific professionalism provided for women to claim authority within professions and the research findings that demonstrated that it was safe for women to pursue extended education and substantial careers, many physicians were not immediately convinced of women's capabilities. The persistence of conventional attitudes toward women is not surprising. My analysis of the professional reception of *Sex in Education*, however, reveals how much of medicine's limiting construction of *woman* was intertwined with physicians' efforts to determine the characteristics and boundaries of their profession. The still-strong connection between science and common sense in the nineteenth century (Bensaude-Vincent 104) might have led physicians to apply "common sense" ideas about women's capabilities in ostensibly scientific contexts. When presented with scientific evidence of women's abilities, some commentators on *Sex in Education* seemed to cling to the older model of medical professionalism, based in the wise (masculine) family doctor, who was an advisor and confidante, not a scientist, to argue that the well-being of individual women and the health of the (white) species dictated that women should approach school cautiously. In some cases, even physicians who otherwise identified with the new scientific approach to medicine relied on conventional models of gender. The adherence by physicians to traditional views of women and men despite emerging evidence that challenged those views coincided with their attempt to define their profession. Consequently, the new ideal of the professional scientific physician, who would objectively accept and act on the findings of convincing studies, including those that demonstrated that women could succeed as members of the medical profession, ran the risk of undermining the moral authority that physicians had enjoyed largely because they were men. Furthermore, when medical leaders asserted superiority over education, they were not simply reflecting the fact that physicians tended to be men and primary and secondary school teachers were increasingly women; they were also participating in a context in which education was constructing a model of professionalism that differed from—by seeking compatibility with women's lives and interests—the model pursued by medicine.

Likewise, education's reception of the construction of gender in *Sex in Education* served as an opportunity to protest unprofessional working conditions. Hall blamed the presence of women as teachers and students for demoralizing and emasculating men teachers, as men and as professionals. For Howard, the (often public) testing teachers were subject to was not only evidence that education did not have professional autonomy over the field's credentialling practices, but it was also inhumane, if Clarke was correct about women's inability to cope with extended periods of stress. If, however, as Thomas argued, women were thriving as career teachers, then women needed a college education to do that work well and to move education toward greater professionalization, displacing less educated and presumably less professionalized women.

As these brief reviews of how *professionalism* and *gender* were constructed in the professional reception of *Sex in Education* suggest, these terms were co-constructed, and the emergence of exclusively masculine professionalism was not inevitable. Instead, elements of the construction of both of these concepts were compatible with women moving into positions of rhetorical and professional authority and expertise. Rather than medicine (and possibly other conventional professions) promoting epistemologies, discourses, and institutions that excluded women, it may be more accurate to say that medicine maintained an affiliation with masculinity despite increasing material and social motivations for women to pursue advanced education and professional careers, despite research methods and findings that resisted received knowledge about women, and despite rhetorical values privileging a neutral stance and valuing expertise regardless of the rhetor's personal characteristics. The persistence of limiting constructions of women and the construction of professionalism as masculine points to the depth of the social and cultural roles of gendering.

The story of education can be re-understood in ways that complicate the idea that the field achieved only weak professionalism because of the predominance of women. The reception of *Sex in Education* suggests other ways the history of professionalization in education could have developed. Following Clarke's description of the field in *The Building of a Brain*, teachers could have claimed authority across schools, domestic life, social life, and exercise, using mind-body connections to craft a holistic view of education (much like what we see today in schools offering wraparound services). Following Thomas's view of the college-educated teacher as "efficient," teachers could have restructured education as a technical process, or "efficiency" could have been defined (for education as well as manufacturing and other processes) as responsive to the humanity of those involved. Following Howard's critiques, education could have asserted greater control over how success would be measured, limiting public involvement in professional activities. Not all of these paths would have been desirable; my point here is that the reception of *Sex in Education* included potential models of professionalism for education in which the femininity of its practitioners was not a liability. The assertion of masculine professionalism by the scientific professions and the consequent exclusion of education from that model of professionalism occurred despite a conversation around *professionalism* and *gender* that suggested other possibilities.

Attending to the reception of *Sex in Education* by professional audiences exposes three features of the debate surrounding this book that are important to rhetorical studies. First, professionalization as we recognize it today emerged through extended discussions involving practitioners well-known and unknown. As part of those conversations, the reception of *Sex in Education* presents an illustration of the collective development of notions of professionalism, even as it proves that the development was inconsistent, with incompatible values and priorities competing for inclusion within intra- and inter-disciplinary models of professionalism. Professionalism has been an important discourse, associated with powerful institutions and status positions, that has shaped individual lives and collective experiences for the last 150 years. Reception is key to understanding the rhetorical construction of this now-central social and institutional role.

Second, although the constructions of professionalism that emerged through the reception of *Sex in Education* were inextricably intertwined with constructions of gender, *professionalism* and *woman* were not constructed in ways that were inherently mutually exclusive. In fact, some of the material, epistemic, and discursive features attributed to professionalism, especially in education but also in medicine to some extent, could have accommodated women. Although the persistence of conventional constructions of *woman* overrode those potential openings in the construction of *professionalism*, this examination of the reception of *Sex in Education* demonstrates that the emergence of the modern professions as masculine institutions was less uniform than it often appears.

Finally, reception can exceed or deviate from the scope established by the received text. As this chapter has demonstrated, the direct reception of Clarke's book often did not engage in research confirming or refuting Clarke's arguments; instead, it frequently served as a space in which writers could advocate for their preferred vision of professionalism.[19] In studying reception, we can see the issues that rhetors *want* to discuss. These receptive rhetors might be those who are less powerful and lack the platform to set an agenda for a discourse community; they might also be powerful rhetors who use reception to appropriate a subversive text and reassert their authority; or they might be rhetors who use the reception of a text as an opportunity

---

19. Many of the studies of women's reproductive processes completed in the early twentieth century indirectly challenged Clarke's claims, but without citing *Sex in Education*. Bittel attributes the research by physician Clelia Duel Mosher and psychologist Leta Stetter Hollingworth, aimed at depathologizing menstruation and demonstrating that women were intellectually capable to "the continuing legacy of Edward Clarke" (232). My focus here, however, is on texts that explicitly name *Sex in Education* as a text the writers engaged with as a form of receptive rhetoric.

to make claims only tangentially related to the argument of the initial text. However the power dynamics of a receptive context unfold, the possibility of using reception as an excuse to talk about something other than the original rhetor's topic is an important aspect of how rhetoric works in ways that may be messy and not at all straightforward but are nonetheless crucial in understanding the emergence and evolution of social change.

4 Silence and Indirect Reception

As the previous two chapters have demonstrated, the texts written in response to Edward H. Clarke's *Sex in Education* were deeply invested in constructing definitions of *gender, science,* and *professionalism* and in shaping the rhetorical and material purposes to which those concepts could be put. As crucial as these rhetorical efforts were in the late-nineteenth-century US, the negotiation of these terms in the published reception of *Sex in Education* represented the concerns of a narrow subset of the US public, mostly those of the white middle and professional classes. In the late nineteenth and early twentieth centuries, African Americans, Indigenous people, immigrants, and members of the working class contributed very little to the discussion of Clarke's book. These silences suggest the limitations of focusing on only the "spoken" elements of reception. In this chapter, I demonstrate that rhetorical studies of silence could be enhanced by viewing silence as a form of reception. In fact, many instances of rhetorical silence are recognizable because they are responses to prior rhetorical acts; therefore, we can better understand silence by considering it as an act of reception. Doing so foregrounds the collective or collaborative nature of many silences, because reception can be understood as shared among and situated in a community. Reception's range of style and purpose across agonism and cooperation aligns with existing feminist scholarship on the varied functions of silence. Silence as a form of reception can be accidental, intentional, or imposed; because reception studies emphasizes the situatedness of receptive acts, we can ask how silent recipients' positionality affects which texts they respond to and how they respond when they do.

In writing a chapter focused on supposed silences by marginalized rhetors, I am acutely aware of the history of scholars assuming that African American women did not participate in nineteenth-century US rhetoric (Royster, *Traces* 252–53). The work of several scholars (including Foner and Branham, Haywood, Logan, Royster, Stancliff, and many others) has demonstrated that African American women were rhetorically active throughout the period I examine. Because of this scholarship, I expected to find texts by African Americans among the reception of *Sex in Education*. The fact that I didn't was surprising to me and should not be taken as conclusive. However, my inability to locate a body of published reception by African American and other marginalized rhetors suggests that *Sex in Education* might have been received quite differently among those groups than it was among white audiences. I wondered why it might have been received differently and what social and material conditions might have affected if and how some potential readers encountered (or not) and chose to respond (or not) to Clarke's book.

It might be argued that Clarke's purpose and audience constitution explain some of the silences in the reception of *Sex in Education*: he claimed to be concerned primarily with health and higher education, which tilted his audience toward educators, physicians, and readers who had a woman in the family with the resources to pursue a college degree. Furthermore, Clarke's motive was ensuring the "evolutionary" success of "the race," which for him was exemplified by relatively affluent white families. In light of Clarke's focus and approach, it perhaps makes sense that those excluded from his purpose and audience would not engage with *Sex in Education*; however, those silences were more than a matter of reader interest. Attending to the silences and the indirect reception (reception framed by and filtered through another person's reception) of *Sex in Education* reveals the extent to which the book and its published reception depended on and reinforced racist and classist beliefs.

Analyzing silence as a form of reception extends existing feminist rhetorical scholarship exploring silence as rhetorical action. In *Unspoken: A Rhetoric of Silence*, Cheryl Glenn is careful to note that not all silences empower the silent rhetor, but she also warns us not to assume that silence is a sign of passivity (xi). Particularly for studies of reception in which the scholar traces what people *do* with a text—how they make meaning with it or deploy it to build or reinforce worlds—noting silences (intentional and empowering or not) can better reveal the contours of the rhetorical landscape. Likewise, Glenn explains that "silence . . . reveals speech at the same time that it enacts its own sometimes complementary rhetoric" (3). Attending to the locations and patterns of silence as part of the full picture of the reception of a text can reveal more about the "spoken" responses than we could learn from studying those responses alone. It can also teach us about the rhetoric being enacted through the silences themselves.

If, as is the case with the African American and working-class women featured in this chapter, the potential (but mostly silent) rhetors were part of historically marginalized groups who had limited access to mainstream rhetorical resources, scholars might be tempted to assume that "nothing" is there. Silence, however, as Glenn explains, does not necessarily mean "nothing": "Containing everything in itself, silence is meaningful, even if it is invisible. It can mean powerlessness or emptiness—but not always. Because it fills out the space in which it appears, it can be equated with a kind of emptiness, but that is not the same as absence . . . . Like the zero in mathematics, silence is an absence with a function, and a rhetorical one at that" (*Unspoken* 4). In studies of reception, it can be easy to see only the "spoken" rhetoric, to forget that other people might have responded to the initial text but did not (or, that the always-incomplete archival record at least suggests that they responded with silence). As Raymie E. McKerrow observes, "There is a natural tendency to gravitate toward that which is observable—that which is present in the social scene. What this principle seeks is a reminder: Absence may be more important, more potent, as a source of information than mere presence" (237). Once a silent reception has been identified, the next step is attempting to interpret why the silence exists and what it communicates.

Three methodological resources can help with the work of identifying and explaining receptive silences. The first is using contextual information to understand the material and social factors that might have affected a potential rhetor's choice to engage in receptive rhetoric. In particular, examining the rhetorical context surrounding the silence—other texts that were related to the topic of the receptive conversation but that did not engage with the focal text itself—might suggest the constraints and interests influencing silent reception. For example, I looked for conversations related to African American women's education that did not engage with *Sex in Education* directly but that illuminated the historical and material circumstances that shaped other (and Others') rhetoric while not centering Clarke and his ideas, instead addressing concerns about women, education, work, and collective well-being in ways that were useful to those rhetors.

The second methodological resource for studying silence as a form of reception is the analysis of indirect reception—commentary that is filtered through or presented in support of the receptive argument of someone other than the person commenting. Indirect reception should be approached cautiously, especially when power or status differentials are involved (as when two physicians reported on working-class women's characterizations of their health in support of the physicians' own arguments about *Sex in Education*). Even as we should be wary of relying on indirect reception, these rhetorical acts can reveal aspects of, or raise questions about, the silences surrounding them.

The third methodological resource, one that weaves through the first two, is "strategic contemplation," identified by Royster and Kirsch as one of the "critical terms of engagement" (19) that emerged from their survey of feminist rhetorical studies:

> Strategic contemplation involves engaging in a dialogue, in an exchange, with the women who are our rhetorical subjects, even if only imaginatively, to understand their words, their visions, their priorities whether and perhaps especially when they differ from our

own. . . . [I]t involves recognizing—and learning to listen to—silence as a rhetorically powerful act. It entails creating a space where we can see and hold contradictions without rushing to immediate closure, to neat resolutions, or to cozy hierarchies and binaries. (21–22)

Because rhetorical research is itself a form of reception and because strategic contemplation is often required to make sense of receptive silences, who the researcher is influences which stories are told, how silence is interpreted, and even if a silence is recognized as meaningful. Given the inherently partial (both incomplete and subjective) nature of explaining historical silences, all three methodological resources—examining historical contextual information, analyzing indirect reception, and engaging in strategic contemplation—lend themselves to provisional, tentative interpretations of silence as a form of reception. They can help us begin to understand some possible rhetorical "function[s]" of the "absence," to use Glenn's words.

In what follows, I examine silence as a component of the reception of *Sex in Education*. Recognizing the wide range of people who could have addressed Clarke's argument, including African American, Indigenous, immigrant, and working-class women, reveals just how narrow, despite its volume, the published reception of *Sex in Education* in the nineteenth-century US was. I pursue this analysis by interpreting the silences themselves based on information about the historical and rhetorical context, analyzing a few problematic cases of indirect reception, and engaging in strategic contemplation. I also explore the silences in the reception of *Sex in Education* by examining what was said by members of dominant groups *about* the marginalized groups who responded to Clarke's book with silence. This discourse contributed to a rhetorical context that likely made speaking up risky or not worthwhile for some potential rhetors, partially explaining their silence. All of this evidence points to my claim for this chapter: rhetorical silence can often be understood as a form of reception, and when it's examined as part of a larger receptive phenomenon, silence can illuminate features of the rhetorical context and of the published reception that might not otherwise appear. In the case of *Sex in Education*, the description and interpretation of receptive silences reveal the discriminatory assumptions and worldviews underlying *Sex in Education* and its published reception. This analysis demonstrates that the published reception (past and present) of Clarke's book, which has predominantly focused on the book's bias against women, participates in the racism and classism at the core of *Sex in Education*.

Receptive Silence as Agential

One notable silence in the reception of *Sex in Education* is the apparent lack of response from African American women. African American women were attending college throughout the time Clarke's book was being debated following its 1873 publication: Mary Jane Patterson graduated from Oberlin College in 1862, Bennett College (co-educational until it became women only in 1926) was founded in 1873, and the Atlanta Baptist Female Seminary (later Spelman College) was established in 1881, along with many other African American colleges founded throughout the country in the nineteenth century (Scott 23; Royster, *Traces* 142). Even before the Civil War, African American women worked in educational administration and teacher preparation (Royster, *Traces* 138–39). African American women, particularly elite women, then, were deeply involved in pursuing education and professionalization in the last quarter of the 1800s. Yet, as Royster explains, African American women were not immune from the belief that women belonged at home, not at college, and "it did not matter ideologically that the cult of true womanhood simply had never held true for the overwhelming majority of poor and immigrant white women or African American women whose experiences throughout their time in the United States had included, unquestionably, work outside the home. All women were held to this standard" (*Traces* 180). Late-nineteenth-century African American women experienced the tension between their educational and professional goals and the gender ideology that was a feature of much of the debate around *Sex in Education*. This makes their silence in response to Clarke's book significant.

Although I have been unable to locate any nineteenth- or early twentieth-century texts in which African American women engaged with *Sex in Education* directly, questions about women's education—its purpose, scope, and relation to women's domestic roles—were part of African American discourse in the late nineteenth and early twentieth centuries. Consequently, I have been able to draw from the historical and rhetorical contexts to propose some tentative interpretations of African American women's silent reception of *Sex in Education*. These are only hypotheses, but they suggest how the features of the rhetorical landscape around the reception of a text—the exigencies, values, and purposes that we notice—can change through attention to silent reception.

One reason African Americans may have chosen not to participate in the debate around *Sex in Education* was their understanding of the purpose and value of women's education. African American commentators wrestled with the challenges that education and careers posed to conventional femininity, but typically put those tensions in the context of serving African American communities. In contrast to Clarke, who saw white women's education as a threat to the evolutionary success of "the [white] race" (*Sex in Education* 139), African American speakers and writers understood women's education as necessary to the material and social success of African Americans, even if they were sometimes careful to limit that education to what they believed to be appropriately feminine levels and careers. For example, in "The Higher Education of Women," Anna Julia Cooper responded to the contention that education "spoiled" a woman's marriage chances, calling it "the most serious argument ever used against the higher education" of women (68).[1] Nonetheless, Cooper encouraged teachers and community leaders to "give the girls a chance!" (78). This (very likely coincidental, because Cooper did not directly engage with *Sex in Education* in this text) echo of the subtitle of Clarke's book (*A Fair Chance for the Girls*) and the question of whether an educated woman would be a suitable wife suggest that Cooper was, like Clarke, addressing the tensions between women's rights and opportunities and the effects of education on women's social and reproductive roles. Shirley Wilson Logan suggests that in raising (and countering) the popular doubts about women, Cooper situated African American women among all women, both in terms of the skepticism they faced about their abilities and in terms of the rights that they merited. According to Logan, Cooper "was careful to place [Black women's] concerns in the global context of neglect and respect for women, showing . . . that the [B]lack woman, a member of this global community, was entitled to no less than other women" (126). Accordingly, Cooper called for higher expectations for young African American women: "Let our girls feel that we expect something more of them than that they merely look pretty and appear well in society. Teach them that there is a race with special needs which they and only they can help; that the world needs and is already asking for their trained, efficient forces" (78). For Cooper, the education of African American women was an opportunity and a responsibility to improve conditions in their communities. Contrary to Clarke's recommendation to limit women's education, Cooper promoted the funding of scholarships for women (79).

---

1. Anna Julia Cooper (1858–1964) was a prominent African American speaker, educator, and scholar. She originally delivered "The Higher Education of Women" before the American Conference of Educators (Washington, DC) in March 1890. In April 1891, she published the speech in *Southland*. It was also included in *A Voice from the South* (1892); citations refer to this version. See Shirley Wilson Logan's *"We Are Coming": The Persuasive Discourse of Nineteenth-Century Black Women* for a fuller discussion of Cooper's speech.

Taking a more conservative approach was Reverend Thomas Nelson Baker,[2] who in 1906 wrote the article "The Negro Woman" for *Alexander's Magazine*.[3] In the section of this article focused on education, Baker asked, "What shall be the education of the Negro woman?" (83). In an argument similar to Clarke's assertion that the progress of "the [white] race" depended on the ability of white women to bear healthy children, Baker asserted the importance of African American mothers to the progress of their race:

> The Negro race like all other races is dependent upon the quality of its mothers. The hope of the race is conditioned not upon the woman on the platform, but upon the woman in the home[;] . . . the hope of the race is conditioned upon that class of women who are too busy with their children to attend conventions where the race problem is solved by resolutions and logomachy; . . . it is upon these women, the mothers of the race[,] that the hope of the race depends. (84)

Both Baker and Clarke would have had women primarily educated for motherhood, but where Clarke warned of the health risks associated with studying "in a man's way," Baker warned against women participating in public activism. He insisted that motherhood was the best work for women: "One thing the education of the Negro woman must not do, it must not educate her away from being a mother—it must not be an education that will make her feel that there is a higher sphere for woman than that of being a mother" (84). However, looking at what he characterized as New England's history of producing the country's "strongest men" because its women were better educated than its men, Baker concluded that "[The African American woman] needs for the sake of the race to be better educated than the Negro man" (84). These mothers would, Baker implied, "unconsciously" teach their sons "justice and fair play" just as the "large hearted, cultured, fair-minded mothers" of New England had taught their sons (84). Echoing the Republican Motherhood ideal, Baker described education for African American women in terms that drew from idealized motherhood in order to promote the success of African American men and, by extension, the progress of the race.

---

2. Thomas Nelson Baker (1860–1940), who was born into slavery, was the first African American to earn a PhD in philosophy in the US. He worked as a minister, speaker, and writer.

3. The editorial masthead described the goal of *Alexander's Magazine* as "the Spreading of Reliable Information Concerning the Operation of Educational Institutions In the South, [and] the Moral, Intellectual, Commercial and Industrial Improvement of the Negro Race in the United States."

Assumptions based on African American women's gender, however, were of course compounded by assumptions made by white Americans about their race. Those assumptions affected both nineteenth-century African American women's experiences attending college and their motivations and goals in pursuing higher education. Royster explains how the history of enslavement affected perceptions of African American women as college students: "Further complicating women's place in higher education for African American women were the stereotypes about character that continued to plague them because of their roles as 'breeders' and rape victims during slavery and because of the images of them as being licentious, amoral, animalistic" (*Traces* 181). The need to "prove" African American women's morality as well as to keep young women safe while living away from home led to strict rules about how students could spend their time. Historian Stephanie J. Shaw describes an educational system for African American women that closely supervised students' time: "Administrators designated recreational hours during the week and on Saturdays, but at all other times students were to direct their attention to serious study and service work" (83). Such a schedule violated Clarke's recommendations to limit the hours women devoted to academic and domestic work. The parents and teachers of African American women, however, had priorities and material circumstances that differed from Clarke's and his white middle-class readers'.

Some of the restrictions on how African American women students spent their time reflected the religious convictions of the institutions' white missionary teachers and the poverty of the schools (which needed men and women students' labor to contribute to the building and upkeep of the facilities). As Shaw explains, however, parents often fully supported the schools' strict discipline: "Finding programs as structured as these gave [parents] and their daughters a kind of insurance against exposure to some of the dangers that [B]lack girls faced in less controllable public environments" (83). Shaw also notes that the well-being of African American students was not only a matter of individual safety, but also communal investment: "Parents supported these stringent measures because their daughters' (perhaps also the family's, and sometimes the community's) futures were at stake. The economic sacrifice of the family and sometimes the community, and the hope that they invested in the young women, made it difficult to suffer the failure of the student owing to indiscretion, naïveté, or even self-will" (85). This sense that a woman's education would benefit her community was quite different from the individual desire for self-improvement or a career that was assumed to motivate white women's education in much of the reception of *Sex in Education*.

According to Royster, African American women sought higher education in order to enter professions, especially teaching, to provide for their families (*Traces* 178). They also wanted to develop the knowledge and abilities to allow African American communities to operate independently of white professionals (*Traces* 195–96). Royster situates the value of elite nineteenth-century African American women's education in what that education meant for their communities:

> With enhanced abilities, over the years after their college and university training, these women were able to transform the communities in which they lived. They were movers and shakers. They were the "race women," the club women, the managers of programs, deliverers of professional and community services. They interpreted African American experiences from their various and sundry professional standpoints and were central players in the sustaining of life and culture. They were people who used language well, as writers and speakers. They got many critical jobs done in their communities, and done very well. (*Traces* 205–06; see also Shaw 75)

The purpose and payoff for education operated differently for African American and white women in the late nineteenth century.

The sense that an African American woman's education was beneficial to her community suggests one possible reason for African Americans' agential silent reception of *Sex in Education*. For Clarke, white women improved the lot of their race through healthy reproduction, and extended education and work endangered that function. In contrast, African American women were understood to improve the conditions for their communities through pursuing education and work. Both during their school years and after they graduated, Shaw explains, African American women were expected to work diligently: "If ever they weakened in their struggle to achieve the education made available to them or in the work they subsequently undertook, they were encouraged to pray not to have easier lives but to be stronger women; not 'for tasks equal to [their] powers,' but 'for powers equal to [their] tasks'" (102; quotes are from nineteenth-century clergyman Phillips Brooks). This approach to women's pursuit of education and labor differed fundamentally from that of Clarke and those who published responses to him.

In addition to the material and social benefits of women's education, some proponents saw even higher purposes for African American women's education, as Shaw explains: "They were not simply to work to bring about equality, justice, and a better standard of living for their people, which was the practical hope of their families and communities, but more broadly they were to work to establish the kingdom of God on earth" (74). This understanding of the goals of higher education for women was very different from Clarke's focus on evolution and the survival of the fittest; although both visions were motivated by collective interests, one depended on women's education for success and the other was believed to be put at risk by women's education. One viewed women's education as part of a Divine plan with significant communal consequences and the other viewed women's education as an often unnecessary and unimportant individual accomplishment, one that might even run counter to God's plan for women. These alternative perceptions of the purposes of women's education likely caused Clarke's ideas about women's health and education to be received differently by members of each audience.

Between the collective valuing of African American women's advanced education and the racism at the core of much of the *Sex in Education* debate (discussed below), there may have been little incentive for African Americans to participate in the discussion of this book. Literary scholar Koritha Mitchell advises us to "look through the lens of achievement, rather than protest," because "[d]oing so quickly reveals that African Americans have always focused more on creating possibility for themselves and each other than on responding to oppression" (3). Shaw describes late nineteenth- and early twentieth-century African American parents' attitudes toward education in terms in keeping with prioritizing "creating possibility" over "responding to oppression":

> Parents deliberately encouraged the pursuit of courses of study that would lead to higher occupations, and they pushed the children to be self-confident, independent high achievers. These parents were neither unrealistic nor irresponsible in rearing their daughters in this way. Nor had they misread society's cues about the social and economic options available to [B]lack women. They simply insisted upon distinguishing between what their daughters were capable of doing and what they might be allowed or expected to do. (14)

Considering Shaw's understanding of African American parents' motivations and K. Mitchell's insistence that "creating possibility" has always been a stronger focus for African Americans than "responding to oppression," one possible explanation for African Americans' silent reception of *Sex in Education* comes into focus: they might have been prioritizing what African American women could accomplish through schooling, rather than engaging in a discourse based on aspirations for evolutionary progress, a discourse founded in racism.

Examining the context surrounding nineteenth-century African American women's education suggests that their silent reception was an agential rhetorical act, one that might be understood as consensual and protective against a racist background as were some of the silences Gwendolyn Etter-Lewis observed in the oral histories she collected from elderly African American women (435). We might also interpret this collective receptive silence as agential in the sense that it created space for young women to pursue educations and careers that would benefit the women and their communities. Royster and Kirsch urge us to think broadly and curiously about rhetors' contexts and motivations, asking "How do we transport ourselves back to the time and context in which they lived, knowing full well that it is not possible to see things from their vantage point? How did *they* frame (rather than *we* frame) the questions by which they navigated their own lives?" (20). When we shift the frame away from middle-class white women and what their education might have meant for them and their communities and toward African American women and their purposes for education, African Americans' silent reception of *Sex in Education* moves to the foreground as an intentional and productive response, not only to Clarke's book, but to their broader context in the late nineteenth century.

RECEPTIVE SILENCE AS IMPOSED

Silence as an indicator of exclusion has a long history. Glenn notes the long-standing connection between citizenship and speech:

> That women and other traditionally disenfranchised groups have been systematically and consciously excluded from public speaking and active listening comes as no surprise: these groups have, since before Aristotle's time, been excluded from full participation in the production of all Western canonized cultural forms, including the production of rhetorical arts. Power and authority in cultural production have customarily been the prerogatives of the male citizen. (23–24)

The silencing associated with exclusion from citizenship can function through formal limits on who can be citizens and on who can speak, but it can also function through informal (but still very powerful) discursive patterns that simultaneously deny a group's right to belong and to speak. Such a discursive pattern of exclusion operated in *Sex in Education* and much of its reception; collectively, these texts silenced African Americans, Indigenous Americans, immigrants, and working-class people through grounding claims about what would be good for women and for the country in the racist and classist tenets of social Darwinism. In this section, I analyze what Clarke and his respondents said about people outside of the white middle class, identifying a pattern of racist and classist exclusion that defined who counted as citizens. This aspect of the social and rhetorical context around *Sex in Education* suggests another interpretation of the largely silent reception by African Americans, Indigenous Americans, immigrants, and members of the working class: they were all actively silenced by the worldview underlying *Sex in Education*.

Proponents of social Darwinism maintained that groups of people (races, nationalities, classes) were subject to the evolutionary concepts of survival of the fittest and natural selection, and they constructed a hierarchy of human races and genders based on their beliefs about which groups of people were more and less evolved. Louise Michele Newman explains that nineteenth-century biologists and social scientists typically understood white women as intellectually inferior to and less variable than white men; according to this model, the "average type of [white] woman exhibited certain characteristics that were also common among 'primitives' or 'lower races': irrational and slow thinking, intuitive or instinctual approaches to knowledge, religiosity, emotionality, and so forth" (*White Women's* 31). Both white women and members of the "lower races" were understood to be "less evolved" than white men.

The belief that white women had achieved less evolutionary progress than white men supported their exclusion from higher education and the professions. However, at the same time, white women's location "higher" on the scale of evolution and civilization, by virtue of their whiteness, was manifested by their differentiation from white men. In other words, the fact that white men and white women supposedly occupied "separate spheres" was understood as evidence of white women's relatively advanced evolutionary status: only in the "most civilized" societies were men and women strongly distinct from each other. Consequently, nineteenth-century definitions of the sexes, grounded in popular evolutionary theory, depended on and reinforced racism (Schuller 105). Accordingly, as Newman observes, the vocabulary used by social Darwinists to highlight gender differences among white people didn't appear in discussions of other races: "'woman' was used to mean an Anglo-Protestant woman; 'lower races' or 'primitives' were used without reference to gender because the theory presupposed that there were no significant sexual differences among primitives" (*White Women's* 31). From this standpoint, the concerns that Clarke raised in *Sex in Education* implicitly applied only to white women: because social Darwinism positioned African Americans and Indigenous people as less evolved, African American and Indigenous women were not believed to suffer as a result of their reproductive physiology the way white women supposedly did. Furthermore, when Clarke worried about the evolutionary survival of "the race," it is clear that he was concerned about the survival and progress of the descendants of particular white Americans.

In viewing gender, race, and education's supposed harm to reproductive potential through the lens of a racist and politically motivated understanding of evolution, Clarke and his respondents defined who "belonged" and who did not, which people could positively contribute to the evolutionary future of the United States and which could not. K. Mitchell describes the act of "insisting that [B]lack women are not women" as a form of "discursive violence" (27), and "violence, whether physical or discursive, has one major purpose: to mark who belongs and who does not . . . . In other words, violence is a performance of the denial of citizenship, an active rejection of the idea that one belongs" (5–6). Clarke and others in the debate around *Sex in Education* ignored African American and Indigenous women's potential as students and characterized them as not suffering from the reproductive ailments that were believed to affect white women. In doing so, Clarke and those who participated in the published reception of *Sex in Education* denied the humanity of those outside of the white middle class, thereby silencing them.[4]

What seemed to pain Clarke the most about identical co-education was the potential it had to harm those young women whom he believed to be the best and brightest, thereby undermining evolutionary progress. He warned his readers that "In our schools it is the ambitious and conscientious girls, those who have in them the stuff of which the noblest women are made, that suffer, not the romping or lazy sort; and thus our modern ways of education provide for the 'non-survival of the fittest'" (112). Clarke described what he perceived to be dire outcomes for "the race" if (white) women's educational methods did not account for their periodicity:

> [I]f the education of the sexes remains identical, instead of being appropriate and special; and especially if the intense and passionate stimulus of the identical co-education of the sexes is added to their identical education,—then the sterilizing influence of such a training, acting with tenfold more force upon the female than upon the male, will go on, and the race will be propagated from its inferior classes. The stream of life that is to flow into the future will be

---

4. Eric D. Anderson observes that, despite the role that Darwinian evolution played in supporting racism in the late-nineteenth-century US, few Black speakers or writers addressed Darwin's theories, in part because they located the origins of racism in beliefs that predated Darwin's work. Given Clarke's reliance on a Darwinian worldview, the African American silent reception of *Sex in Education* might be considered an extension of their silence in response to Darwin.

Celtic rather than American: it will come from the collieries, and not from the peerage. (139–40)

In a nineteenth-century US context where Irish immigrants were not understood to be "white" and were at times characterized in ways that white Americans found "repulsive" (Duffy 61), Clarke's suggestion that future Americans might descend from Irish coal miners invoked not only anti-immigrant sentiment and classism, but racism as well. If young white, middle-class women, their parents, and their teachers were not frightened enough by the risks to individual health posed by pursuing education "in a boy's way," dread of immigrants, the working classes, and racial "others" might have motivated them to seek alternative educational methods.

The reception of *Sex in Education* relied on racist themes, just as the book itself did. For instance, in *Sex* and *Education* (1874), Julia Ward Howe referred to nationality, race, and climate in her refutation of Clarke. Howe summarized Clarke's "prognosis" as she understood it, possibly exaggerating his claims in order to make them appear ridiculous:

> The result will be a physical and sexual chaos, out of which the Doctor sees no escape save in an act akin to the rape of the Sabines. Tennyson's line suits with his mood:—
> "I will take some savage woman, she shall rear my dusky race." (16–17)

In her synopsis, Howe highlighted an assertion Clarke made in *Sex in Education*: in the chapter describing the cases he had seen of women who had lost their health after too much study, Clarke cited the legendary abduction of Sabine women by Roman men in an attempt to increase the population of early Rome. Clarke predicted a parallel need for white population growth in the US if white women continued to undermine their fertility through extended schooling: "it requires no prophet to foretell that the wives who are to be mothers in our republic must be drawn from trans-atlantic [sic] homes. The sons of the New World will have to re-act [sic], on a magnificent scale, the old story of unwived Rome and the Sabines" (63). Both Clarke's original text and Howe's glossing of it with Tennyson's line (from "Locksley Hall") referencing the narrator's daydream about a life among the "noble savages" illustrated racist and sexist ideas about US citizenship. All women were cast as a means to increase the number of citizens, not as citizens themselves, and the women who would serve this purpose if white women did not were characterized as "inferior" and subject to violence to achieve the population goals of white middle-class men. Although Howe might have been mocking Clarke for exaggerating the risk to "the race" resulting from women's education, her choice of this line of poetry indicates her comfort with the racist hierarchy underlying Clarke's work.

For Howe, climate was the driving force influencing "the human organism." She insisted that the climate of a location affected whole families, not just individuals (and certainly not just women). She cited Nova Scotia, India, China, and Turkey as places that had changed the physical characteristics of American and English families. In the process of demonstrating that education was not the primary shaper of women's health, Howe proposed a model of nationality based on physical malleability, suggesting that bodily acclimatization to a new country was possible. Notably, and in contrast to Clarke's vision of who counted as a "real" American, Howe claimed that immigrants to the US became physically "American" relatively swiftly: "The potent American climate works quickly in assimilating the foreign material offered to it. Two generations suffice to efface the salient marks of Celtic, Saxon, French, or Italian descent." Yet even Howe could not imagine the full incorporation of African Americans into the US: "The Negro alone is able to offer a respectable resistance" to the American climate (27). This one firm limitation on Howe's model of how climate affects the body also named a limit on who she could imagine being included in the US citizenry.

Perhaps in response to claims from medical and nonprofessional readers (like Howe) that he had not accounted for the influence of climate on health, Clarke opened *The Building of a Brain* (1874), his sequel to *Sex in Education*, with a long discussion of the challenges the North American continent posed to the evolutionary success of European settlers. This elaboration of the factors affecting reproductive and evolutionary fitness opened another avenue for imposing silence, this time by dismissing Indigenous people's long history on the continent and their experiences with European settlers. Clarke began by asserting that North America had always been hostile to human life:

> No race of human kind has yet obtained a permanent foothold upon this continent . . . . On this continent, races have been born and lived and disappeared. Mounds at the West, vestiges in Florida, and traces elsewhere, proclaim at least two extinct races. The causes of their disappearance are undiscovered. We only know that they are gone. The Indian, whom our ancestors confronted, was losing his hold on the continent when "The Mayflower" anchored in Plymouth Bay, and is now also rapidly disappearing. It remains to be seen if the Anglo-Saxon race, which has ventured upon a continent that has proved the tomb of antecedent races, can be more

fortunate than they in maintaining a permanent grasp upon this Western world. (13–14)

In Clarke's retelling of North American history, human life on the continent had always been tenuous, due to features of the continent itself (of course, he ignored the ongoing effects that European settlers had had on the continent's existing civilizations).

Clarke went on to argue that education (especially the education of women) was key to "Anglo-Saxon" persistence in North America: "One thing, at least, is sure,—[the Anglo-Saxon race] will fail, as previous races have failed, unless it can produce a physique and a brain capable of meeting successfully the demands that our climate and civilization make upon it" (14). Survival, however, was not Clarke's final goal; he sought evolutionary progress for his "race": "But the Anglo-Saxon will not be satisfied, and ought not to be, with simply securing a permanent foothold here. He will not rest content with mere acclimation and existence. The sponge and the oyster can exist, and perpetuate their kind. He must do more than they: he must ascend in the scale of being, as well as exist" (14–15). In calling for European settlers to seek evolutionary "progress," Clarke attributed an evolutionary inferiority to the previous inhabitants of North America, those who, he claimed, failed even to survive.[5] Education played a significant role in Clarke's vision of how "Americans" were to survive and "ascend in the scale of being." He asserted that "humanity demands, and our education must give, both the highest development of the individual, and the perpetuation of individuals thus developed, or, as it is commonly expressed, the perpetuation of the fittest" (15). Clarke maintained that simultaneously achieving these two goals required white women to protect their reproductive development, to pursue intellectual growth only to the extent that it did not limit their reproductive potential.

In telling this history of human life in North America to establish the exigence for his argument about the detrimental effects of white women's education, Clarke quite dramatically silenced Indigenous voices by erasing the long history of their civilizations, their current existence, and the ongoing violence perpetrated by European settlers against them. In keeping with his social Darwinist perspective, Clarke constructed human life (individual and cultural) in North America as a function of survival of the fittest; the "strong" races would survive in North America, while the "weak"

---

5. Of course, Clarke is incorrect in his characterization of the history of Indigenous North American civilizations: the mound-building cultures that Clarke cited existed in North America for approximately five thousand years, and humans have lived in North America for tens of thousands of years.

races would not. Again, in the effort to define the best education for white women, one that would not undermine the survival and "ascent" of the white race, Clarke and his supporters (the passages above were reprinted and positively commented on in several periodicals) silenced and committed discursive violence against members of groups they believed to be "less evolved."

The silencing of people perceived to be "less evolved" in the published reception of *Sex in Education* mirrored their exclusion from full citizenship, because silence is contrary to democratic citizenship. This examination of the rhetorical context around a collection of silences in the reception of *Sex in Education* brings to the fore the racism, classism, and hostility toward immigrants underlying a text that most often has been read by scholars as an example of nineteenth-century popular and medical misogyny (see chapter five for further discussion of the contemporary reception of *Sex in Education*). Perceiving silence as part of a larger body of receptive rhetoric allows that silence to "speak" by illuminating the logics that were accepted and forwarded in the published reception, the same logics that silenced those who might otherwise have spoken.

Indirect Reception

Working-class women stood to lose a great deal—income and very likely their jobs—if Clarke's recommendation that women reduce their workload to accommodate their "periodic" nature were adopted in workplaces. In her 1874 response to *Sex in Education*, reformer Caroline H. Dall identified the threat that Clarke's ideas posed to working women:

> It would seem as if Dr. Clarke can hardly yet understand what a blow his essay deals at the industry of woman . . . . Thousands of women are thrown upon themselves for self-support at the age of fourteen. The moment that school-tasks are remitted three days out of thirty, clerks will leave the desk, servant-girls their accustomed work, shop-girls their counters. It is not too much to say that male labor must replace service as intermittent as this. ("V." 105–06; see also Duffey 117–18; Elmore 180)

The question of how women could support themselves—of whether employers would hire employees who needed so much time off—if the need for periodic rest were broadly accepted points to a difference between the context of the reception of *Sex in Education* for working-class women and college-bound women.

Clarke was inconsistent on the issue of working women's health in *Sex in Education*, stating at one point that working women were less prone to the reproductive ailments that supposedly plagued the woman student:

> There are two reasons why female operatives of all sorts are likely to suffer less, and actually do suffer less, from such persistent work, than female students; why Jane in the factory can work more steadily with the loom, than Jane in college with the dictionary; why the girl who makes the bed can safely work more steadily the whole year through, than her little mistress of sixteen who goes to school. (131)

The first reason Clarke offered was that working women were typically mature enough to have well-established reproductive systems (Dall, cited above, and Ames, cited below, contradicted this claim); in contrast, students often attended college at younger ages, before reproductive development was complete (131). The second explanation Clarke gave for working women suffering less than students did was "because [female operatives] work their brains less." Citing Herbert Spencer, who had articulated the doctrine of social Darwinism, Clarke continued:

> "That antagonism between body and brain which we see in those, who, pushing brain-activity to an extreme, enfeeble their bodies," does not often exist in female operatives, any more than in male. On the contrary, they belong to the class of those who, in the words of the same author [Spencer], by "pushing bodily activity to an extreme, make their brains inert." Hence they have stronger bodies, a reproductive apparatus more normally constructed, and a catamenial function less readily disturbed by effort, than their student sisters, who are . . . trained to push "brain-activity to an extreme." (133–34)

In his classist explanation of why physical labor was safer for women than schooling, Clarke suggested that his advice to reduce overall workload and to take periodic intermissions from work did not apply to working-class women.

Despite maintaining that working women did not face the same risks as students did, Clarke faulted working women for engaging in continuous labor:

> Female clerks in stores strive to emulate the males by unremitting labor, seeking to develop feminine force by masculine methods. Female operatives of all sorts, in factories and elsewhere, labor in

the same way; and, when the day is done, are as likely to dance half the night, regardless of any pressure upon them of a peculiar [reproductive] function, as their fashionable sisters in the polite world. All unite in pushing the hateful thing out of sight and out of mind; and all are punished by similar weakness, degeneration, and disease. (130–31)

This inconsistency in Clarke's argument was reinforced by his choice, in a book supposedly focused on education, of a shop clerk and an actress as two of his seven clinical cases of disease resulting from continuous effort. Both lost health because they "worked on courageously and steadily in a man's way and with a woman's will" (74). Because of her position as a bookkeeper in a mercantile house, Miss C— spent six days each week standing, making no accommodations "for the periodicity of her organization" (76–77). Miss B—, an actress, followed Clarke's advice and regained her health; Miss C— did not, leading Clarke to conclude "Latterly I have lost sight of her, and, from her appearance at her last visit to me, presume she has gone to a world where backache and male and female skeletons are unknown" (77). The consequence of working in a man's way, no less than studying in a man's way, could be death.

Despite the potential consequences to working women's health (if Clarke's theories were correct) and to their material conditions (if they lost income or their jobs because they took time off periodically) suggested by *Sex in Education*, I have been unable to locate any instances of working-class women, parents, or employers responding directly and independently to *Sex in Education*. Furthermore, the potential implications of *Sex in Education* for working women evoked minimal discussion in the public and medical presses. It seems there was simply very little said about how working outside the home might have interfered with women's reproductive physiology and development.

The near silence on the subject of working women in the reception of *Sex in Education* might have reflected the complex attitudes toward the protection of white women in the late nineteenth-century US. Newman argues that women's rights advocates responded paradoxically to concerns about working women[6] and to women seeking education. When it came to education, proponents of women's rights denied that white middle-class women needed protection, but when it came to labor, they supported the idea that white working-class women would benefit from protective legislation in-

---

6. Because the labor market was segregated racially and sexually (Newman, *White Women's* 96), the employees whom white New England reformers were concerned about were predominantly white women.

tended to improve facilities, limit working hours, or increase pay for women (*White Women's* 87). These seemingly contrary responses to similar concerns suggest the "class and racial dimensions [that] were central but rarely articulated explicitly" in nineteenth-century notions of women's protection (*White Women's* 87). Newman describes the advantages and disadvantages of protection, explaining why women might have sought and rebuffed it in paradoxical ways:

> Protection was a problematic strategy in woman's movement politics, implying dependency, victimhood, and vulnerability on the one hand but also privilege, high status, economic well-being, and personal security on the other hand. In the context of late-nineteenth-century U.S. political culture, to accept the status of the protected implied a certain lack of autonomy, a curtailment of freedom and economic opportunity, even as protection supposedly insulated white women from the sullying aspects of competition and worldly activity. (*White Women's* 101)

Protective legislation could be understood as a necessary corrective to exploitive and dangerous working conditions. It also, however, functioned as a way to reassert women's domesticity, either by allowing them to spend more time at home because they could earn sufficient income in fewer hours or because implementing protective measures would make women too expensive to employ (96).

These competing motivations may have contributed to the near silence in the reception of *Sex in Education* on the book's implications for working women. For middle-class activists to assert that working women did not require periodic rest would have meant closing off one pathway to better working conditions for women, conditions in keeping with the ideas of femininity that even women's rights advocates often adhered to. Supporting periodic rest for working women, however, would have undermined the efforts to open more educational and professional opportunities to middle-class women. Likewise, working-class activists may have pursued a strategic silence in response to *Sex in Education* because accepting the notion that women could not work continuously would have limited women's earning potential; asserting that women were all capable of continuous labor, however, would have masked the real physical challenges often posed by nineteenth-century US working conditions.

Because my search for responses to *Sex in Education* that focused on the book's implications for working women had yielded no texts by working-class women themselves and only a handful of texts by middle-class advocates of working women, I initially classified the working-class reception of

Sex in Education as a silence. However, when confronted with silent receptions, especially when the silence involves people who have not been widely or deeply studied, we must ask if their reception might look different (in genre, content, or purpose) than we expect, based on our experience studying the rhetorical acts of speakers and writers with whom we are more familiar. In other words, we need to consider the possibility that what appears to be silence is actually the result of the researcher not looking in the right places. In the case of the reception of *Sex in Education*, I eventually found working-class women's voices embedded in texts written by more powerful rhetors who were writing for purposes that in some cases differed widely from the messages conveyed by the working women themselves.

The two most substantial explorations of working women's reproductive health in response to *Sex in Education* were books by physicians Azel Ames, Jr. and Mary Putnam Jacobi. Although both Ames and Jacobi relied heavily on their medical expertise and described working women's health in terms that aligned with their attitudes toward women's social roles (with Ames advocating traditional domesticity and Jacobi favoring broader opportunities for women), they both also incorporated working-class women's perspectives into their texts. In these contexts, working class women's messages addressed the issues raised by *Sex in Education*, but they did not engage with Clarke or his book directly; instead, their comments served as evidence supporting arguments made by Ames and Jacobi in their reception of *Sex in Education*. From the information available, it is not clear whether the women cited by Ames and Jacobi had even read Clarke's book. It is clear, however, that their characterization of their working lives contributed to the conversation around *Sex in Education*. Consequently, working-class women participated indirectly in the reception of *Sex in Education* but in ways that they did not control.

Citing *Sex in Education* as inspiration (3), Azel Ames, Jr., the Special Commissioner of Investigation with the Massachusetts Bureau of Statistics of Labor, published *Sex in Industry: A Plea for the Working-Girl* in 1875. Unlike Clarke, Ames contended that paid work could be just as intellectually rigorous as study was: "in the intricacy of much modern machinery, the intrinsic mental demands of many processes of employ, and the special mental peculiarities of others, it is obvious that no inconsiderable amount of brain exaction is involved" (16). Additionally, Ames cited "the monotony, depression, bodily fatigue, and 'constrained position'" that made much labor more difficult than study. Ames also refuted Clarke's claim that women did not enter the workplace until they were past puberty: "The statistics adduced clearly give a very large per cent as certainly yet under the usual age at which the menstrual function asserts itself, who are employed in the industries of the nation" (16). In challenging Clarke's claims that labor was not as harmful to women as education was, Ames laid the groundwork for his argument that working women's reproductive potential required protection, just as women students' did.

Ames studied a range of workplaces likely to employ women: "These inquiries have been especially into the effects of factory employments, typesetting, telegraphy, sewing-machine operation, basket-making, the counting of money, strands, etc., with casual examination into other lines" (62). He found that jobs that required standing all day (54–59) or following the constant actions of machinery (47–48) were dangerous because they did not allow the regular rest necessary for the "normal establishment" of the menstrual function (45). Other dangerous occupations were those that "require[d] a higher degree of intelligence than most mill-work" (83), such as telegraphy and typesetting. Ames worried most about work that combined mental and physical labor (111), noting that "the disturbance [of the menstrual function] will be proportionate, in the rapidity of its advance and degree, to the degree of concentration, celerity, and continuity of employ" (123). Like Clarke, Ames argued that mental effort detracted from the development of the female reproductive system. Although he acknowledged that other aspects of working conditions—the hot rooms, the availability and quality of restrooms, the close contact with men, the confined spaces, the poor posture—contributed to overall reduced physical health, Ames prioritized the effects of combined mental and physical effort on women's reproductive health.

As evidence supporting his claims, Ames incorporated the words of working women into his text. For example, in his discussion of typesetting, Ames quoted six people employed as compositors or as managers in printing offices. One informant, Miss J—, was identified as "a lady compositor." She described several ailments that she attributed to her work as a typesetter:

> I have been at this work five years, but have been frequently obliged to give up for vacations, from peculiar [reproductive] troubles and general debility.... I was well until I had set type a year, when I began to be troubled with difficult periods, and have been, more or less, ever since. When I go away, I get better; but, as often as I return to my work, I am troubled again. Have wholly lost color, and am not nearly as fleshy and heavy as when I began work. I have now a good deal of pain in my chest, and some cough, which increases if I work harder than usual. I am well acquainted with many other lady compositors who suffer as I do. (92)

From the testimony of typesetters, their supervisors, their employers, and their physicians, Ames concluded that there was a "physico-mental influence upon the peculiar function [menstruation] of woman" (95). Miss J—, however, described health concerns that included, but extended well beyond, her "difficult periods." Ames's selective interpretation of Miss J—'s characterization of her work and her health reflected his purpose and argument in *Sex in Industry*; it also demonstrates the challenges working women faced in attempting to interrupt silence when they lacked control over the rhetorical uses to which their words would be put.[7]

Just as he asked typesetters about the effect of their work on their health, Ames likewise inquired among telegraph operators, who reported that their health broke down after about a year of steady work. When he asked the women what caused their poor health, Ames did not immediately get the answer he was looking for:

> On being interrogated as to the special causes and effects of prostration in telegraph-offices, the first reply of nearly all young "lady operators," perhaps not unnaturally, is to the effect, that the close confinement, over-heat of rooms, and position, are principally operative; but more direct inquiry, calling out the more active and self-examining thought, invariably produces the reply, that the "nervous debility," "cold feet and hot head," and dizzy headache, make up a good part of the results; while particular inquiry, in a large proportion of cases, establishes the fact, *always*, in the larger offices, that menstruation occurs more frequently than it ought. (99–100)

The women's reluctance to associate their work with menstrual irregularity could reasonably be attributed to the modesty expected of nineteenth-century women; however, the fact that Ames had to ask three times before women mentioned menstruation suggests the possibility that the telegraph operators saw their initial complaints about cramped, overheated working conditions as more pertinent to their health than any menstrual symptoms they may have experienced.

As in the passage above, some of Ames's informants took the opportunity of being asked about their work and their health to describe their difficult working conditions. For example, one woman, identified as "Miss —," who was "in charge of the female department of one of the largest [telegraph] of-

---

7. Of course, I am also interpreting Ames and his informants for my own purposes. My point is not that interpretation, even motivated interpretation, is always wrong; instead, I'm suggesting that interpretation can complicate, reinforce, and even mitigate existing silences.

fices in the country" listed several complaints, most of which had little to do with reproductive physiology:

> One year is as long as one can work in a busy office without a good vacation. The confined position, constipation, heat, and dizzy headache, I think, are the most noticeable troubles of "lady operators" who are "grown up." The hours are too long for such strained employment. From eight, A.M., to six, P.M., with only an hour for dinner, makes too long a day for the kind of work. I am sorry to say some of our girls eat their lunch in the room, not going out at all. A woman can do as much as a man in this business, and do it as well, but does not get the same pay for it. A skilful [sic] "lady operator" here will sometimes have from two hundred to two hundred and thirty messages a day; *but she could not stand that rate more than a month.* Most of our chief-office "lady operators" are from twenty-three to twenty-four years old . . . . They generally begin to learn from sixteen to eighteen years of age, and *the youngest, of course, feel it most.* I think, that, with those of our age, the chief menstrual trouble is with its occurring too often. (101–02[8])

Miss — identified several issues with telegraphers' working conditions and compensation. Because nineteenth-century US physicians tended to attribute menstrual difficulties to a wide range of behaviors and circumstances (including having cold feet, dancing too late, and attending school continuously), Ames would not have been alone in asserting that most of the working conditions Miss — described contributed to reproductive disorder. In looking in particular at silences, however, we can see that Ames did not amplify Miss —'s broader complaints about how telegraphers worked and were compensated. Miss — spoke, but because Ames had other purposes for his book, Miss — was effectively silenced.

In fact, in addition to choosing to foreground menstrual difficulties and downplay other material and health concerns, Ames even went so far as to contradict one informant's characterization of the health of her co-workers. In the appendix to *Sex in Industry*, Ames included a letter from "a lady operator with whom I had held conversation as to the special effects of telegraphy." This woman clearly distanced telegraphy from menstrual disorder:

> I made inquiries of the ladies employed in my room, as you requested; and all, with one exception, declared the business had no damaging effect upon the menstrual function; in *that* respect they

---

8. Ames did not indicate whether Miss — emphasized the italicized passages herself or whether he highlighted them because they supported his argument.

> have experienced no change since they entered the business. Take it as a whole, I believe telegraphy exerts no unfavorable influence in that direction, although it would seem to be a natural result on account of the nervousness inseparable from the business. Those I have consulted say every other function will be affected *except* the menstrual. (157)

In response to this assertive denial of any connection between telegraphy and menstrual difficulties, Ames observed that the women in the writer's office were all over twenty years of age (and so had "established" reproductive systems). He also refuted the writer's evidence: "a careful inquiry has established the fact . . . besides the disturbances spoken of above, two at least are sufferers from dysmenorrhea, and two from occasional menorrhagia which always improves on taking a vacation" (158). In this passage, the telegrapher's indirect reception of *Sex in Education* appears alongside of Ames's direct reception, making visible the contradiction between the two; although the informant denied that Clarke's claims applied to working women, Ames insisted on their validity. Considering this exchange in the broader context of the near silence around the question of the effect of continuous out-of-home work on women's reproductive health, it appears that the informant used the opportunity Ames gave her to state unequivocally that telegraphy did not affect women's menstrual cycles, while Ames relied on alternative evidence and medical discourse to deny her statement. In effect, Ames invited the "lady operator" to speak but then invalidated her comments, silencing her perspective to assert his own.

Based on his medical expertise and knowledge of female reproductive physiology, on authoritative statements from other physicians, and on the (interpreted) accounts of working women, Ames concluded that businesses should be forbidden from employing girls until after they had reached puberty (46) and that working hours should be determined by a woman's age and ability (61). Ames proposed changes to industry based on "A scientific gradation of pursuits as to their salubrity or non-salubrity, [and] their physiological effects," that would "govern, to a great degree, the participation therein of the forming female" (130). He also called for men to be better paid so that women would not be required to work (133–34). Other reforms Ames advocated were reduced working hours (137) and, consistent with his informants' observations, laws regulating working conditions enforced by inspectors (140). Finally, in accordance with the belief that female reproductive physiology required regular rest to function correctly, Ames recommended that working women "be permitted a 'periodical absence,' without pecuniary loss" and "additional vacations of sufficient extent" for women in jobs "which require high degrees of mental concentration, with physical energy" (142). Although he believed that women's most valuable work occurred in their roles as wives and mothers, Ames proposed these reforms with the knowledge that many women needed the income their labor provided; his proposals were intended to adapt working conditions to the demands of women's reproductive systems.

In *Sex in Industry*, working women participated indirectly in the reception of *Sex in Education*. What we "hear" in their contributions to Ames's book is, however, not a coherent message about the effects of continuous work on women's reproductive health. The inconsistency possibly reflects the variety of values and authorities at work in the drafting of *Sex in Industry* and in working women's lives. Gender ideology might have prompted not only Ames but also some of his informants to describe women as weak and prone to reproductive ailments. The status differences between the physician Ames and his working-class informants might have shaped interviewees' responses. Feminine modesty, possibly mitigated by Ames's profession, might have limited what women were willing to say about their bodies. The respondents' desire for better working conditions might have been complicated by fears that employers would penalize them for complaining or for achieving improvements that might be costly to businesses. Finally, as we have seen, Ames's control over if and how his informants' words appeared in his text might have distorted and undermined the women's messages. Working women's quotations used as evidence in *Sex in Industry* reveal that they were not silent on the question of how constant labor affected their reproductive health, but their words also demonstrate the limitations and complications of relying on someone else—especially someone who does not share your status and purpose—to deliver your message.

While Ames's argument depended on and reinforced a conventional model of domestic femininity, Mary Putnam Jacobi operated from an unconventional model of femininity, reflecting her status as one of the US's earliest, most accomplished, and best-known women physicians. As discussed in the previous chapter, *The Question of Rest for Women During Menstruation* (1877) relied on survey responses from women across occupational and educational backgrounds, making this book, like *Sex in Industry*, an instance of working women's indirect participation in the reception of *Sex in Education*. In part to demonstrate that there was no correlation between a woman's efforts at school or work and her reproductive health, Jacobi included among her participants women with a range of educational and work backgrounds: housewives, teachers, writers, physicians, factory workers, clerks, and domestic servants (33). She argued that, contrary to nostalgic ideas about women's domestic roles, women had always worked outside the home (16), and she cited data from the 1870 census to demonstrate that one-sixth of US women participated in "the paid industry of the country" (19). Jacobi excluded the 373,832 women engaged in agricultural labor, however, explaining that "of these the immense majority is in the Southern States, and probably consists of negroes, who for our purposes may be excluded from the reckoning" (19). Although Jacobi did not explain why "our purposes" justified omitting agricultural workers from her calculations, one hypothesis is that she was participating in the pervasive and racist exclusion of African American women from the discussion of factors, including coeducation and labor, that might affect their reproductive health. This exclusion might have coincided with a lack of interest (which Ames shared) in the outdoor physical farm labor of women of any race because it was perceived to be less dangerous to female physiology than work that required women to leave home, took place inside hot or overcrowded rooms, or restricted a woman's physical movements.

Although Clarke focused his attention on the effects of education, Jacobi pointed to the large number of white working women to justify their inclusion in deliberations over women's need of rest during menstruation. According to her calculations (which excluded farm workers, most of whom she assumed were African American), "1,221,451 white women [were] engaged in work of sufficient regularity and importance to render the question of monthly vacations a serious one" (19). By including working women in her study, Jacobi pointed to some of the wider implications of Clarke's argument that women required periodic intermissions in their (academic) labor. This was not just a question of a few thousand women attending college;[9] it was a question of over a million women who contributed to the national economy and to their families' support.

In contrast to *Sex in Industry*, where working women's views were presented in lengthy discursive passages, *The Question of Rest* incorporated working women's perspectives in tables, where their survey responses were aggregated with others into numerical reports or excerpted to single words or brief phrases. For example, "Table XVII.—Maximum Capacity for Exercise" presented survey responses to the question "Strength, as measured by capacity for exercise. How far can you walk?" as averages, separated into groups according to the degree of menstrual pain they experienced and their general health (27; see Figure 1). In the nearby text, Jacobi explained that because some participants responded to this prompt with numbers and others with descriptive terms, she had converted some of her participants' ver-

---

9. Solomon, citing Newcomer, states that eleven thousand women were enrolled in higher education in 1870 (63).

bal survey responses into numbers. For example, for one subset of her data, Jacobi explained that she had made these conversions: "'Blank' is estimated at two miles, 'Little' at one mile, and '[M]any' at five" (50). Table XVII reported averages based on Jacobi's translation of words to numbers and combined responses from women across occupations and social and educational backgrounds.

Group 1. No Pain.	Group 2. Severe Pain.	Group 3. Slight Pain.
Average of entire group: 435 miles, or 5 a piece.	Average of entire group: 228 miles, or 3¼ a piece.	Average of entire group: 82 miles, or 4⅝ a piece.
Average healthy section: 405 miles, or 5⅝ a piece.	Average healthy section: 114 miles, or 4⅖ a piece.	Average healthy section: 64 miles, or 5¼ a piece.

Figure 1: "Table XVII.—Maximum Capacity for Exercise." Mary Putnam Jacobi, *The Question of Rest for Women During Menstruation*, p. 51. Courtesy of HathiTrust.

"Table XII.—Family Health of Group I," presented survey participants' reports of their family health in their own words (see Figure 2). Group I was made up of the participants who reported no menstrual pain, and their characterization of family health ranged from the general ("Poor") to the specific ("Chorea and hemiplegia as child"), from the descriptive ("[Childhood] frail, mother consumptive") to the vague ("Sisters invalids"). The table data suggested the varieties of ways women perceived their own health and the health of their families, but they did not provide a full sense of women's understandings of the relationships among health, work, education, and family tendencies.

Because examining the effects of working-class labor on menstrual health was not Jacobi's purpose, she combined the survey responses of all her participants—housewives, physicians, clerks, teachers, factory workers, and domestic servants—in the tables. As a result, even though the voices of women collectively were incorporated into the medical reception of *Sex in Education* (Wells 173–76), the voices of working-class women were muted. The tables do not report, for instance, if factory workers and clerks reported suffering more or less with menstruation than did housewives and physicians. Through *The Question of Rest*, working-class women's voices were included in the reception of *Sex in Education*, but we have no way of knowing exactly what they were saying.

In her analysis, Jacobi argued that the kind of rest women needed to maintain health was frequent and brief rather than concentrated in a few days each month. She asserted that women's choice of occupation reflected the patterns of work and rest that truly benefited them:

> [T]here is nothing, at least in the evidence before us, to show that *exclusively* menstrual rest is capable of exerting a curative influence. The kind of rest needed by women consists in interruptions to employment every two or three hours, not every three or four weeks. The immense preponderance of domestic service over every other form of female labor, we mean of labor demanding the same degree of capacity, is in itself an indication of preference for work involving more hours but frequent interruptions, over work more compactly arranged, in an unbroken series of hours, though these terminated earlier. (206)

Notably, in characterizing women as benefiting from breaks arranged throughout the day, Jacobi decreased the difference between women and men as workers, because all workers could be well served by rest interspersed throughout the working day. Although her claim that women preferred domestic service because it afforded the necessary pattern of work and rest appeared to imply that women were naturally inclined to domestic labor, her later suggestion that "in higher employments, eight hours steady work is felt as a severe burden, when we believe . . . two sessions of work, of four hours each, would entail little fatigue" (206) demonstrated that other forms of work could be arranged to incorporate brief breaks, thus accommodating women workers. Consequently, there was nothing inherently "feminine" about domestic service; it just happened to follow a pattern amenable to women's health, and other forms of labor could easily be similarly organized.

Despite her repeated insistence that women benefited from frequent, short breaks rather than longer breaks timed according to their menstrual cycles (232), Jacobi had to admit that her assessment applied only to healthy women. Unfortunately, according to Jacobi's statistics, inherited disease, insufficient exercise, and behavioral choices (diet, dress, etc.) produced menstrual pain in a substantial proportion of women. For those women, Jacobi admitted, rest might be indicated: "It remains true . . . that in our existing social conditions, 46 per cent. of women suffer more or less at menstruation, and for a large number of these when engaged in industrial pursuits or others, under the command of an employer, humanity dictates that rest from work during the period of pain be afforded whenever practicable" (232). Notable here is that Jacobi did not link rest to menstruation; women were to rest "during the period of pain," whenever that might be. Also notable is Jacobi's reference to "industrial pursuits" and "employers," making it clear—in the final sentence of her book—that her study and argument were not limited to women seeking advanced education but instead included, and even focused on, women at work.

	Good.
58 cases, or 63⅔ per cent. (1 excellent, 2 perfect).	
	Poor.
	33, or 36⅓ per cent.
4	Mother, cancer.
2	Very delicate.
5	Chorea and hemiplegia as child.
13	Mother consumptive, childhood delicate.
17	Not very strong.
18	Sister epileptic.
22	Father consumptive.
28	Mother scrofulous.
29	Delicate.
30	Poor.
36	Mother and brother consumptive.
35	Sisters invalids.
39	Mother consumptive.
14	Very poor.
43	Not robust. Rheumatism.
46	Childhood delicate.
47	" frail, mother consumptive.
48	" " " rheumatic.
49	Mother consumptive.
51	Delicate childhood.
54	Eczema in family.
50	"Bilious."
53	Uterine disease.
60	Consumptive. Gout.
67	Poor.
68	Very delicate child.
70	Delicate.
76	Poor.
80	Delicate.
81	Poor.
82	Father head disease, sister consumptive.
85	Mother and sister delicate.
88	Mother rheumatic.

Figure 2: "Table XII.—Family Health of Group I." Mary Putnam Jacobi, *The Question of Rest for Women During Menstruation*, pp. 43–44. Courtesy of HathiTrust.

Both Jacobi and Ames incorporated working-class women's voices into their responses to *Sex in Education*, and the results in both cases were problematic. Women spoke more fully in *Sex in Industry*, but their assertions were frequently undercut by Ames. On the other hand, individual women were masked in averages and limited in what they could say in their excerpted responses to restrictive survey prompts in *The Question of Rest*, but Jacobi insisted that menstruation itself was not pathological, potentially freeing women to pursue their work.

An examination of working-class women's indirect reception of *Sex in Education* reveals complications of key rhetorical elements, including purpose (as complaints about working conditions were pushed aside by Ames's focus on menstruation), voice (as individual comments were combined into averages or converted into terms that fit the method of Jacobi's study), and authority (as the experiential expertise of working-class women was leveraged by physicians with their own agendas). Attending to working-class women's indirect reception of *Sex in Education* further illuminates the rhetorical landscape surrounding Clarke's book. It highlights the relationships between professionals as researchers and non-professionals as research participants in the early days of qualitative research. It identifies the material and physical well-being of working women as an under-recognized component of nineteenth-century women's rights activism. Finally, it reveals the rhetorical limitations and opportunities in attempting to speak "through" someone with greater access to rhetorical resources.

Near silences and indirect reception can operate in several ways; the example of Ames's and Jacobi's research represents just two models of how these forms of reception can function rhetorically. For example, a near silence might be strategic on the part of the nearly silent person as a way of exerting agency or of protecting oneself; it might also be used against others as a means of silencing or excluding them. In the context of reception, consider how a piece of news might be received near silently in different contexts with phrases like "no comment" to protect the speaker; "Oh, I could say a lot about that, but I won't" to increase the status of the speaker; or "And you know what that means!" to establish some listeners as insiders and some as outsiders. Or a better-established colleague might offer an indirect response to some policy change on behalf of less-secure colleagues. Importantly, near silence and indirect reception share many of the functions of silence—exerting agency, excluding people, restricting the ideas and perspectives that circulate—and so attending to them as forms of reception furthers the project of learning about the full breadth of human rhetorical activity.

Conclusion

The most obvious way to study rhetorical reception in historical contexts is to analyze archived responses to a primary text, but silence, which resists the archive, is also a crucial form of reception. Glenn asserts that "Any theory of rhetoric must also have a concomitant theory of silence" (153), and I maintain, likewise, that any analysis of reception that does not attend to silence is incomplete. Receptive silence not only conveys its own meanings but also reveals features of its rhetorical context—the ideological, political, material, and social situations influencing whose reception was recorded and who received a text silently, if at all.

First, a receptive silence can illuminate the different social and rhetorical values at work among those who comment publicly on a text and those who don't. For example, African American women's silence in response to *Sex in Education* pointed to ways of valuing education and of women's contributions to their communities that differed from those of Clarke and his white, middle-class readers. In this case, silence might have been self-protective, and it might have enacted priorities important to African American women. A receptive silence can also highlight the warrants underlying a text's argument, as the silences among African Americans and Indigenous Americans exposed the racism on which Clarke's argument was based. These silences were imposed, as Clarke's and his white readers' beliefs about who was and was not valuable excluded some potential recipients from the collective discussion around the future of the "American" population. Receptive silence might also point to different sets of rhetorical values and material resources. For instance, receptive silence might occur when the genres and discourse communities serving as the primary sites of reception do not allow some potential recipients to say what they need to say, perhaps because their forms of knowledge are not recognized; those sites might also exclude those who lack the material resources to engage in the discussion.

Second, reception's tendency to be multiply voiced paves the way for understandings of silence as collectively composed. A nearly unanimous receptive silence, as I (provisionally) found among nineteenth-century African American women *not* responding to *Sex in Education*, suggests consistency in their shared perspective on women's education. It also suggests the comprehensiveness of the racism imposing silence on potential recipients, a malicious collaboration like that fostered by *Sex in Education* and many of its published responses. Receptive near silence and indirect reception can demonstrate a range of collective rhetorical activity. One form might look like what Ames and Jacobi produced when they incorporated white working-class women's perspectives into their texts but tightly constrained, or even dismissed, what they said. A multi-voiced indirect reception might also be agential; for instance, a spokesperson might be designated to present a group's response to a policy in order to allow others to maintain a protective silence. Just as "spoken" reception might contain perspectives across the continuum from supportive to agonistic, receptive silence might also be understood to be multiply "voiced" in a similar way: even in the context of a collective receptive silence, that silence might not mean the same thing from everyone.

Third, understanding silence as a form of reception helps us broaden our focus to include not only those with the social and rhetorical resources to respond publicly, or even in more private forms like diaries and letters, but also rhetors who, for reasons reflecting their agency or their constraints, received texts silently or nearly silently. For instance, the restricted access working-class women had to platforms for commenting on *Sex in Education* demonstrates how the agendas of powerful people shaped the reception of Clarke's book. There are almost always many more receptive silences and near silences than "spoken" receptive acts, and identifying and exploring those silences expands our understanding of who is participating "aloud" and what rhetorical factors preclude others from participating in that way in a particular receptive scene.

Interpreting historical incidences of receptive silence, near silence, and indirect reception is difficult, because silence often means the absence of direct evidence. However, tools like analyzing the historical and rhetorical context, studying indirect reception, and engaging in strategic contemplation offer rhetorical historiographers ways to elucidate—carefully and always tentatively—the reasons for, motivations underlying, and effects of silence. Identifying and interpreting receptive silences illuminates the rhetorical work of silence itself, as well as revealing the situations of those who were silent/silenced. It also deepens our understanding of the rhetorical work performed by the initial text and its "spoken" reception. In the context of the nineteenth- and early twentieth-century reception of *Sex in Education*, an examination of the receptive silences reveals the racist underpinnings of a book that defined *woman* biologically and socially for many Americans, even those who disagreed with Clarke's conclusions about education for women. Importantly, many contemporary scholars (including me) have cited *Sex in Education* as an exemplar of nineteenth-century medical and popular misogyny without acknowledging the text's racism. The historical receptive silences around the book should serve as a warning to contemporary scholars who might be tempted to point to "separate spheres" as a convenient explanation for nineteenth-century women's social and rhetorical behavior without acknowledging that the model depicts social Darwinist notions of racial differences as well as gendered differences. Silence is a form of reception that is crucial to looking beyond what voluble rhetors want audiences to notice so that we can perceive the assumptions and implications that might not be foregrounded in published discourse yet are nevertheless essential to a full understanding of the social and rhetorical landscape.

5 The Receptive Repurposing of *Sex in Education*, 1973–2023

In the preceding chapters, I have examined the rhetorical work done in the popular, professional, and silent reception of Edward H. Clarke's *Sex in Education* in the years immediately following its publication in 1873. In this chapter, I analyze the reception of *Sex in Education* in more recent years, from 1973 to 2023. The initial respondents to Clarke's book understood the issues of women's education and women's social roles to be live questions, and their acts of rhetorical reception contributed to the debate over women's rights. For writers in the late twentieth and early twenty-first centuries, however, women's right to pursue an education was not an open question, so their reception of *Sex in Education* took a different form than did that of earlier audiences. Among all the texts that I have located, no one citing Clarke from 1973 to 2023 debated the book on its own terms by seeking to confirm or refute the propriety of identical co-education. Instead of engaging with the claims in *Sex in Education* as late nineteenth- and early twentieth-century writers did, recent writers treated the book as an artifact, as an item of historical interest.

Although *Sex in Education* was hotly debated when it was first published, the controversy surrounding it was short-lived. The increasing numbers of women attending high school and college (Tyack and Hansot, *Learning Together* 163–64; Solomon 63); the Morrill Land Grant Acts, which funded public colleges that admitted women;[1] and the growing demand for women to serve as elementary and high school teachers all reflected a rejection of *Sex in Education* in practice, even if some Americans still believed in its principles. Also limiting the long-term influence of *Sex in Education* were material conditions, including many schools' dependence on tuition from girls and women as well as the impracticality of operating a school according to Clarke's recommendation that all young women should reduce their workload or stop studying entirely while menstruating.

---

1. The Morrill Land Grant Acts of 1862 and 1890 did not require that the colleges receiving federal allocations admit women as students, though the acts did not exclude women, either. Women's rights advocates argued that as citizens, women had the right to attend institutions funded with public money, and the land-grant colleges and universities gradually opened to women (Solomon 52–53).

Because of these and other considerations, by the early 1900s, few people referenced *Sex in Education*. In the late 1960s, however, nearly one hundred years after it was first published, references to Clarke's book re-emerged. With second-wave feminism's investment in recovering women's history and with multiple reprints making *Sex in Education* accessible to contemporary readers (including one from Arno Press in 1972 and another from Heritage Press in 1974), scholars and feminists began weaving analysis of Clarke's ideas into their studies of women's historical and modern-day experiences.[2] But why refer to and recirculate a discredited and harmful text? One answer lies in reception studies' tenet that as cultural values change, the ways that readers value a text and the features that they attend to will also change (Agnew 7). In other words, because readers are active recipients of texts who interpret and use texts in their own socio-historical contexts, the very meanings, values, and rhetorical functions ascribed to texts change as they circulate in various contexts. In the case of *Sex in Education*, its reception over the fifty years from 1973 to 2023 featured references to the book that supported arguments at odds with its own content, values, and claims.

Of course, nineteenth-century receivers of *Sex in Education* also used the book to serve ends other than those Clarke intended: to articulate the preferred characteristics of popular scientific rhetoric (chapter two), to describe the rhetorical and epistemological features of the newly emerging professional (chapter three), and to assert entirely different frameworks for valuing women's education and work (chapter four). The tendency to use a text for reasons the writer never anticipated is inherent in reception. What makes the reception of *Sex in Education* between 1973 and 2023 different from the book's initial reception, however, is that the early receivers worked beyond Clarke's purpose while still engaging with his argument; even as they made claims peripherally related to the content of *Sex in Education*, they did so while also addressing the question of the effects of extended education on women's reproductive physiology. Receivers in the late twentieth and early twenty-first centuries did not need to debate whether or not continuous schooling would harm women or their offspring, so they put *Sex in Education* to uses even further afield from the question of identical co-education. Although all instances of reception involve both doing things *with* and doing things *to* the text in different proportions, the reception of *Sex in Education* over time featured a shift between these two receptive functions.

---

2. Many of the book-length responses to *Sex in Education*, including George Comfort and Anna Manning Comfort's *Woman's Education, and Woman's Health* (1874/1978), Julia Ward Howe's collection *Sex and Education* (1874/1972), and Mary Putnam Jacobi's *The Question of Rest for Women During Menstruation* (1877/1978) were also reprinted around this time.

The early receivers of *Sex in Education* primarily performed social and rhetorical work *with* Clarke's book as they engaged with it on its own terms. In repurposing *Sex in Education* to serve ends completely disconnected from the debate over women's higher education, however, its receivers since 1973 have primarily done things *to* the text.

In their study of the reception of photographic images, Jens E. Kjeldsen and Ida Andersen observe that reception studies acknowledges that even in what is ostensibly a single rhetorical act, power flows in multiple directions. Not only is "power . . . something that utterances exercise, but it is also something that audiences bestow on utterances" (309). This means that even as rhetoric can "do something to audiences," audiences also "have the power to do something to the rhetoric they encounter" (311). While one understanding of the purpose of tracing the reception of a text over time might be to determine the effect that text had on generations of readers, this is, according to Kjeldsen and Andersen, a relatively narrow conception of what the rhetorical analysis of reception might uncover: "The aim is not to establish a single source effect and connect this to the discourse or sender, or to establish strict, causal links between rhetorical utterances and changes in opinions or behaviour. The aim is to understand the complex interaction between the rhetorical situation, the characteristics of the utterances, and the audience uptake and its negotiation of the rhetoric" (311). The reception of *Sex in Education* 1973–2023 exemplifies just the sort of "complex interaction" among the rhetorical situation, the power that Clarke's book continues to exert over readers, and the power that audiences have to "do something to" *Sex in Education*.

In my analysis of over three hundred articles, books, websites, and podcasts addressing both academic and popular audiences that discussed *Sex in Education* between 1973 and 2023, I have found that there were four purposes to which most writers put their references to Clarke's book: as a synecdoche representing the historical misogynistic medical-social attitudes hindering women's individual and collective aspirations, as evidence that Clarke inadvertently improved conditions for women, as representative of erroneous ideas from the past that continue to threaten women today, and as a target for mockery. These four purposes, which I discuss separately for clarity, overlap in practice, reinforcing one another. Collectively, these rhetorical acts of reception demonstrate that even if *Sex in Education* exerted power over women in the past, readers—many of them women—in the late twentieth and early twenty-first centuries exerted their own power over the book by changing its meaning, value, and rhetorical function.

Among the scholarly texts citing Clarke's book, a variety of academic disciplines are represented, including anthropology, architecture, bioethics, dance, disability studies, economics, education, film studies, history (of agriculture, art, education,[3] immigration, medicine, race, science, sports, and women), law, library studies, literacy studies, literature, nursing, political science, population studies, rhetoric, sociology, and sexuality and gender studies. I want to be careful here to say that I present these instances of reception not to criticize them; indeed, much of the research and thinking presented through these texts has been crucial to my own understanding of *Sex in Education* and its historical context. Instead, my discussion of the recent reception of *Sex in Education* takes the form of rhetorical analysis meant to illuminate the ways that attending to reception reveals the interactions among text, audience, and rhetorical situation, interactions that determine (and change) what a text means.

Because my goal is rhetorical analysis, I treat the texts cited as primary-source evidence in this chapter the same way I treat the historical texts that I analyzed in preceding chapters, providing publication dates in parentheses so that readers can situate them in their historical contexts. To help readers visualize the frequency of the receptive patterns discussed in this chapter, I group the receptive texts by categories in tables, in addition to quoting representative examples. This mode of presentation demonstrates the overlap among receptive purposes as some texts appear in multiple groups within and across tables. It also foregrounds the collective nature of reception and its effects. The revisions to *Sex in Education*'s meaning, value, and rhetorical function were achieved across numerous receptive texts written throughout the fifty years studied here. Grouping the evidence of receptive patterns into tables (rather than listing them in lengthy parentheticals or endnotes) foregrounds the collective rhetorical effort that can be involved in "doing things" to texts receptively.

To explore the dynamic nature of rhetorical influences among *Sex in Education* and its modern-day receivers, I first describe the four ways that writers receiving *Sex in Education* from 1973 to 2023 repurposed the text. Then, I discuss my own reception of *Sex in Education* in order to illustrate the complex, embodied, situated processes involved in the text "doing something to" the audience while the audience is also "doing something to" the text. Finally, I consider how the notion that audiences and texts "do something" to each other addresses feminist values such as collectivity, subjectivity, and resisting gendered binaries. I conclude that attending to reception as

---

3. Notably, and in keeping with the patterns identified in chapter four, histories of African American education and African American women almost never cite *Sex in Education*. One exception is Patricia Bell Scott's article "Schoolin' 'Respectable' Ladies of Color: Issues in the History of Black Women's Higher Education" (1980), which referred to Clarke, but only in a parenthetical citation.

a rhetorical process is necessary to understanding the breadth of human rhetorical activity and to pursuing feminist interests in rhetorical scholarship.

RECEPTIVE PURPOSE: SYNECDOCHE FOR HARMFUL HISTORICAL BELIEFS ABOUT WOMEN

By far the most common reason recent writers discussed *Sex in Education* was to explain the nineteenth-century context, especially as it affected white, middle-class, literary or professional women (see Table 1). These texts tended to be histories, written by academic historians, historians of literature, journalists, or popular writers telling stories of the past. In their texts, *Sex in Education* appeared as the exemplar of the nineteenth-century attitudes and arguments used to limit women's potential. In other words, this book functioned as a synecdoche, a trope of substitution in which a part represents the whole, or as Quintilian put it, a trope that allows us to comprehend "many things from one, the whole from a part" (VIII.vi.19). For instance, in her introduction to a collection of historical essays on sexuality, literary scholar Regina Barreca (1995) called *Sex in Education* "[a] blueprint for establishing the nineteenth-century conviction of the spiritual, intellectual, and moral inferiority of women" (xviii). She went on to suggest that Clarke was responsible for a widely held worldview: "In the cosmology established, accepted, and exacerbated by his 'research,' women were in a fixed relationship to men" (xviii–xix). According to Barreca, *Sex in Education* modeled nineteenth-century attitudes about women.

Likewise, Susan E. Cayleff (1992) explicitly presented *Sex in Education* as representative of late nineteenth-century beliefs: "Clarke's views, although the best known on the subject of the incompatibility of education and proper physiological development for girls, were demonstrative of a widely held nineteenth-century medical belief which posited that women's entire system was built around, and relentlessly affected by, her ovaries" (229). These writers seemed to understand *Sex in Education* as harmful in its initial context but also as rhetorically useful to them a century later as a way of characterizing and critiquing the constellation of late nineteenth-century beliefs limiting white women's opportunities. These beliefs included medical understandings of women, sustained by suspect research; social and medical perceptions of the role of reproductive potential in determining women's value and options; and popular conceptions of men's and women's roles as defined in opposition to each other.

A similar synecdochic construction appeared among writers who commented on the role of *Sex in Education* in shifting the public's rhetorical values toward science. These writers positioned Clarke and his book as representative of a new scientific rationale for limiting women's opportunities. For example, Sharra L. Vostral (2008) credited *Sex in Education* with shaping the discourse around women's health for years, opening up for public argument what was previously a personal matter:

> Edward Clarke immediately spurred debate and defined the terms of scientific menstruation for more than an entire generation. His work became the touchstone for further cultural criticism as well as medical research, and [it] raised the stakes concerning the meaning of menstruation. Physicians, educators, and policy makers embraced Clarke's work at a particular historical moment so that menstruation became politicized. As a political topic it became the subject of debates. (29)

Although her perspective on the damage inflicted by Clarke's argument differed from Vostral's, historian Sue Zschoche (1989) similarly characterized *Sex in Education* as the originator of what would become a powerful anti-women's rights argument. She wrote that, in grounding women's capacity in their biology, "Clarke altered the terms of a familiar debate, and perhaps more to the point, he proposed to end that debate once and for all" (549). *Sex in Education* was referred to synecdochally in these cases by making the book stand in for the whole line of science-informed arguments about women's roles in which it participated.

In crafting a history around *Sex in Education*, contemporary writers often characterized it as a result or extension of texts, events, and social trends that preceded it. In these texts, *Sex in Education* also functioned as a synecdoche for its intellectual context. Writers citing *Sex in Education* most often positioned it as a descendant of the theories of Charles Darwin and Herbert Spencer; some also contextualized Clarke among his medical contemporaries, such as British psychiatrist Henry Maudsley, American neurologist William Hammond, and American physician Silas Weir Mitchell of "rest cure" fame. Some noted Clarke's debt to the theory of the conservation of energy (the first law of thermodynamics), which justified his claim that women could not afford to "waste" energy on education because that energy was required for their reproductive development. Others characterized *Sex in Education* as a reaction to social developments, such as the women's rights movement, the increasing number of women attending college, perceptions of white, middle-class women's health as poor, and declining birthrates among elite white women. Contemporary writers also frequently pointed to an immediate exigence for *Sex in Education*—demands by women to be admitted to Harvard University, Clarke's own institution.

One example of a text that situated *Sex in Education* among the social tensions of the mid- and late-nineteenth century was journalist David Baron's *American Eclipse: A Nation's Epic Race to Catch the Shadow of the Moon and Win the Glory of the World* (2017). Baron described Clarke's book as representative of several post-Civil War concerns:

> *Sex in Education* found a receptive audience in an America unsettled by shifting gender roles. The Civil War, having tragically killed well over half a million men, left many women unmarried, forcing them to enter the workforce. Meanwhile, the successful effort to abolish slavery had inspired women to seek their own full citizenship, including the right to vote, which was no longer denied—at least in theory—to freed [B]lack men. American society was changing so irrevocably that it seemed women were in danger of no longer being women, and men would soon be emasculated and cease to be men. Clarke's book foretold this horrid future. (39–40)

Like any rhetorical act, *Sex in Education* responded to the ideas and concerns of its context. One reason Clarke's book might have been cited so frequently by recent writers is the way that it pulled together so many issues current in the 1870s, particularly issues of continuing interest: women's rights (many of the texts cited here participated in or followed from feminism's second wave), racism and anti-immigrant sentiment, the effects of scientific theories and discoveries on public health, and the role of professionals in shaping collective decision-making. Because *Sex in Education* reflected and furthered nineteenth-century thought on all of these topics, the book served historians as a convenient way to represent not only a variety of social issues, but also how all of those issues intersected with and reinforced one another.

Indeed, in his essay on "Interpretation in History," Hayden White characterizes historiography as dependent on the four master tropes (metaphor, metonymy, synecdoche, and irony). Synecdoche in particular allows the historian to move "towards integration of all apparently particular phenomena into a whole" (73). As Frank D'Angelo explains, referring to White, "As the historian seeks to understand the relationship between parts and parts, and parts and wholes, he or she must necessarily use figurative language because figures represent the power of the imagination to grasp the world figuratively" (206). The pattern among recent writers of relying on *Sex in Education* as an exemplar of not only a set of attitudes toward women but also an emerging nineteenth-century epistemology grounded in science fits the notion of historiography functioning through synecdoche. The writers' choice to use *Sex in Education* synecdochally, then, could be seen as a reasonable response to their rhetorical situations, especially the challenge of condensing the vast complexity of a past world into something comprehensible to modern-day readers.

It is important to note, however, that in using *Sex in Education* as a synecdoche, those receiving the book in recent years changed its meaning, value, and function. They treated it not as a text attempting to persuade readers to take a side on an open question, but as a text representing a collection of erroneous, harmful, and/or prejudiced ideas from the nineteenth-century US. In their reception of the book, recent readers recast the value of *Sex in Education* so that it was no longer valuable as a presentation of physiological theory authorized by a respected physician. Its value instead lay in its helpfulness as a shorthand that aided modern-day writers and readers as they sought to understand a complex historical moment.

Along with relying on *Sex in Education* to represent nineteenth-century medical and social attitudes, many of those who cited the book also reported on its popularity, the number of editions published, and the speed with which copies were sold. For example, Karin Bergstrom Costello's introduction to an excerpt from *Sex in Education* included in a collection of primary sources called *Gendered Voices: Readings from the American Experience* (1996) concluded, "Immensely successful, the first edition sold out in one week and went through 17 editions in 13 years. Despite criticism, Clarke's ideas remained popular and influential for years to come" (306). Kimberly A. Hamlin (2014) was among several writers who reported that "At the newly coeducational University of Michigan, two hundred copies [of *Sex in Education*] reportedly sold in one day" (73). Writers also pointed to the copious response to *Sex in Education* as indirect evidence that it was widely read. For example, Zschoche (1989) reported that in the fifteen years after it was published, "*Sex in Education* generated a small cottage industry in publishing as each of its additional sixteen editions called forth yet another round of rebuttals, counterassertions, and conflicting testimonials 'certifying' either the health or the invalidism of the college woman" (547). Likewise, Lynn Peril (2006) described the immediate response to the book, noting its popularity despite lacking modern means of generating interest in a new publication: "A flood of journal articles and at least four books replying to Dr. Clarke followed—most impressive when one remembers there were no morning talk shows, no Internet discussion groups, no electronic media whatsoever to whip the waves of controversy" (231). Quantifying the popularity of *Sex in Education*, Naomi Oreskes (2019) reported that more than twelve thousand copies of the book had been printed by the turn of the century (77).

In addition to acknowledging that *Sex in Education* was a bestseller, many writers also admitted that the book did worry some nineteenth-century women and their families. Bryn Mawr president M. Carey Thomas's 1908 declaration was frequently quoted: "We did not know when we began whether women's health could stand the strain of college education. We were haunted in those early days by the clanging chains of that gloomy little specter, Dr. Edward H. Clarke's *Sex in [E]ducation*" ("Present Tendencies" 69). Together, claims about the intellectual effects of *Sex in Education* along with reports of its popularity established the book as influential in its historical context. I tend to agree with these writers; however, as chapter four demonstrates, it is also true that *Sex in Education* was concerned with a relatively small and elite subset of nineteenth-century women in the US. Furthermore, ample evidence exists to demonstrate that *Sex in Education* had minimal effect on the number of women pursuing higher education. Recounting histories involves many acts of selection, particularly when one text, person, or event is made to stand synecdochally for a constellation of historical actors, so we might ask why recent writers so often chose to discuss *Sex in Education* as not only part of their historical narratives, but as the representative text of nineteenth-century sexist thought. What made reading and writing about *Sex in Education* synecdochally such a popular rhetorical choice for writers in the late twentieth and early twenty-first centuries?

One answer may be that Clarke made a good villain for heroic nineteenth-century (white, often professional or literary) women to overcome. Many of the texts citing *Sex in Education* were accounts of women, individually or collectively, achieving professional goals despite the obstacles posed by the attitudes exemplified by *Sex in Education*. For example, in her biography of novelist and reformer Cornelia James Cannon (2011), Maria I. Diedrich used *Sex in Education* to describe the challenges educated women faced:

> In addition to [the] absence of viable professional opportunities, women with aspirations were terrorized by a medical profession that targeted white middle-class women with their racialized eugenic assignments. As early as 1873 Harvard's Edward Clarke warned in *Sex in Education* that as a woman's brain expanded from her exposure to learning, her uterus inevitably shrank and her reproductive capacity diminished. Eminent scientists such as Clarke, R. R. Coleman, and Charles B. Davenport, supported by eugenically programmed politicians, reformers, and the media, criminalized women's educational efforts by associating them with race suicide. (32)

Immediately following this description of the hostility among scientists toward educated women, epitomized by *Sex in Education*, Diedrich stated, "This was the context in which the Jameses prepared their daughters for adulthood" (32). It is clear from this account that anyone who achieved an advanced education (as Cannon did) despite being "terrorized," "targeted," and "criminalized" by people who were "eugenically programmed," had accomplished something that they, and we, should be proud of.

Relatedly, some writers contended that *Sex in Education* was intended as an obstacle to women who sought to study and work as scientists. These women not only challenged conventional gender roles but also threatened men's monopoly on the sciences. For example, Renée L. Bergland (2008) grouped Clarke among the "Late nineteenth-century scientists [who] tried frantically to establish a simple, true sex, to define true women as intellectually inferior, and to bar them from scientific institutions because modern scientific theories threatened to diminish masculine certainty in painful and frightening ways" (82). Such accusations venture into inferring Clarke's motivations (was he intentionally trying to criminalize women's education and bar women from science, or were those outcomes simply the consequence of a misguided attempt to protect women's health and reproductive potential?), but the tendency to characterize Clarke in this way may reflect the historian's need to explain how the past became the present. If overwhelming opposition to women's education existed in the late nineteenth century, how have we become a society in which women can earn advanced degrees and pursue a variety of careers? One rhetorical strategy for addressing this exigency might be to concretize abstract social beliefs synecdochally in the form of an individual person, one who could be overcome or defeated. Casting Clarke as the villain in their histories, recent writers repositioned Clarke in a way that coincided with their characterization of his book as representative of misogynist and eugenicist attitudes. These worldviews, quite naturally, were promoted by a villain.

Analyzing how *Sex in Education* was used to craft a historical narrative—one that often presented the book as a synecdoche for a confluence of nineteenth-century US social features—demonstrates the ways that, through reception, an audience can alter the meaning, value, and function of a text. Those who received *Sex in Education* from 1973 to 2023 also (and here I'm crafting my own narrative) reclaimed a misogynist and eugenicist book as part of a feminist success story, one in which the popular treatise and its villainous writer (and all the books, articles, speeches, writers, and scientists they represented) were defeated by women determined to seek educations and careers. Recasting Clarke as a villain and the book as an obstacle that modern academic and professional women have overcome fundamentally changed the meaning of *Sex in Education*, and it is one way that recent readers repurposed the book to serve their own rhetorical ends.

Table 1. Recent Receivers Who Repurposed *Sex in Education* as a Synecdoche for Elements of Its Context

Sex in Education as a synecdoche for broad nineteenth-century arguments used to limit women	Barreca (1995) xviii–xix; Cayleff (1992) 229.
Sex in Education as representative of a new scientific rationale limiting women	Kenschaft (2005) 157; Vostral (2008) 29; Zschoche (1989) 549.
Sex in Education as an extension of its intellectual context (evolution, medicine, thermodynamics)	Barker (1998) 140; Barreca (1995) xv–xvi; Bem (1993) 10; B. Bender (1993) 82; Birkle (2015) 88; Bohan (1990) 213; Browner (2005) 151; Burstyn (1980) 85–86; Clancy (2023) 82; DeLuzio (2007) 58, 66, 68; Dodd and Gorham (1994) 12; Eschbach (1993) 84–85; Fehr (2008) 102; Fisher (2014) 187; Gianquitto (2013) 276–77; Hamlin (2014) 70; Hayden (2013) 83; Kates (2001) 45; La Vergata (2019) 47; Lowe (2003) 2; May (2006) 632–33; May (2008) 45; McWilliam and Brannock (2001) 9; M. Mitchell (2007) 144; Myers (2010) 41; Noddings (1990) 407–08; Oreskes (2019) 76–77; Park (1991) 62; Park (2007) 1587; Richardson (2003) 40; R. Rosenberg (1982) 6, 9; R. Smith (1997) 294; Solomon (1985) 56; Strange (2000) 613; Tuttle (2000) 129; Tyack and Hansot (1990) 147–49; Vertinsky (1990) 51–52; Warsh (2019) 25; Wood (1973) 37, 43.
Sex in Education as a reaction to its social context (Civil War, women's rights movement, perceptions of women's health as poor, declining fertility among elite white women)	Baron (*American* 2017) 39–40; Bell and Offen (1983) 425–26; Bem (1993) 9; Bem (1996) 38–39; Briggs (2000) 250; Clancy (2023) 81, 93; Dan and Lewis (1992) 229; DeLuzio (2007) 57, 70; Fellman and Fellman (1981) 67; Horowitz (2008) 18; May (2008) 44; C. Smith (2016) 161–62; Sorber (2018) 151; Tyack and Hansot (1990) 152; Vostral (2008) 27; Warsh (2019) 25, 206.

Sex in Education as popular and therefore as representative of public interests and attitudes	Cayleff (1992) 229; Cazden (1983) 170; Costello (1996) 306; DeLuzio (2007) 51; Dorenkamp et al. (1985) 43; Drachman (1990) 2438; Gordon (1987) 213; Griffin (1984) 38; Hamlin (2014) 73; Hubbard (1979) 251; Inness (1995) 12; Lander (1988) 33; Lindemann (2012) 39; Mastrangelo (1999) 62; Myers (2010) 41; Nickliss (2018) 235; Nix (2016) 60; Oreskes (2019) 77; Palmieri (1995) 6; Peril (2006) 231; Perkins (1996) 537; Radke-Moss (2008) 2; Rothman, et al. (1995) 92; Schultz (2014) 51; Showalter (2016) 197; C. Smith (2016) 159; Tavera (2018) 8; Vertinsky (1987) 19; Vertinsky (1990) 51; Walsh (1977) 124; Warsh (2019) 26; Zschoche (1989) 547.
Sex in Education as causing concern and therefore as representative of the challenging context for women (including references to Thomas's "clanging chains" quotation)	B. Adams (2014) 110; Baron ("A Woman" 2017); Deacon (1998) 272; Drachman (1984) 55; Eschbach (1993) 113; Gordon (1987) 213; Hamlin (2014) 73–74; Horowitz (2008) 26; Hubbard (1979) 251; Hubbard (1990) 39; Inness (1995) 1–2; Lander (1988) 43–44; Morantz-Sanchez (1985/2000) 55; Morantz-Sanchez (1999) 123; Nix (2016) 60; Oreskes (2019) 78; Palmieri (1987) 55; Palmieri (1995) 218; Pau on Lau (1978) 20; R. Rosenberg (1982) 12; Russett (1989) 206; Spears (1986) 144; Tyack and Hansot (1988) 37; Tyack and Hansot (1990) 151; Walsh (1977) 124; J.W. Warren (2005) 61–62; Zschoche (1989) 547.

Receptive Purpose: Evidence That Clarke Inadvertently Improved Conditions for Women

Using *Sex in Education* as a synecdoche to describe the historical context was sometimes paired with claims about the unexpected material effects of Clarke's book. Despite a consensus that *Sex in Education*'s purpose was to limit women's opportunities, some writers who recounted the consequences of the book asserted that *Sex in Education* inadvertently prompted efforts that increased women's educational and occupational prospects (see Table 2). These writers received *Sex in Education* not in isolation, but alongside evidence (such as college curricula and staffing patterns, women's clothing, architecture, and medical and social scientific research) that indicated that

Clarke's book unintentionally improved women's educational and career opportunities. For instance, several books and articles from 1973 to 2023 reported that women's colleges, concerned by the threat that *Sex in Education* posed to their existence and participating in the widespread anxiety about white middle-class women's health, incorporated lectures in physiology; courses in physical education, hygiene, and anatomy; and extra-curricular athletics. In highlighting the improved conditions and opportunities for women that resulted from efforts to protect them from the very threats Clarke identified, these writers used their reception of *Sex in Education* to repurpose the text from a factor limiting women's education to a factor that inadvertently improved women's education.

For instance, in her history of women's college education, popular writer Liva Baker (1976) maintained that *Sex in Education* produced effects contrary to Clarke's goals: "The publication of *Sex in Education* served unintentionally to unite *not* those who would cloister women but those who would establish modern health practices. Women, declared Dr. Clarke's opponents, required more, not less exercise" (75). Baker continued, "as a result of the vigorous and widespread debate, co-educational and the newly developing women's colleges, self-consciously perhaps but not the less enthusiastically, focused an extraordinary amount of attention on the health of their students" (76). Likewise, sport historian Roberta J. Park (1991) used the timing of the establishment of collegiate athletic and physical education programs to draw a direct line from *Sex in Education* to women's access to physical education: "Whereas [extra-curricular] athletics had preceded [curricular] physical training for males at most institutions, physical training for females owes its initiation at Bryn Mawr, Goucher, the University of Michigan, University of Wisconsin, and elsewhere in substantial measure to the issues which Clarke had raised in *Sex in Education*" (44). Writing in *Harvard Magazine*, Sophia Nguyen (2018) interpreted late-nineteenth-century women's athletic clothing alongside *Sex in Education*. She asserted that in the late 1800s, "athletics were central to female students' lives," because women's colleges perceived physical exercise as protection against the kinds of poor health Clarke predicted: "In his 1873 bestseller, *Sex in Education*, Harvard Medical School professor Edward H. Clarke had warned that intellectual exertion would damage a young woman's childbearing capacity, 'deranging the tides of her organization' by diverting blood-flow to the brain. In response, women's colleges insisted on fitness." In their reception of *Sex in Education*, recent writers asserted that the book had unintentionally prompted conditions that, instead of dissuading women from attending college because of the threat that higher education allegedly posed to their health, actually improved access to institutional resources for college women's physical education.[4]

Other recent writers examined hiring patterns at colleges in the late nineteenth and early twentieth centuries, leading them to the conclusion that *Sex in Education* increased professional opportunities for women, despite the book's implicit exclusion of women from any career that might require constant intellectual work. For example, Carla Yanni (2017) observed that one response to *Sex in Education* was the hiring of new administrators responsible for ensuring college women's well-being. In turn, these administrators "pressed for safe, secure, and attractive housing"; significantly, "through their efforts, women's needs rose in the hierarchy of college concerns" (28). In other words, Yanni posited that *Sex in Education* indirectly led to the creation of professional positions for women, the construction of appealing residence halls for women students, and greater institutional attention to women's needs. Likewise, some recent writers received *Sex in Education* alongside evidence that women's colleges regularly hired women physicians. These writers observed that because women's colleges required their students to undergo routine physical examinations to ensure that they were not suffering as a result of their studies, the institutions hired women physicians to perform the examinations and oversee students' health. These new positions contributed to increased demand for women physicians (Morantz-Sanchez [1985/2000] 156). According to these writers, rather than exclude women from professional careers, *Sex in Education* inadvertently provided justification for the creation of professional positions for women.

Just as some recent commentators on *Sex in Education* characterized the book as unintentionally improving career opportunities and college experiences for women, others cast it as a boon for political reformers. For example, Gail B. Griffin (1984) credited *Sex in Education* with increasing support for women's rights: "While Clarke's book had enormous currency, it also elicited great anger, drawing into the fray men and women who might not otherwise have joined in" (38). In some cases, negative reactions to *Sex in Education* were described more generally, as in June Johnson Bube's (1997) literary scholarship: "women responded to these apparently scientifically sound pronouncements [by Clarke] with competing images of women's nature and roles, with different, often contradictory, ideas of who women are and what they should be able to do in society" (58). In this case, *Sex in Edu-*

---

4. Although many historians credited the *Sex in Education* controversy with spurring on physical education and athletics programs for women college students, some attributed reluctance to allow women to participate in sports to the circulation of *Sex in Education*; those making this argument included Bell (2007); Craig (2017); Stanley (1995) 423.

cation was re-imagined, not just as an anti-woman book, but as motivation to develop copious descriptions of womanhood, a feminist enterprise inherently at odds with Clarke's emphasis on reproduction as women's primary function and value.

The recent reception of *Sex in Education* also cast the book as a motivation for research into women's health, menstruation, and female adolescence. Writers making this argument cited Mary Putnam Jacobi's *The Question of Rest for Women During Menstruation* (1877; see chapters three and four), Clelia Duel Mosher's "Normal Menstruation and Some of the Factors Modifying It" (1901) and *Woman's Physical Freedom* (1923), as well as the work of several women serving as resident physicians at women's colleges. These writers maintained that this scholarship constituted a new body of work that "challenge[d] on scientific and empirical grounds the somatic definition of woman's nature and . . . push[ed] toward innovative and less biologically constricting approaches to female health and hygiene" (Morantz-Sanchez [1985/2000] 56). In fact, *The Question of Rest* was credited by one writer with "help[ing to] define the parameters of the scientific method by establishing that laboratory tests counted more than anecdotes" (Hamlin [2020] 12–13). In other words, these writers concluded that *Sex in Education* had initiated research into female reproductive physiology that not only "out-scienced" Clarke, but also justified women's medical training and occupied women as biomedical researchers, opening employment opportunities for women who had completed advanced training despite Clarke's warnings.

Finally, recent writers also referred to survey research, such as that conducted by the Association of Collegiate Alumnæ (1885; see chapter three) and by physicians Rachel Bodley (1881) and Emily F. Pope, Emma L. Call, and C. Augusta Pope (1881), as evidence that Clarke's influence was ultimately quite weak. These surveys demonstrated, with statistics that contemporaries found persuasive, that women college graduates and women physicians were healthy. In focusing on the surveys conducted in response to *Sex in Education*, this thread in the book's recent reception positioned it as a motivation for women to engage in the sociological research that was just emerging in the late nineteenth century. Combined with other writers' claims about improved conditions for women college students, increased occupational opportunities, and justification for women's medical research, the identification of women's pursuit of sociological research asserted that, despite the justified anger and fear women past and present have felt in response to *Sex in Education*, it was, unintentionally, an important prompt toward material changes that ultimately benefited women.[5] In using *Sex in Education* for the receptive purpose of identifying it as an inadvertent improver of conditions for women, recent audiences fundamentally changed the meaning, value, and function of *Sex in Education*, an extreme instance of the audience "doing something" to a text.

Table 2. Recent Receivers Who Repurposed *Sex in Education* as a Text That Inadvertently Improved Conditions for Women

Sex in Education as prompting colleges to include coursework in physiology and opportunities for physical fitness for women	Appel (1994) 30; Baker (1976) 75–76; Bix (2013) 13; DeLuzio (2007) 89; Gordon (1990) 27; Gordon (1997) 481; Howell (1995) 84–85; Lowe (2003) 3–4; Nguyen (2018); Nix (2016) 61; Park (1991) 44; Radke-Moss (2008) 190–91; Shattuck (1992) 97, 104; Zieff (2010) 1220–221.
Sex in Education as justifying professional opportunities for women	Conable (1977) 72; Dorn (2017) 137; Lowe (2003) 3–4; Morantz-Sanchez (1985/2000) 156; Prescott (1997) 285–86; Yanni (2017) 28.
Sex in Education as increasing support for women's political rights	Griffin (1984) 38; Herndl (1993) 112.
Sex in Education as motivating medical and social scientific research into women's health	Bittel (2009) 232; Brumberg (1993) 102; DeLuzio (2007) 89; Drachman (1986) 64–65; Hamlin (2020) 12–13; Hayden (2013) 227–28, n. 5; Horowitz (1993) 281; Morantz-Sanchez (1985/2000) 55–56; R. Rosenberg (1982) xv; Showalter (2016) 198; Walsh (1977) 131–33; Wein (1974) 32.

---

5. Although many of those who have cited *Sex in Education* since 1973 have focused on the book's unintentionally positive effects on women's opportunities, others have traced its eugenicist rhetorical influence on later writers, speakers, and political figures, including Theodore Roosevelt (see, for example, Diedrich [2011] 76; Ehrenreich [1974] 619).

Receptive Purpose: Connecting Present Sexism to Historic Sexism

A third thread in the recent reception of *Sex in Education* traced the implications of Clarke's argument up through the present, suggesting that modern-day prejudices against women draw from the same faulty information that was presented in *Sex in Education*. Receiving *Sex in Education* in this way, audiences exerted their power over Clarke's text by resituating it in modern debates as the ancestor of recent instances of sexism, including doubts about women's abilities (see Table 3). For example, the title of Rebecca Onion's *Slate* article "America Has Always Seen Ambitious Women as Unhealthy" (2016) summarized what Onion identified as an ongoing pattern in which *Sex in Education* participated. Onion contextualized the popular media coverage of then-presidential candidate Hillary Clinton's pneumonia in the history of attitudes toward women:

> The long record of American beliefs about women's bodies and health sheds some light on this week's overreaction to Clinton's illness. In the United States, powerful women who make bids for education, status, and position have long been seen as sick: weak, sterile, overweight, ugly, or broken. These ideas may seem antediluvian; this week proves they are still very much alive.

Onion then quoted historian Jacqueline Antonovich, who drew a direct line from Clarke to the present: "'Many of these conversations about women, work, and education can be traced back to good old Dr. Edward H. Clarke,' historian Jacqueline Antonovich . . . wrote to me." The article's conclusion confirmed the application of Clarke's sexist ideas in recent political culture: "The idea that female success is a crime against the natural order has had a startlingly long shelf life in American culture . . . . [Clinton] has desired a position she doesn't deserve and she isn't suited for; she *must* be paying with her flesh." In Onion's analysis, *Sex in Education* represented attitudes that, though ostensibly refuted, continue to affect women's opportunities.

In a similar vein, Radha Vastal (2017) recounted the history of women's success around 1900 in the professions, including as college professors and physicians, but especially in filmmaking, and the subsequent decline in their numbers. In part, Vastal attributed the shrinking numbers of professional women after 1920 to books like *Sex in Education*. She concluded her article by suggesting that the inconsistent progress of professional women could still be linked to beliefs similar to those expressed by Clarke:

We've come a long way from Clarke's views, but not as far as we might hope. Pernicious undercurrents of gender bias continue to undercut professional women's accomplishments . . . . Realizing that progress ebbs and flows, that gains made at a particular moment in time aren't automatically protected, that they may be lost and have to be won again, is both demoralizing and inspiring.

In Vastal's analysis, *Sex in Education* is not fully relegated to the past, because its arguments about women's limited capabilities could reemerge at any time.

Sex in Education was also cited in several articles and book chapters exploring gender issues in modern education. For the writers of these texts, prejudices and questions (especially, "Do single-sex or co-educational schools serve students better?") that emerged in recent years echoed the prejudices and questions that motivated Clarke. In one case, Michelle Commeyras (1999) reported on a survey seeking to learn about literacy educators' beliefs about gender. She located these beliefs along a continuum marked by five different perspectives on gender, using *Sex in Education* as part of her description of the "essentialist perspective" (354). She went on to observe that Clarke's ideas were simultaneously outdated and present in modern society: "While these ideas seem ridiculously antiquated to most of us in the 1990s, there are people who find biological determinism to be the best theory for explaining differences between the sexes" (355). In the context of advanced scientific education, Leonard Sax (2005) connected Harvard president Lawrence H. Summers's questioning of women's abilities in math, science, and engineering to *Sex in Education* by saying that Summers "followed in Clarke's footsteps." For these writers, *Sex in Education* was not just a historical text; its ideas were still current in society. In citing *Sex in Education* in their responses to recent events, contemporary receivers of Clarke's book characterized current attitudes about women as outmoded, particularly attitudes that affected women's access to education. In other words, the ideological failure very clearly (to these readers) associated with *Sex in Education* also adhered to recent essentialist attitudes toward women's abilities.

As the examples above demonstrate, repurposing *Sex in Education* as an ancestor of modern-day sexism was typically used to dismiss those attitudes. This receptive rhetorical strategy also figured into Ruth Bader Ginsburg's majority opinion in *United States v. Virginia* (1996; reprinted in *Justice, Justice*), in which she cited *Sex in Education* as part of a continuing pattern of doubts about women's abilities in order to question the veracity of those doubts, past and present. In *United States v. Virginia*, the US Supreme Court considered whether the admissions policy excluding female applicants from the Virginia Military Institute (VMI) violated the Equal Protection Clause of the Fourteenth Amendment. The Court found that Virginia could not constitutionally "reserv[e] exclusively to men the unique educational opportunities VMI affords" (110). Ginsburg referred to *Sex in Education* and other texts critical of women's abilities to demonstrate that both historical and contemporary experts were wrong when they insisted that women were not capable of higher education.

After asserting that "Today's skeptical scrutiny of official action denying rights or opportunities based on sex responds to volumes of history" (119), Ginsburg cited *Sex in Education* as evidence that at the time VMI was established, higher education was believed to be dangerous for women (123–24). She also cited David Riesman, an expert who had testified on behalf of VMI. Riesman asserted that if VMI admitted women, the institution would be forced to shift from an "adversarial system" of education to one "that provides more nurturing and support" (129, n. 12). Deborah A. Widiss (1998) explained the significance of this pair of citations:

> All these experts claimed that certain gender-based developmental differences made some modes of learning inappropriate for women. A century ago such statements were used to deny women access to almost all forms of higher education; VMI sought to use them in the same way today to deny access to the adversative method. But readers will recognize that the nineteenth-century experts were wrong. Allowing women to learn with men neither interferes with their reproductive functions nor endangers their health. More than one hundred years of coeducation have made this clear . . . . Disallowing integrated learning because experts think it may be bad for the women is wrong now just as it was wrong in the past. The negative precedent discredits the present claims. (254)

In Ginsburg's reception of *Sex in Education*, Clarke's book served, as it did for other recent writers, as a synecdoche encapsulating the long history of experts' underestimations of women's capabilities. Ginsburg's reception, however, went one step further to foreground the commonality between past and present attitudes toward women: in 1873, as in 1996, experts asserted that women were unsuited for certain models of higher education. That similarity, though, allowed her to argue that so-called "experts" on women's capabilities were not to be trusted, at any time. Ironically, in Ginsburg's hands a book intended to limit women's access to higher education contributed to a justification for increasing women's access to education.

In another application of *Sex in Education* to legal decision-making that relied on asserting a common thread between past and present sexism, Leslie Bender (1988) explained that "tort law has been developed in the language of male orderings, values, power structures, and interests" (37). In other words, past sexism shaped the development of the principles of tort law, which resulted in sexist legal understandings that influence judicial decisions today. Bender traced "a continuous tendency in our Western culture to define 'woman' by an absence of developed rationality or, at best, by an inferior capacity to reason" through a historical lineage that included *Sex in Education* (24). Bender then identified the problem that this construction of femininity posed in the context of tort law: "If we have been culturally and socially informed by a concept of 'woman' that does not correlate with notions of reason or reasonableness, then how is the phrase 'reasonable person' or the notion of 'reasonableness' as a tort standard of conduct going to connote women's thinking, values, attitudes, or approaches to problem solving?" (24–25). In Bender's, Ginsburg's, and other legal receptions of *Sex in Education*, the book served as a reference point to explain gender constructions that were historically embedded in our institutions and that are still part of our lives today. Such a use of *Sex in Education* illuminates how the audience exerted power over Clarke's book to position it as evidence justifying a thorough revision of the often-unspoken sexist beliefs entrenched in our institutions.

Although some feminists today might want to dismiss *Sex in Education* as a temporary obstacle to women's progress, there is a rhetorical advantage to using the book to connect present sexism to historic sexism. According to the writers cited above, *Sex in Education* is part of a longstanding history of experts casting doubt on women's abilities. In their reception of Clarke's book, *Sex in Education* served as a synecdoche for this tradition, demonstrating how wrong the experts have been about women in order to assert modern-day women's capabilities—to run for office, to work in professions, and to attend VMI. These writers received *Sex in Education* as an ancestor of ongoing prejudice against women, gender essentialism, and sexism embedded in tort law. The fact that *Sex in Education* was obviously flawed in the eyes of most modern readers was used to argue for increased rights for contemporary women, on the grounds that if historical experts had failed to characterize women's abilities accurately, current restrictive beliefs about women were likely wrong, too.

Table 3. Recent Receivers Who Repurposed *Sex in Education* as a Precursor to Present-Day Sexism

Sex in Education as influencing modern-day sexist attitudes	Bullough (1975) 298; Clancy (2023) 82; Ognibene (1983) 12; Onion (2016); Vastal (2017).
Sex in Education as relevant to gender issues in contemporary education	Allison (1995) 180–81; Anfara and Mertens (2008) 52; Commeyras (1999) 354–55; Griffiths and Saraga (1979) 20; Hallman (2000) 62–63; Hansot and Tyack (1988) 760; May (2008) 2; McWilliam and Brannock (2001) 9, 12; Noddings (1990) 407–08; Picker (1984) 93; Rury (1987) 49; Salomone (2003) 64–65; Sax (2005); Weaver-Hightower (2008) 160; Weiler (2002–2003) 16; Williams (2016) 40–42.
Sex in Education as evidence in contemporary legal questions	Bender (1988) 24; Coughlin (1994) 40; Erickson (1989) 241; Ginsburg (1996) 123–24; Rhode (1991) 1737; Siegel (1992) 280; Strum (2003) 340; Widiss (1998) 254.

Receptive Purpose: Target for Mockery

Most references to *Sex in Education* from 1973 to 2023 argued that its physiology was inaccurate, that it did not slow the progress of women's education, and that it was sexist (in addition to the writers cited above, see Bullough [1973] 237; Burstyn [1973] 89; Frankfort [1977] 87; Kirschmann [2004] 63; Rossiter [1982] 13; Stanley [1996] 50). What is perhaps surprising is how often modern writers, even in scholarly texts, moved beyond criticizing *Sex in Education* to mocking the book and its ideas. Receivers' derision encouraged other readers to receive it as, in at least some cases, a laughably inaccurate assessment of women's capabilities. These writers participated in repurposing *Sex in Education* in a fourth way—as a target for mockery (see Table 4). Along the way, they reshaped Clarke's ethos from authoritative to ill-informed or even malevolent.

Hostility toward *Sex in Education* often appeared in humorous or bitter asides, as in Barreca's introduction to her collection, *Desire and Imagination: Classic Essays in Sexuality* (1995). In describing *Sex in Education*, Barreca used a parenthetical comment to ridicule what she saw as a logical flaw in Clarke's argument: "Women are bound by the cycles of their bodies, according to Clarke, who asserted that if a woman 'put her will into the education of her brain,' she necessarily withdraws it from her reproductive organs (presumably where it is in constant demand, even for an unmarried virgin)" (xv). Later, she again used parentheses, this time to scoff at Clarke's deployment of "physiology" to justify his claims: "Surely it is difficult to ignore the point that any number of words could and perhaps should be substituted for *physiological*, (*dominant, oppressive,* and *tyrannical* leap to mind)" (xix). Scholars' derision of Clarke and his work also manifested in scare quotes, as in Ellen Skinner's (2003) characterization of the obstacles faced by early advocates of higher education for women: "In pursuit of a college education, M. Carey Thomas and other women of her generation had to surmount the pervasive assumption that women were intellectually inferior as well as the dismal medical warnings of 'experts' like Edward H. Clarke that intellectual activity strained the weak female brain and nervous system leading to the eventual collapse of the reproductive organs" (109). In his time, even Clarke's harshest critics were likely to agree that he possessed expertise; Clarke might have been wrong, but there was little question that his profession and distinguished career qualified him as an expert. The doubt cast on Clarke's expertise through these quotation marks reflected E. Skinner's disdain for Clarke's position, and it prepared modern-day readers to view his ideas with suspicion.

Perhaps with more of an attempt at humor, but nevertheless pointedly, Oreskes (2019) asked how Clarke's theories might apply to men:

> [Clarke's use of thermodynamics] was . . . asymmetrical, because for some odd reason it only applied to women. Admittedly, Clarke had an explanation for this: he suggested that the female contribution to reproduction was uniquely demanding, and he did allow the possibility that overexertion could be harmful to both boys and men as well. Yet, while stressing the claim that if a woman was educated, her uterus would shrink, he evidently never paused to ask: if men were educated, what part of their anatomy would shrink? (138)

The pattern of recent scholars' derisive reception of *Sex in Education* was so prevalent that Virginia G. Drachman (1990) noted it in her article on the history of women lawyers: "The outrage of many nineteenth-century women at *Sex in Education* has been echoed by contemporary historians, who have interpreted Clarke's book as a dangerous threat to women's rights" (2438, n. 72). In considering these acts of mockery and derision as part of the long-term reception of *Sex in Education*, these hostile reactions to the book illustrate how, through reception, an audience constructs a text's meaning, value, and purpose. Clarke did not set out to publish a punching bag, but readers—even otherwise staid academic writers—in recent years have made it into one.

Among books intended for popular audiences, the scorn directed at Clarke and his work was even more pointed. Journalist Rachel Swaby (2015) described *Sex in Education* as "one doctor's nutty ramblings" (3). Verging into sarcasm, Barbara Ehrenreich and Deirdre English (1979) challenged Clarke's reasoning: *Sex in Education*, they wrote, "concluded, with startling but unassailable logic, that higher education would cause women's uteruses to atrophy!" (127–28). The derision toward Clarke might have made it easier for some popular writers to mischaracterize his argument, as when Natalie Shure (2017) conflated the supposed effects of education on women's reproductive health with the act of learning about menstruation. She wrote that Clarke "argued against educating girls during their periods. (His reasoning? Learning about their own bodies would wreak havoc on their cycles by diverting blood flow to their brains)." Although Shure's characterization of Clarke's physiological claims was inaccurate, her parenthetical question, "His reasoning?" paired with a misrepresentation (Clarke did not warn against women learning about their own anatomy and physiology) conveyed a sense that Clarke's reasoning was highly illogical. The tone of these and other popular texts commenting on *Sex in Education* was often one of "Can you believe that people used to think this?" Such an implicit question encouraged recent readers to receive *Sex in Education* as an expression of preposterous beliefs about women and their physiology. Incorporated into the derisive reception of Clarke's book were the implications that the people of the past were not as well informed as the people of the present are and that no one in the nineteenth century could have critiqued *Sex in Education* the way we can today, because they lacked physiological knowledge that is now commonplace.

Some of the texts that mocked *Sex in Education* aimed to be funny, such as the podcast "Edward Clarke vs Girls" (2017) in which the hosts, Dave Anthony and Gareth Reynolds, made fun of the book's premises, conclusions, and even Clarke's own health issues. Other ostensibly humorous references to *Sex in Education* took the form of online lists of historical misunderstandings of female reproductive physiology. For example, "9 Bizarre Facts About Your Period Nobody Ever Told You" (2021) by Alexandra Churchill explained Clarke's argument this way: "[H]e was asserting that if a young woman attended college, all the blood in her body would be diverted from her uterus to stimulate her brain. Sounds like this guy slept through a med lecture or two (or seven) himself." Although both historical and recent objectors to *Sex in Education* rejected Clarke's thesis and sometimes adopted sarcastic stances toward the book, the early-twenty-first-century efforts to get the audience to laugh at Clarke, his ideas, and his book differed from the nineteenth-century reception of *Sex in Education*. This difference perhaps reflects advances in physiological knowledge, but it might also reflect an assumed acceptance of women's rights among recent writers, in contrast to the controversy the topic generated among Clarke's contemporaries. Furthermore, the recent derision directed toward Clarke and his book might also have functioned to demonstrate that those who read and wrote about *Sex in Education* in the late twentieth and early twenty-first centuries were better educated and more egalitarian than Clarke and his allies. Yet the frequency with which *Sex in Education* continued to be discussed (and mocked) suggests that the issues the book raised still had some relevance for recent readers.[6]

Table 4. Recent Receivers Who Repurposed *Sex in Education* as a Target for Mockery

Sex in Education as the subject of bitter comments and disbelief	Barreca (1995) xv, xix; Ehrenreich and English (1979) 127–28; Oreskes (2019) 138; Shure (2017); E. Skinner (2003) 109; Swaby (2015) 3.
Sex in Education as the subject of humor	Anthony and Reynolds (2017); Churchill (2021); Hickson (2016); Smothers (2018).

Reception and the Personal

As the last few pages demonstrate, the reception of *Sex in Education* from 1973 to 2023 took the form of rhetorically repurposing Clarke's book by altering Clarke's ethos (from expert doctor to villain) and the exigencies the book addressed (from participating in the debate over whether or not women should go to college to serving as a synecdoche for a set of nineteenth-century attitudes about women, as an inadvertent improver of conditions for women, as an ancestor of modern-day sexism, or as the target of derision). I have identified these patterns of repurposing from a large body of published texts that referred to Clarke or his book. But of course, I am also engaged in the rhetorical reception of *Sex in Education* myself, repurposing it for my own rhetorical ends and shaping how others will receive it. Examining reception means being aware that the researcher participates in the phenomenon she studies.

---

6. Indeed, Anthony and Reynolds compared *Sex in Education* to twenty-first century white supremacy and climate-change denial.

Naturally, my reception of *Sex in Education* reflects my personal experiences and commitments. Feminist theory confirms the value of knowledge grounded in the personal. As Lisa Ede, Cheryl Glenn, and Andrea Lunsford explain, "feminist theory has consistently challenged any public/private distinction, arguing that knowledge based in the personal, in lived experience, [should] be valued and accepted as important and significant" (412). Personal knowledge, however, does not develop in isolation. It is embedded in and responds to complex contexts: "From a feminist vantage point . . . it is impossible to take the subjectivity of the rhetor for granted, impossible not to locate that subjectivity within the larger context of personal, social, economic, cultural, and ideological forces, impossible not to notice not only the context itself, but also who is absent from this context as well as what exclusionary forces . . . are at work there" (412). Each receiver's individual experiences and the ways she is embedded in a variety of intersecting social forces cannot help but shape how she receives and acts on texts, though some texts may draw on more or fewer features of someone's personal history and context. These subjective and perhaps idiosyncratic responses to a text can nonetheless affect its broader reception, as those personal measures of a text's effects (or usefulness) determine whether or not (and how) a reader chooses to cite or otherwise recirculate it so that it reaches a wider audience.[7]

If, as Kjeldsen and Andersen maintain, rhetorical reception studies recognizes that texts and audiences both "do something" to each other (311), then feminism encourages us to go a step further and acknowledge that the site in which that encounter occurs is an embodied, situated, messy human being. Attending to the individual, situated factors influencing one's reception illuminates the tug-of-war between the text and the reader over what the book means and what its purpose is. In what follows, I describe the professional and personal exigencies, experiences, and social-material conditions affecting my reception of *Sex in Education*, then I consider how other writers' personal histories might have shaped their reception of Clarke's book, too. I make no claim to being representative of other readers of *Sex in Education*; instead, what I hope to offer is one example of what Kjeldsen and Andersen call "the complex interaction between the rhetorical situation, the characteristics of the utterances, and the audience uptake and its negotiation of the rhetoric" involved in rhetorical reception (311). In particular, I aim to end this chapter, which has been focused on how receivers have done things to *Sex in Education*, by revealing how the text has acted

---

7. The power to influence how, and even if, texts—especially those by people of color—are received and recirculated is at the heart of discussions of the "politics of citation" (Ahmed; Delgado).

on me as I have acted on it and by suggesting that others who have received and repurposed *Sex in Education* may have engaged in their own versions of this "complex interaction." Such a perspective is entirely in keeping with feminist rhetorical studies, with its commitments to recognizing the value of the personal, the affective, and the positional. Any theorization of how rhetoric acts on people should account for the interplay among the text and the audience (individually and/or collectively) occurring in embodied, situated, subjective contexts.

I first came across *Sex in Education* in my research on the rhetoric of nineteenth-century US women physicians. The book was relevant to that project because Clarke's argument that women should take periodic breaks from mental exertion would have hindered not only women's ability to complete medical training but also their reliability as healthcare providers. After I finished that project, I grew increasingly curious about how scientific reasoning, evidence, and authority became part of public decision-making. *Sex in Education* addressed all the intersections to which my previous scholarship and my subsequent research interests had drawn me: women's rights rhetoric, nineteenth-century medical rhetoric, and scientific-professionalism as an emerging rhetorical resource in the nineteenth-century US. I was also interested in how rhetoric works—how it actually achieves social change. *Sex in Education*'s mixed record—intensely popular but with little effect on women's education—seemed like a good case through which to study rhetorical impact. I was familiar with feminist analyses of rhetorical success as dependent on factors other than the skill of the rhetor (Campbell; V. Collins; Hallenbeck, "Resituating"; Ritchie and Ronald), and my reading of history had shown me that social changes often occurred because of factors other than persuasive speeches and essays. Economic necessity, technological innovation, and demographic shifts have all at times seemed to be more influential than rhetoric in instigating social change. I started to wonder about rhetoric's role among of a constellation of factors prompting change.

I knew *Sex in Education* had been controversial (though I did not know before I started collecting texts how voluminous the debate was), and I knew that Clarke had not achieved his goal of establishing a model of education that accommodated women's supposed periodic nature. I was interested in the feminist potential of analyzing collective rhetorical action, such as the resistance to *Sex in Education*, as a counterpoint to the autonomous rhetors so often canonized. The breadth and variety of subjects addressed or implicated by *Sex in Education* and its reception have given me plenty to write about, allowing me to write this book, which serves my intellectual curiosity and my career goals. On a practical level, my reception of *Sex in Education* (and its reception) has been influenced by my department's expectations for scholarly production; my university-sponsored access to books, online databases, and research time; and a network of supportive colleagues across institutions. My material context has afforded me many of the resources I needed to read and write about *Sex in Education*. Just as *Sex in Education* acted on me intellectually, prompting me to identify connections among several scholarly interests, I have acted on the text and possibly on its future readers through the connections, observations, and analyses I have pursued in this book.

As elements of my personal life intersected with Clarke's argument, however, I felt *Sex in Education* asserting its power over me. Like many of the contemporary scholars who cited *Sex in Education*, I am the modern-day version of the women Clarke wrote about: white (though my Irish heritage might have given Clarke pause), highly educated, and willing to spend long hours studying and working. I even manifested some of the concerns Clarke feared would result from women's extended education; even by twenty-first-century standards, I was late to marry and have children. I studied *Sex in Education* through the years I was pregnant and caring for young children. In the difficult days of miscarriages and breastfeeding challenges, I wryly wondered if Clarke had been right. Had my extended education and commitment to an academic career undermined my ability to have and nurture children?

Although *Sex in Education* did not achieve its purpose in that it did not convince me to reduce the hours I spent working and learning, it is fair to say that the book affected me, sometimes by making me feel judged and sometimes by making me grateful that medical knowledge about reproduction had advanced since the 1870s. I often think of the nineteenth-century women who read *Sex in Education* while or after struggling to conceive or carry a child to term, of how Clarke's book might have made them blame themselves or feel selfish for having invested themselves in pursuits other than motherhood. In this sense, putting my own experiences alongside of my reading of *Sex in Education* allowed me to feel a sense of commonality, to identify with the historical women affected by the book and to hope that they knew, through personal experience, the support of friends, or an innate resistance to believing their gender limited them, that Clarke was wrong. That a thoroughly discredited, 150-year-old text still seemed to echo in my personal life suggests the rhetorical power *Sex in Education* continues to wield.

Still, I knew Clarke was wrong, and I was certain he was wrong because I knew what my "real" problem was—I was too old to have babies. All around me, news articles, medical websites, and other sites of popular culture were warning women not to wait "too long" to start their families, sometimes sympathizing with women trying to conceive in their late thirties or forties, sometimes implying that we had gotten ourselves into this situation and needed to accept the consequences. At some point in my study of *Sex in Education*, it occurred to me that the "don't wait too long" advice directed at women today is the modern-day equivalent of *Sex in Education*'s argument. Instead of reproductive organs failing to develop because too much energy was directed toward schooling or work, twenty-first century women are warned that their eggs will not be viable if they spend too much time pursuing educational and career goals before trying to start their families. According to both the nineteenth- and the twentieth-first-century explanations, my miscarriages were my fault, the result of too much school. If I had spent less time on my education and career and started my family sooner, I would have had several easy pregnancies. My argument here is not that modern research into the effects of age on fertility is wrong just as Clarke's theory about women's physiology was; instead, I'm observing similarities in how I received both sets of advice. *Sex in Education* and its modern-day counterparts acted on me by making me doubt my choices and by drawing my attention to the persistence of advice to women to minimize or avoid commitments to education and career. In positioning (in my mind and in this published reflection) *Sex in Education* as analogous to contemporary advice to women, however, I acted on the book, engaging in a receptive purpose very similar to the rhetors cited above who used *Sex in Education* to connect present sexism to historic sexism. In other words, in connecting these two pieces of advice, I have "done something" both to Clarke's book and to the recommendation not to "wait too long."

My experience witnessing political rhetoric in the twentieth- and twenty-first-century United States also influenced my reception of *Sex in Education*, just as my familiarity with *Sex in Education* shaped my reception of political rhetoric around fertility. Both *Sex in Education* and contemporary advice to women to protect their fertility by prioritizing reproduction over education and career convey judgments about which women's fertility is valuable. Commentators' concerns about "missing out" on bearing children do not seem to apply to poor women who might be accused of exploiting the welfare system by having "too many" babies or to immigrant women charged with manipulating the immigration system through their reproductive choices. Clarke's fear that "the race will be propagated from its inferior classes" (139) has its parallel in today's "replacement" theories and in efforts to restrict access to abortion that are rooted in white supremacy (for discussions of these ideas in popular media, see Gaynor; Goodwin; Hartmann). Positioning *Sex in Education* in this ongoing lineage of racist beliefs about fertility forces us to read Clarke's biological construction of *woman*— a construction that has been very influential in understanding nineteenth-century women's roles and rhetorical activity—as not just a sexist, but also a racist construction. His concern about (white) women's fertility was not only (or even primarily) for the sake of their own health and reproductive goals, but also for the sake of the "advancement" of "the race." This realization fundamentally changed how I read and wrote about the meaning, value, and function of *Sex in Education*, and I used my power as a receiver of Clarke's book to likewise affect how my readers understand his text.

Of course, any account of the factors influencing an individual's reception of a text is inescapably partial; there is simply no way to characterize all the experiences, cultural events, values, and social institutions that shape a text's reception, even for just one person. Although it is impossible to trace all the aspects of an individual's receptive context, even an incomplete outline can suggest factors in the process of reception that may not otherwise be visible. For instance, when I first read *Sex in Education* in graduate school, my own initial identification with the educated women Clarke sought to repress made me indignant; in this sense, I suspect I understand at least some of the motivations behind the writers cited earlier in this chapter who ridiculed Clarke (I did, after all, derisively text my sister several of Clarke's particularly offensive and patronizing lines as I came across them). Later, as I re-read *Sex in Education* and studied its reception during and after my own experiences with what Clarke might have called "the sterilizing influence of [my educational] training" (*Sex in Education* 139), my feelings shifted more toward sympathy for the women who, because of Clarke's book, might have blamed themselves for their own poor health, infertility, or feeble babies; I also understood the zeal with which educated women sought to disprove Clarke, and perhaps the urge to cast him as a villain today. Finally, constantly witnessing the evidence of modern-day racism, classism, and hostility toward immigrants has made me sensitive to Clarke's reliance on those systems and to how they continue to play out in reproductive rhetoric today. Both individual and broader cultural aspects of my rhetorical situation affected my reception of *Sex in Education*, shaping how I have written about it here.

Every act of reception, even a professional response to a text, is to some degree personal, as the receiver filters what is said through her own interests and experiences. My own story of receiving *Sex in Education*, though not intended as representative, suggests that other writers' personal experiences likely shaped their reception of Clarke's book. For instance, some of the writers cited in this chapter were among the women pursuing graduate education in the 1960s and 1970s; the resistance and doubts they probably faced likely affected their reading of *Sex in Education*. Some of these writers were pioneers in writing academically about sexuality; those experiences likely influenced how they characterized *Sex in Education*. Reception in professional genres often minimizes the personal experiences that might have motivated audience members to read a text or the exigency they felt to right past wrongs, but those elements certainly influence any text's reception.

One scholar whose reception of *Sex in Education* did foreground personal experience and positionality was Monique L. Snowden, who published "'Bettering Her Education and Widening Her Sphere': Betwixt and Between Coeducational Experiences" in 2011. This article, which described and modeled a qualitative research method, incorporated anecdotes from Snowden's life, recounting her experiences as an African American woman at Texas A&M. She used *Sex in Education* as one of her "grounding texts" (933), and she quoted it as part of her examination of her intersectional experiences:

> On one side, I had long since acknowledged the possible impositions that my "[B]lackness" might present at *my* historically white university. On the other side, however, I was less aware of the constrictions that my perceivable gender and socially constructed womanhood inflicted on he who might feel that his claimed and rightful space was reprehensibly narrowed by what Dr. Edward Hammond Clarke, a prominent Boston physician, framed in 1873 as the "bettering of her education and widening of her sphere." (931)

This quotation, from the introduction to *Sex in Education*, was followed by additional quotations from Clarke's book and other historical sources commenting on collegiate (gender) co-education. For Snowden, *Sex in Education* was rhetorically useful as part of her process of outlining an approach to research exemplified through her interpretation of a racist and sexist encounter from her past.

Like others who have rhetorically received *Sex in Education*, Snowden did something *with* and *to* the book. She explained that she used *Sex in Education* and other texts "to facilitate [readers'] understanding of how I experienced and thus perceive my coeducation" in part by quoting "subjectively significant—dominant . . . and persistent . . . —texts and discourses" (935). Snowden positioned *Sex in Education* (along with other texts) as contributing to her experience of feeling unwelcome in college. She foregrounded the book's real effects on real people, even more than a century after it was published. Snowden's individual experience as a college student reinforced her scholarly reception of *Sex in Education*; she did what she did to the text in part because of what the text had done to her.

My account of the personal factors influencing my reception of *Sex in Education*, Snowden's article placing her story of a racist and sexist encounter alongside quotes from *Sex in Education*, and the individual experiences with sexism that might be inferred from the hostility and derision directed toward Clarke and his book all demonstrate the power that *Sex in Education* continues to exercise on its readers as well as the power that audiences have to change the text—to reinterpret and revalue it. In asserting the value of paying more attention to how audiences receive texts, Kjeldsen argues that such studies "are not only a way of understanding the power of the audience, [they are] also a way of understanding the power of rhetoric—in situ and in general" (7). Although it is not practical, and perhaps not even useful, to interrogate the individual experiences, commitments, and social contexts affecting all acts of rhetorical reception, it is worth remembering that the ways an audience (collectively or individually) receives a text may be grounded in personal, often emotional, connections to the text and what it represents. In other words, the process of negotiating what the text does to an audience and what the audience does to the text occurs in complex social and individual contexts. Even when what texts and audiences do to one another is not as agonistic as much of the recent reception of *Sex in Education* has been (audiences in fact frequently welcome the effects some texts have on them!), it is worth recognizing that those receptive processes are always embodied and situated in human experiences.

Conclusion: Feminist Receptive Repurposing

In their reception of *Sex in Education* over the years 1973 to 2023, writers have "done things" to the text, repurposing it for their own rhetorical ends, transforming Clarke's ethos from authoritative physician to misogynistic villain, circulating it among audiences Clarke never imagined, and filtering it through their own experiences. Reception is a rhetorical act, occurring in a situation and for a purpose that might be similar to or very different from the conditions in which the text was originally composed. To some extent, repurposing is a natural effect of receiving a text in a new context. However, receiver-writers make choices in their repurposing, and those choices can be rhetorically significant.

Although we have long understood that meaning-making happens among the rhetor, text, and audience, this analysis of the reception of *Sex in Education* presents that process as it has occurred on a scale that is simultaneously larger and more intimate than is typical for much rhetorical scholarship. The two frames work together, as the individual reminds us that the collective is not an indiscriminate mass; it is instead made up of people with their own motivations and experiences. Both the large frame, focused on the collectivity of receptive rhetorical action, and the small frame, focused on the subjective, messy individual, shift attention away from the conventional autonomous rhetor. They also suggest that reception may be more of a rhetorical *process* than a rhetorical *act* in many cases, as the collective efforts to repurpose a text accumulate and develop over time and as an individual's reception of a text evolves in response to and in concert with her subjective experiences and interests.

In addition to exploring the rhetorical implications of feminist values like collectivity and subjectivity, this chapter's attention to reception as a means by which audience members have "done things" to *Sex in Education* applies the feminist commitment to resisting binaries to rhetorical conceptions of textual production and reception. In identifying the ways that audience members have changed the meaning, value, and rhetorical function of Clarke's book, the binary that aligns rhetorical production with power and masculinity in opposition to reception, passivity, and femininity collapses. Rhetorical production is meaningless without reception to amplify, enact, or recirculate the message: an eloquent speech has no effect if it's delivered to an empty room. Production and reception are both sites for the exercise of rhetorical power, as rhetors seek to persuade audiences and as audience members reinforce, revise, and subvert initial rhetorical acts. Reception can affect the future reception of a text itself, as when, for instance, a reader of *Sex in Education* encouraged future readers to approach the book as laughable. Reception can also affect public attitudes toward the topic of the text more broadly, as some of Clarke's readers (past and present) made their own claims about co-education in response to *Sex in Education*.

Femininity has conventionally been characterized as passive and receptive: biologically (the passive egg awaits fertilization by the active sperm; see Martin), culturally (women gather while men hunt; women stay home while men explore, fight, and work), and intellectually (women are intuitive and imitative, while men discover, invent, and advance knowledge[8]). Just as these biological, cultural, and intellectual binaries have been challenged— the egg is now understood to play a role in selecting sperm (Arnold), in some cultures gathering yields more calories than hunting (Kelly), and numerous women have contributed to research across fields—the associations among women, rhetorical reception, and rhetorical passivity continue to be challenged as well. As the reception of *Sex in Education* from 1973 to 2023 demonstrates, women have been actively involved in reshaping the meaning, value, and rhetorical function of Clarke's book and in insisting

---

8. See Darwin (*Descent* 326–27) and Stillé (qtd. in Fishbein 83).

on equitable attitudes toward women across education, law, and occupation. They have done that rhetorical work (alongside men) through reception. Rhetoric's inattention to reception parallels its inattention to women as rhetors. Just as fully understanding human rhetorical activity requires understanding men *and* women as rhetors, fully understanding human rhetorical activity requires understanding production *and* reception as reciprocal rhetorical processes.

Conclusion: Pathways for Feminist Rhetorical Reception Studies

Throughout *Rhetorical Reception*, I have demonstrated that attending to rhetorical reception has much to offer feminist rhetorical studies, using the 150-year history of the reception of *Sex in Education* as an example. *Sex in Education*, however, is far from representative of all receptive phenomena: Edward H. Clarke's book and its reception feature characteristics that made the exploration of certain kinds of research questions possible. The questions I asked and the research methods I pursued in responding to them were shaped by the content *Sex in Education* addressed (medical science, women's rights, and social Darwinism), its historical context at a time with abundant publication opportunities (many of which have been archived and digitized), and its surprisingly long "lifetime" for a text that has been disproven physiologically and roundly condemned for its misogyny. Other receptive scenarios, however, feature different affordances, and other researchers will have different questions and interests. In this conclusion, then, I highlight some of the potential that I see in feminist rhetorical reception studies, suggesting some of the pathways that might be possible with additional research and theorizing that brings together these two important ways of explaining rhetorical action. I present these pathways in two overlapping groups, one that foregrounds feminist rhetorical theory and another that focuses on feminist rhetorical research methods and methodologies. The possibilities described in this chapter are meant to be suggestive, not exhaustive. I hope that one outcome of the reception of this book will be an exploration of the many forms that feminist rhetorical reception studies might take.

FEMINIST RHETORICAL RECEPTION THEORY

The explanations of rhetorical activity developed through feminist rhetorical reception studies contribute to the broader feminist theoretical project of accounting for women's communicative practices and contexts. Foregrounding the reception of texts, rather than or alongside of their production, offers feminist rhetoricians additional angles from which to view issues that have long been of interest to the field. It also suggests new concepts for feminist rhetorical theory to explore. In what follows, I discuss six theoretical pathways that can be illuminated by attention to reception and that align with and/or extend feminist interests:

- Theorizing the rhetorical construction of gender;
- Theorizing collaborative and collective rhetorical activity;
- Theorizing rhetoric in ways that broaden the range of texts that count as *rhetoric* and of the people to whom we attribute rhetorical action;
- Theorizing emotion and positionality as components of rhetorical activity;
- Theorizing the means by which rhetorical values are articulated and new topics are raised; and
- Theorizing the roles of *rhetor* and *audience* in ways that complicate or even eliminate the boundaries between them and that interrogate the active and passive connotations sometimes associated with them.

This list is not meant to be exhaustive, but rather suggestive of the theoretical possibilities inherent in recognizing the rhetorical work done through reception. I explore each of the pathways below.

Theorizing the rhetorical construction of gender. Feminist rhetorical scholars have analyzed how rhetoric has been involved in developing the concept of *gender* itself, in assigning particular behaviors and social roles to men and women, and in valuing or devaluing certain rhetorical acts because of their gendered associations (Enoch, "Finding" and "Releasing"; Dow; Jack, "Acts of Institution"). As I demonstrated in chapter one, incorporating the role of reception in the uptake of gender construction enhances our theorization of this rhetorical process. The gender constructions formulated in *Sex in Education* were accepted by some, rejected by some, and modified by others in their reception of Clarke's book. These and similar processes of negotiating gender present a complex, multifaceted picture of gender construction as it has been embedded in various social systems, such as (in the case of *Sex in Education*) education, professionalism, and racism, which may themselves be co-constructed reciprocally with gender. Because the characterization of gendered social positions, behaviors, and bodies is often contested and dynamic, not settled with one text or speech, it is a discursive process that is deeply embedded in reception and cannot be fully understood without attending to reception. In other words, a single text rarely completely establishes the expectations for gendered existence; those expectations emerge through an iterative process that includes the reception of that text, the reception of texts written in response to the initial text, responses to those responses, and so on. In order to fully comprehend gendering as a rhetorical practice, we need to perceive it not as an *act* that results solely from rhetorical production but as a *process* that includes reception, and possibly several layers of reception.

Once we start looking at the construction of gender in the context of reception, we can also see how this rhetorical process intersects with other rhetorical processes, including audience constitution, where audiences might be constituted as primarily masculine or feminine or as believers in a certain model of gendered social roles. Gender construction also intersects with the development of rhetorical values, which are themselves negotiated through reception. Importantly, some rhetorical values might be more or less accessible to differently gendered individuals. Likewise, some kinds of rhetorical performances might only be acceptable from rhetors occupying certain gendered positions. Finally, emerging rhetorical values might present new opportunities for or constraints on gendered behaviors, rhetorical or otherwise. For instance, because using science to influence public decision-making was a relatively new rhetorical phenomenon in the nineteenth-century US, women could, through their receptive rhetoric, advocate for evidentiary standards that, many of them believed, would result in a construction of *woman* that was compatible with education and professional work.

The rhetorical construction of gender is also deeply implicated in the development of social institutions, something that might not be visible through analyzing a text alone but emerges through attending to its reception. For example, the reception of *Sex in Education* demonstrated the complex interplay between the characterization of *woman* and the characterization of *professional*, as new scientific models of research proved women's capacities at the same time as the professions sought prestige by excluding women. Likewise, the question of the purpose of education—for broad edification, for specialized expertise, or for the benefit of one's community—intersected with debates about the nature of women's brains, souls, and social roles as raced individuals. None of these aspects of the construction of gender are observable in *Sex in Education* itself, but the examination of its reception in chapters three and four proves that the book propelled forward a conversation that drew all of these features together. In other words, interrogating the rhetorical construction of gender in light of reception allows scholars to understand how gender construction—as an iterative rhetorical process—often intertwines with the development of rhetorical values and social institutions.

Theorizing collaborative and collective rhetorical activity. Pushing back against the model of the independent, powerful rhetor whose goal is to exert influence over others and recognizing that marginalized people very often need to work together to achieve their goals, feminist rhetorical scholarship has accounted for many varieties of collaborative and collective rhetorical activity (for example, Ede and Lunsford, *Singular Texts*; Buchanan; Foss and Griffin; Fillenwarth; Sharer). Although a study of reception could focus on how one individual read and responded to a text, it's very likely that many instances of reception will involve several people, making them good sites for investigations of collective rhetorical activity.

Analysis of reception invites the examination of a large-scale corpus, beyond a single text or rhetor, possibly even beyond a group or movement, or beyond a single rhetorical situation. Such a scope offers the potential for new understandings of collective rhetorical activity. As chapter five's analysis of the reception of *Sex in Education* more than one hundred years after its initial publication demonstrates, collective rhetorical activity can stretch across time (as Clarke's modern-day critics "collaborate" with his nineteenth-century opponents) and can dramatically affect how a text is perceived (as twenty-first century rhetors recast *Sex in Education* as ridiculous and so not a true threat to women's education). When many people participate in a text's reception over time, that collective rhetorical activity takes on some of the features of "social circulation," which Jacqueline Jones Royster and Gesa E. Kirsch describe as providing "leverage for understanding complex rhetorical interactions across space and time" (98). Because reception can span geographic, cultural, and temporal locations, it offers us a means for studying collective rhetorical activity across a range of social and material contexts.

As forms of reception, silence and indirect reception should also be considered components of collective rhetorical activity, components that can deepen understandings of the relationships within collaborative and collective rhetorical acts. As chapter four demonstrates, silence and commentary delivered indirectly through others reveal a great deal about power and ideology. Seeing them alongside more freely "spoken" components of reception may uncover rifts within collective rhetorical activity, even when that activity seeks similar ends. For example, those who were silent or nearly silent in their reception of *Sex in Education* may have shared the opposition to Clarke's claims that was expressed by some of those who published their responses to his book. However, they might have had different reasons for their opposition, or they might have lacked access to the material and social resources necessary to comment publicly and independently on *Sex in Education*. While some of the silent reception of *Sex in Education* likely marked objections to Clarke's argument, it's important to remember that most of the silence may well have been among those who agreed with him.

Considering reception as a means of engaging in collaborative and collective rhetorical activity offers scholars a way of identifying and theorizing collective efforts (as responses to a particular text) that might not otherwise be identifiable. Patterns of silence, whether intentionally chosen by or imposed on rhetors, can likewise be identified and analyzed by looking for rhetors who it seems are not participating in the reception of a text.

Theorizing rhetoric in ways that broaden the range of texts that we perceive as rhetorical and of the people to whom we attribute rhetorical action. Because of the power and access to resources involved in giving an important speech or publishing a prominent text, these productive rhetorical acts have often been composed by members of dominant groups. Receptive rhetorical acts, on the other hand, can be smaller and less expensive, and they often draw less attention to the rhetor than does claiming the podium or press to make an initial statement. These features often make reception more compatible with the resources and social roles of marginalized rhetors. A focus on reception may serve as a means of recognizing the contributions of more people, including those who collectively played important roles in promoting and resisting various kinds of social change.

Although academics, particularly feminists, have long cast doubt on "great man" approaches to studies of rhetoric, history, and social movements, developing conceptions of social change that foreground the involvement of large numbers of often unremembered people seems especially crucial now, as many of the challenges we face depend on collective action. Crafting narratives of past social change that recognize that "great speakers" did not effect change on their own but that receptive rhetorical acts were necessary for the widespread uptake of, revision of, or resistance to alternative worldviews has the potential to shift how members of the public understand their roles in today's events. This is an important perspective in the context of pervasive social media, in which people receive (by reading, liking, reposting, commenting on, and remixing) numerous messages every day.

Reception, then, offers a pathway by which we can identify the contributions of less powerful people to social movements. Importantly, through reception, we can see women's participation in mainstream rhetorical activity, their involvement in "loose, dispersed networks of women and men as well as material arrangements of space, time, and objects" (Hallenbeck, "Toward a Posthuman" 17). Although identifying the characteristics unique to women's rhetoric (as a counterpoint to the conventionally masculine rhetorical tradition) is crucial work, it runs the risk of suggesting that historical women spoke and wrote outside of the social and rhetorical movements of their times. Consequently, women can be cast as bystanders to or victims of dominant social trends rather than as contributors to those changes. Situating women's rhetorical activity within mainstream contexts is an important counterbalance to the necessary work of isolating women's rhetoric in order to better describe its unique features.

For instance, chapters two and three describe women's involvement in the emergence of science as a component of public discourse and in the development of medicine and education as modern professions. Women are often characterized as victims of both of these social-rhetorical changes, so identifying them as contributors to these developments prompts important observations. For instance, some women must have seen promise in science-informed public rhetoric as a mechanism for increasing their rights. Recognizing that the women involved in articulating both scientific rhetorical values and the nature of the ideal professional were very often white and of the middle or professional classes, however, raises questions about these women's desire to maintain their classed and raced privileges through exclusionary mechanisms like professionalization.[1] Attending to reception not only foregrounds the rhetoric of the less powerful and situates it in mainstream contexts, but it also prompts us to ask how rhetors of various gendered, classed, and raced positions furthered the exclusion of others from dominant discourses and institutions. As Barbara Biesecker reminds us, "the critic taking up the project of rewriting the history of Rhetoric would be required to . . . address the real fact that different women, due to their various positions in the social structure, have available to them different rhetorical possibilities and, similarly, are constrained by different rhetorical limits" (157; see also Tonkovich). Because reception was often an accessible means by which marginalized (though variously privileged) rhetors could engage in major social and rhetorical movements, studying reception constitutes a means of broadening the kinds of texts that count as rhetoric, the range of people to whom we attribute rhetorical action, and our recognition of the role of positionality in rhetorical participation.

Theorizing emotion and positionality as components of rhetorical activity. Countering common textbook advice (grounded in the privileging of science) to appear objective and to base arguments exclusively on logic, feminist rhetoricians acknowledge and even celebrate the roles of emotion and positionality in the production and reception of rhetoric (for example, Glenn, *Rhetori-*

---

1. Although most nineteenth-century women physicians in the US were white, several African American women, such as Rebecca Crumpler, Rebecca J. Cole, and Halle Tanner Dillon, not only practiced medicine but also claimed professional status in their writing (C. Skinner, *Women Physicians*). Numerous African American women pursued careers in education in the nineteenth century.

cal Feminism; Ratcliffe, "A Rhetoric"). Feminist rhetorical scholarship even valorizes the "passionate attachments" that we have as embodied and situated researchers (Royster, *Traces* 280), and it recognizes the connections and imagined dialogues we might have with those we study (Royster and Kirsch 21). Analyses of reception can further these commitments by attending to how the identifications and emotions evoked by a text prompt or influence a person's response. Likewise, an analysis could explore the role of an audience member's social position and personal experiences in her interpretation of a text. We are often told that when it comes to persuasion, what the rhetor feels matters less than what she makes her audience feel; as an intersection between audience and rhetor roles, text-to-text reception (Willis 35) is a site in which what the audience feels and what the rhetor feels unite, motivating and affecting the interpretation and possible production of rhetorical acts.

Chapter five reflects on the role of the audience's—including my own—emotion and positionality in shaping reception. It may seem logical to say that rhetors evoke emotions intentionally to shape reception and that an audience member's emotional state, her prior experience, and her social position affect how she interprets a text. Looking past these commonsense observations, however, allows us to ask how a text might call forth emotions that the rhetor did not intend, either because she could not anticipate the experiences audience members might bring to a text or because the text has been received in contexts the rhetor did not imagine. We might also explore how reception involves the creation of emotional bonds between audiences and rhetors across time and space, and how through reception, audiences re-present historical texts as emotionally significant in ways that were not understood in their original context (for example, as admirable where they were once dismissed, or as contemptible or ill-informed when they were once respected). Attending to reception extends our commitment to valuing emotion and positionality as components of rhetorical activity by allowing us to theorize reception as a site connecting rhetors and audiences and as a site in which the emotions and positionality of an audience member can motivate and shape future rhetorical activity.

Theorizing the means by which rhetorical values are articulated and new topics are raised. In chapter two, I present evidence that the popular reception of *Sex in Education* was a site for negotiating the rhetorical values that nineteenth-century audiences would expect when writers used science to intervene in public debates. Particularly when a text does something innovative or controversial, as *Sex in Education* did, how readers receive it—what they praise and what they resist—reflects and even develops rhetorical values. Considering reception as a site for the development of new or the confirmation of existing rhetorical values suggests several questions that are relevant to feminist rhetorical theory, including, who participates in rhetorical value-setting through reception? What is the nature of collective, even diffuse, decision-making about rhetorical values? Which texts are fruitful sites for the collective articulation of rhetorical values through reception, and why?

Just as reception can offer rhetors an opportunity to articulate rhetorical ideals that challenge existing values, reception can also function as an excuse to address topics other than those raised by the initial text. Once a text has been published or an address has been spoken, the rhetor has little control over what audiences do with it. This feature of reception is important for marginalized rhetors, who may use receptive rhetoric as an opportunity to raise topics that powerful rhetors haven't recognized or that they wish to repress. Through reception, the initial text can be used to serve any purpose to which the audience can make a connection. As chapter three demonstrates, professional readers of *Sex in Education* used their reception of Clarke's book to articulate the characteristics and behaviors of physicians and teachers, even though the nature of professionalism was not a topic Clarke took up in his book. With this example in mind, we might investigate other instances in which reception went far afield from the content and purpose of the text being received. In some cases, marginalized rhetors might use a receptive situation to raise a topic that more powerful rhetors have ignored or dismissed. In other cases, reception can serve as a site of appropriation, where the topic raised by a marginalized rhetor is usurped, diluted, or minimized through receptive acts by those who are uninterested in or threatened by the content of the original text.

We might try to learn if there are characteristics of texts that make them suitable for (or prone to) reappropriation in these ways. We might try to identify patterns—in topics, composers, or genres—among texts that serve as excuses to talk about something else. With the ease with which digital texts can be remixed, copied-and-pasted, or turned into memes, the question of how texts operate rhetorically well beyond their original context and purpose is particularly relevant today. In essence, identifying the role of reception in articulating rhetorical values and in raising topics outside of those privileged by dominant rhetors allows scholars to theorize rhetorical and social change.

Theorizing the roles of "rhetor" and "audience" in ways that complicate or even eliminate the boundaries between them and that interrogate the active and passive connotations sometimes associated with them. Reception, especially what Ika Willis calls text-to-text reception (35), often involves an audience member in the act of reading as a prelude to becoming a rhetor who writes her own text. Consequently, a focus on reception highlights the temporary and fluid nature of distinctions between the categories of *audience* and *rhetor*. The merging of reading and writing, of audience and rhetor, has been explored by Ellen Gruber Garvey in her book on Americans' collections of newspaper clippings in scrapbooks, where she characterizes scrapbooking as "a form of active reading that shifts the line between reading and writing" (47). Likewise, Andrea A. Lunsford and Lisa Ede observe that their "two different strands of research—one on audience, another on collaboration—have all but merged during the last couple of years as [they] have seen how frequently writers become audiences and vice versa," particularly in the context of digital media (58).[2] Reception—often the node between reading and writing, as one reads in order to write—is a site in which the interconnections between the roles of *rhetor* and *audience* can be explored in ways that reflect feminist resistance to hierarchy and domination. Instead of perceiving the rhetor and audience as inherently at odds (as in the most agonistic models of persuasion), we can retheorize the relationship between the roles, which may lead to retheorizing what people do as writers, speakers, readers, and listeners.

For instance, considering reception as part of rhetorical practice means asking what it means to effectively and ethically compose-for-reception (to compose in ways that anticipate a variety of receptive contexts) as well as effectively and ethically receive-as-composition (to receive a text with the intention of composing a response). In his article calling for increased attention to delivery and circulation in writing instruction, John Trimbur points to the social and ethical implications of what happens to a text after it is composed (191), noting that different circulatory routes reflect and confer different degrees of esteem and authority (209). Feminist thinking has already begun to engage with the question of how to receive and be received effectively and ethically. For instance, analyses of the racism and sexism built into citation practices are substantially critiques of which texts and writers are received, and through citation, re-received.[3] Likewise, conscien-

---

2. Even as some scholars have recognized the convergence of reading/writing and audience/rhetor, Deborah Brandt maintains that "reading and writing can be in competition with each other[;] . . . they can be antagonistic to one another, [and] the uses and practices that grow up around the one might challenge and change the other" (162).

3. Sara Ahmed explores "Sexism and racism as citational practices," characterizing them as "a catering system" that functions "as a form of reassurance, a way of keeping things familiar for those who want to conserve the familiar" (151). Another contribution to this work is Temptaous Mckoy's concept of "amplification rhetorics"; Mckoy writes that "Feminists who are dedicated to moving from White

tious efforts to amplify what marginalized individuals say in meetings or on social media are attempts to manage reception ethically. Beginning with the rapid expansion of the periodical press in the nineteenth century and the greater access it gave to more people to read and to write in response to what they read, up through today's social media, managing and participating in reception effectively and ethically has become an increasingly important component of rhetorical practice, social change, and democracy. Efforts to retheorize the roles of *rhetor* and *audience* and the work performed through those roles might ask, what is the nature of the rhetorical work of anticipating, encouraging, or managing the reception of a text, by immediate or distant audiences? How is it done effectively and ethically? How do rhetors depend on reception? How is reception itself done effectively and well? How do rhetors work together, knowingly or unknowingly, to forward or repress the reception of others' texts and ideas?

Reception also foregrounds the mutability of the text, as audiences "do something" to it (Kjeldsen and Andersen 311), even changing its meaning, value, and function, as chapter five demonstrates. In this sense, audiences not only become rhetors in using what they read to write their own new texts, but also re-writers of the texts they read. This collapse of the rhetorical triangle, where audience, rhetor, and message are typically positioned at distant corners, undermines the individualistic nature of conventional rhetoric, or as Sarah Hallenbeck puts it, "the clean and constant demarcation between rhetor and surround" ("Resituating" 81). Studies of reception offer another pathway through which to explore the inevitably collaborative nature of communication, to account for the material context that affects rhetorical activity, and to articulate concepts and theories that better account for the blurred boundaries among literate roles and acts.

Ultimately, attending to reception as a rhetorical act also invites interrogation of the categories of *production* and *reception*. Although these terms are convenient, they are misleading, because every act of rhetorical production in some way responds to previous texts, and because acts of rhetorical reception are also productions composed to serve particular purposes and interests. Reception is active and intentional, not passive and automatic. Acknowledging the agential nature of reception raises several questions, in-

---

feminism to more inclusive feminisms must look for ways to pass the mic to other scholars and public intellectuals, forging a space for other narratives to be included in the charge for resistance against institutionalized systems of patriarchy" (Mckoy et al. 75). The statements and policies developed by journals in rhetoric, composition, and literacy also participate in the work of forwarding conscientious and inclusive practices for citation, and therefore, for reception. See, for example, the "Submissions" page for *Literacy in Composition Studies*.

cluding, in what ways does the naming of *production* and *reception* depend on and reinforce gendered, raced, classed, and other constructed forms of access to resources and authority? Relatedly, how might scholarly attention to reception complicate, challenge, and/or enrich our ideas of rhetoric by identifying the rhetorical, social, and material work performed by reception? Rethoerizing the boundaries around reading, writing, audience, rhetor, rhetorical production and rhetorical reception in the context of feminist rhetorical reception studies will allow scholars to continue to explore feminist concepts like relationality, situatedness, the everyday, and resistance to hierarchy. It will also provide us with a means of identifying and explaining the rhetorical and agential work performed through reception, which might otherwise be understood derogatorily as "feminine"—passive and reactive—and set in opposition to conventionally privileged ("masculine") forms of rhetorical production.

Research Methods and Feminist Rhetorical Reception Studies

In addition to opening possible pathways for feminist rhetorical research and theory, focusing on reception rather than (or alongside of) production presents some methodological opportunities. Because the scope and purpose of research into reception can vary widely, there is no single method for studying reception. The reception of *Sex in Education* happened to take place in published books and periodicals, and I was interested in how that reception affected public thinking, so this study focused on reception as it manifested collectively in hundreds of published texts over a 150-year period. Research into reception need not focus on such a large corpus, however; reception scholarship in other fields sometimes considers an individual's reactions to a text as they were recorded in a diary or letter. The potentially wide scope for receptive sites—from individual to collective and from private to public—means that there is a great deal of possibility in studies of reception: possibility in topics for study, in questions to pursue, and in methods of gathering and analyzing evidence. In this section, I present several methodological innovations that might be fostered by further research in feminist rhetorical reception studies.

Scholarship that focuses on reception may require us to rethink archival processes that have been developed to illuminate rhetorical production. For instance, we might ask what research tools and strategies will yield a useful dataset for a researcher using archives to study reception. We might also ask about the benefits and limitations of conventional archives, digital archives, and online search tools (both those that index physical archives and those that index digital archives) in studies of reception. The often-diffuse nature of reception means that it can be difficult to know where to look for texts. Unlike a project in which a researcher can focus on an individual's or an institution's papers because she knows of (or at least suspects) their involvement in the topic of interest, an investigation into reception may require looking across the records of numerous people and institutions, and the act of reception (which might be perhaps only a brief mention) may not be indexed in finding aids. Rhetorical studies of reception, then, pose some challenges to existing methods of archiving and of accessing archives. Some of these challenges are familiar to feminist historiographers, who are accustomed to questioning the social and material conditions that led to the archiving of some texts and not others.

Although digital archives, which can often be searched by keywords or phrases, are likely more accessible than conventional archives for some investigations of reception, they present limitations specific to this kind of work. Balancing the desire to stay open to the unexpected with the need to limit what might otherwise be an overwhelming number of search results—what Jessica Enoch and Jean Bessette refer to as "archival abundance" (638)—can be difficult. One approach to managing the number of search results—specific keyword searches—reduces opportunities for stumbling onto a crucial find while browsing. Although this limitation of digital archival research affects studies in any subject, this challenge is especially pertinent to investigations of reception because it can be difficult to predict what form reception might take, particularly when people respond to the idea behind the primary text without citing the text directly. For instance, some nineteenth- and early twentieth-century rhetors wrote about the effect of education on women's health without naming *Sex in Education* or Clarke. In these cases, we might ask what constitutes reception of *Sex in Education*. Would a rhetor even need to have read Clarke's book, or could she receive it indirectly, through general discussions of women's education that were informed by *Sex in Education*? Although I chose to limit my own study to texts that explicitly referred to Clarke or his book, that might not be the best choice for other research contexts, particularly those with less prolific archived receptions.

Of course, reception did not occur only in the past. Online communication, where a single message can receive thousands of likes and responses, offers a potentially vast dataset for those interested in contemporary reception. Such a project would pose its own methodological dilemmas, including the ethics of accessing and quoting online comments, the question of where to draw boundaries among seemingly endless chains of posts being shared and reshared, and the decisions about how to interpret the various kinds of responses possible online, from likes to emojis to memes to the numerous platform-specific ways of responding to what someone says. Qualitative studies offer another methodological opportunity for feminist researchers interested in contemporary reception. Jens E. Kjeldsen names interviews, focus groups, protocol analyses (such as think-aloud readings), and surveys as means of "making data" for reception scholarship (as opposed to "finding data" in the archives) (9). Although these research methods may be unfamiliar to many rhetorical historiographers, they present opportunities for intentionally collecting data that accords with feminist interests and research practices.

Whether research examines the past or the present, receptive silences present an important methodological challenge. Feminist rhetorical reception studies should develop research methods that identify, explain, and account for silence. How can we systematically look for silence in a receptive context? How might approaches like critical imagination (Royster, *Traces* 83–84) and strategic contemplation (Royster and Kirsch 21–23) help us better identify and understand receptive silences? Where can we look for reception that may *seem* absent but perhaps took an unexpected form, maybe even a form not recorded in existing archives? In other words, how might we account for apparent silences that exist not because no one responded but because our ways of looking for, listening to, and recording rhetorical acts have failed to acknowledge those forms of reception?

Another way that studies of reception might open up the scope of feminist rhetorical scholarship is through tracing reception over periods of time beyond a single generation, a form of engaging in what Deborah Hawhee and Christa J. Olson call the "pan-history." For Hawhee and Olson, "Pan-historiography can . . . refer to studies that leap across geographic space, tracking important activities, terms, movements, or practices as they travel with trade, with global expansion, or with religious zealotry" (90). Following the trends in how a text has been received over centuries and across cultures would complement existing feminist readings of classical rhetorical texts and of transnational rhetoric.

Given the challenges inherent in collecting a large sample of receptive rhetoric, whether the sample is historic or contemporary, these kinds of projects might prove to be ideal opportunities for collaboration. Archival research is often a solitary act (though it is, of course, supported by archivists and others who make the research possible). Collaboration might be especially appropriate if the instances of reception are stored in conventional archives across geographical distance, if reception occurred in several languages, or if interpreting the reception requires specialized knowledge. In other cases, the sheer volume of receptive acts may necessitate collaboration. The possibility for developing large-scale, collaborative research projects built around reception presents an exciting opportunity for feminist rhetorical scholars to engage in new kinds of research, to ask new kinds of questions, and to reap the benefits of drawing together different perspectives that collaboration offers.

Although rhetorical reception studies presents numerous opportunities to feminist researchers, it also poses a substantial challenge to feminist commitments. Notably, pursuing studies of reception risks re-centering a dominant text that has been received. I have struggled with the tendency of a study of reception to re-center dominant voices in my choice to write a feminist book that takes a text that is hostile to women, to immigrants, to Indigenous people, to African Americans, and to working-class people as its starting point. I have repeatedly asked myself what I am doing in giving Edward Clarke more of our attention, of in fact extending the reception of his book through my study. I eventually concluded that feminist rhetorical reception studies may be one of the most effective ways of challenging the dominance of rhetors like Clarke, because it is not just modern-day researchers who have been resisting readers (Bizzell). Marginalized people throughout history have resisted the worldviews promoted by powerful texts. Feminist studies of reception offer one way of identifying those acts of rhetorical resistance. We can also ask how various privileges grant some people, but not others, access to some forms of reception. Additionally, as chapter four demonstrates, we can explore silence as a form of resistant reception. If we do not analyze the reception of widely circulated texts because we fear reinstating their centrality, we risk discounting the importance of reception as a crucial factor in how rhetoric works.

In fact, attending to the reception of dominant texts may ultimately puncture the idea of the autonomous, meritorious text and rhetor. A text that history tells us was crucial to some moment was likely made effective and memorable by its reception. Recognizing that, we can ask what kinds of receptive rhetorical acts ensured that text's importance in its moment and to history? How do we identify those acts and adequately account for their role in rhetorical history? In studying the reception of canonical texts, we can identify the ways that their success was a matter not necessarily of their composers' independent genius, but instead depended on recipients who shaped how others interpreted the texts, how their ideas were enacted, and how their phrases were made memorable. Reception can also provide a window into how a now-canonized text was challenged or rejected by some audience members in its immediate context. In other words, through feminist rhetorical reception studies, we can better understand the complex and varied ways that readers over time have viewed those texts and rhetors that our history books tell us are central. The challenge remains, however, of developing research methods that resist reinforcing the harmful power that some texts and rhetors have held as we examine their reception.[4]

When a text is received across a diverse audience, researchers need to consider how best to represent the receivers' various subject positions and how those positions might affect their responses. Those who commented on *Sex in Education* consisted of a mix of elite, less privileged, and even unnamed individuals. I have tried to provide identifying information for historical figures whenever possible and to take their positions into account as I interpreted what they said about *Sex in Education*. One of the promising features of studying reception is the way that it humanizes what might otherwise be an abstract audience. I saw some receivers taking petty, personal jabs at Clarke; some obviously protecting their own interests; some (intentionally or unintentionally) misrepresenting what Clarke said; some responding through the lens of their prejudices; some reading Clarke's book very carefully; some anticipating the implications of his claims for women who were less privileged than they were; some responding very evenhandedly to what they saw as the strengths and weaknesses of Clarke's argument; and some situating *Sex in Education* and their responses to it in the context of what it means to be human and what kind of society they wanted to live in. In other words, the reception of *Sex in Education* was very human, with all the nobility and imperfection that that entails. How to characterize all of that variety, how to identify patterns without problematically erasing the instances that defy those patterns—these are issues that arise in almost any research project, because the data always exceed the narrative that can be told about them. The potential, however, of navigating among a wide-ranging set of texts and rhetors that arises with research into reception makes these questions especially pertinent to this kind of research.

Conclusion

As I said above, I hope that one form the reception of *Rhetorical Reception* will take is the exploration of new pathways for feminist rhetorical scholarship made possible by investigating reception as a rhetorical act. Such pathways would recognize reception as an active and agential (not *passive* in the pejorative sense) form of rhetoric. They would also acknowledge that reception is a necessary component of how rhetoric works; in other

---

4. Thanks to Sarah Hallenbeck for helping me think through the costs and benefits of studying the reception of texts that reinforce dominant, exclusionary worldviews.

words, they would characterize reception as a crucial element in how rhetoric contributes to social continuity and change. The possibilities described in this chapter are necessarily limited, growing out of my own experiences researching and writing this book. I am confident that other scholars, with their own topical interests and approaches to research, will create pathways for studying rhetorical reception that I can't even imagine.

I will conclude with an observation, which I have mentioned elsewhere in *Rhetorical Reception*, that is simultaneously theoretical and methodological: rhetorical scholarship is itself a kind of reception. This is true even of scholarship that foregrounds rhetorical production rather than reception. Rhetorical recovery work is very much the work of changing how a text is received. Articulating new concepts relevant to the rhetoric of marginalized people and developing new frameworks in which to understand previously ignored texts are also efforts to affect reception. Even a relatively straightforward rhetorical analysis aims to draw the reader's attention to particular aspects of the text, shaping how the reader interprets it. Understanding rhetorical scholarship as a kind of reception aligns with the self-reflective nature of much feminist rhetorical scholarship, and I made use of this interconnection in chapter five, where I discussed my own reception of *Sex in Education* alongside of what other writers have said and thought about the book in the late twentieth and early twenty-first centuries.

Even without incorporating one's personal experience of reception into scholarship (and I think that the expectation that scholars should always do so would be extremely harmful), we should consider how, as specialized receivers, we change the meaning and value of the texts we study, simply by analyzing them and by drawing our colleagues' and students' attention to them. Recognizing that rhetorical scholarship is a specialized form of reception entangles us in our own scholarship. Awareness of one's involvement in the reception and re-circulation of texts has ethical implications. Which texts should get more attention? How should texts be framed to prepare others for their reception? Who would benefit from receiving a text, and who needs to receive it differently than they have in the past? Because we know about the long history of women and their texts being "respoken" through rhetorical accretion (V. Collins 148), our responsibility in shaping the reception of texts is acute. Although being aware of rhetorical scholarship as a kind of reception adds another layer to what can already be complex work, this awareness also reminds us of our privilege, as specialized receivers, in helping one another better understand the fascinating ways that humans and texts (of all kinds) interact to create and change our world.

Works Cited

Adams, Bluford. *Old and New Englanders: Immigration & Regional Identity in the Gilded Age.* U of Michigan P, 2014.
Adams, Tracey Lynn. *A Dentist and a Gentleman: Gender and the Rise of Dentistry in Ontario.* U of Toronto P, 2016.
Agnew, Lois. "Demosthenes as Text: Classical Reception and British Rhetorical History." *Advances in the History of Rhetoric*, vol. 19, no. 1, 2016, pp. 2–30.
Ahmed, Sara. *Living a Feminist Life.* Duke UP, 2017.
Allison, Clinton B. "Gender and Education: How Are Gender Biases Reflected in Schools?" *Counterpoints*, vol. 6, 1995, pp. 161–94.
Ames, Azel, Jr. *Sex in Industry: A Plea for the Working-Girl.* Boston, James R. Osgood and Co., 1875.
Anderson, Eric D. "Black Responses to Darwinism, 1859–1915." *Disseminating Darwinism: The Role of Place, Race, Religion, and Gender*, edited by Ronald L. Numbers and John Stenhouse, Cambridge UP, 1999, pp. 247–66.
Anfara, Vincent A. and Steven B. Mertens. "What Research Says: Do Single-Sex Classes and Schools Make a Difference?" *Middle School Journal*, vol. 40, no. 2, 2008, pp. 52–59.
Anthony, Dave, and Gareth Reynolds. "Edward Clarke vs. Girls." *The Dollop* from All Things Comedy, 2017, www.youtube.com/watch?v=qRo46fyrah0.
Appel, Toby A. "Physiology in American Women's Colleges: The Rise and Decline of a Female Subculture." *Isis*, vol. 85, no. 1, 1994, pp. 26–56.
Arnold, Carrie. "Choosy Eggs May Pick Sperm for Their Genes, Defying Mendel's Law." *Quanta Magazine*, 15 Nov. 2017, www.quantamagazine.org/choosy-eggs-may-pick-sperm-for-their-genes-defying-mendels-law-20171115/. Accessed 4 Nov. 2022.
"Art V." *The North American Review*, vol. 118, no. 242, Jan. 1874, pp. 140–52.
Association of Collegiate Alumnæ. *Health Statistics of Women College Graduates.* Boston, Wright & Potter Printing Co., 1885.
Bacon, Jacqueline. "'Acting as Freemen': Rhetoric, Race, and Reform in the Debate over Colonization in *Freedom's Journal*, 1827–1828." *Quarterly Journal of Speech*, vol. 93, no. 1, 2007, pp. 58–83.
Badger, Ada Shepard. "IV." *Sex* and *Education: A Reply to Dr. E.H. Clarke's "Sex in Education,"* edited by Julia Ward Howe, Boston, Roberts Brothers, 1874, pp. 72–86.
Baker, Liva. *I'm Radcliffe: Fly Me!: The Seven Sisters and the Failure of Women's Education.* Macmillan Publishing Co., 1976.
Baker, Thomas Nelson. "The Negro Woman." *Alexander's Magazine*, vol. 3, no. 2, 15 Dec. 1906, pp. 71–85.

Barker, Deborah. "The Riddle of the Sphinx: Elizabeth Stuart Phelps's *The Story of Avis*." *LIT: Literature Interpretation Theory*, vol. 9, no. 1, 1998, pp. 31–64.

Baron, David. *American Eclipse: A Nation's Epic Race to Catch the Shadow of the Moon and Win the Glory of the World*. Liveright, 2017.

—. "A Woman in Eclipse: Maria Mitchell and the Great Solar Expedition of 1878." *Undark*, 17 Aug. 2017, undark.org/2017/08/17/wilo-maria-mitchell-astronomer-eclipse/. Accessed 11 Nov. 2022.

Barreca, Regina, editor. *Desire and Imagination: Classic Essays in Sexuality*. Plume, 1995.

Bateman, Katharine Saunders. Sex in Education: *A Case Study in the Establishment of Scientific Authority in the Service of a Social Agenda*. 1994. Dartmouth College, MA thesis.

Batstone, William W. "Provocation: The Point of Reception Theory." *Classics and the Uses of Reception*, edited by Charles Martindale and Richard F. Thomas. Blackwell, 2006, pp. 14–20.

Beedy, Mary E. "Girls and Women in England and America." *The Education of American Girls: Considered in a Series of Essays*, edited by Anna C. Brackett, New York, G.P. Putnam's Sons, 1874, pp. 211–55.

Bell, Richard C. "A History of Women in Sport Prior to Title IX." *The Sport Journal*, vol. 10, no. 2, 2007, https://thesportjournal.org/article/a-history-of-women-in-sport-prior-to-title-ix/. Accessed 11 Nov. 2022.

Bell, Susan Groag, and Karen M. Offen, editors. *Women, the Family, and Freedom: The Debate in Documents*. Stanford UP, 1983.

Bem, Sandra L. *The Lenses of Gender: Transforming the Debate on Sexual Inequality*. Yale UP, 1993.

—. "Transforming the Debate on Sexual Inequality: From Biological Difference to Institutionalized Androcentrism." *Gendered Voices: Readings from the American Experience*, edited by Karin Berstrom Costello, Harcourt Brace College Publishers, 1996, pp. 38–49.

Bender, Bert. "Darwin and 'The Natural History of Doctresses': The Sex War between Howells, Phelps, Jewett, and James." *Prospects*, vol. 18, 1993, pp. 81–120.

Bender, Leslie. "A Lawyer's Primer on Feminist Theory and Tort." *Journal of Legal Education*, vol. 38, no. 1/2, 1988, pp. 3–37.

Bensaude-Vincent, Bernadette. "A Genealogy of the Increasing Gap between Science and the Public." *Public Understanding of Science*, vol. 10, no. 1, 2001, pp. 99–113.

Bergland, Renée L. "Urania's Inversion: Emily Dickinson, Herman Melville, and the Strange History of Women Scientists in Nineteenth-Century America." *Signs*, vol. 34, no. 1, 2008, pp. 75–99.

Biesecker, Barbara. "Coming to Terms with Recent Attempts to Write Women into the History of Rhetoric." *Philosophy and Rhetoric*, vol. 25, no. 2, 1992, pp. 140–61.

Birkle, Carmen. "Capitals of Medicine: North American Medical Women and Their Encounters with Europe (1850s–1930s)." *Narratives of Encounters in the North Atlantic Triangle*, edited by Waldemar Zacharasiewicz, Österreichische Akademie der Wissenschaften Verlag, 2015, pp. 85–107.

Bittel, Carla. *Mary Putnam Jacobi and the Politics of Medicine in Nineteenth-Century America.* U of North Carolina P, 2009.
Bix, Amy Sue. *Girls Coming to Tech!: A History of American Engineering Education for Women.* MIT P, 2013.
Bizzell, Patricia. "Opportunities for Feminist Research in the History of Rhetoric." *Rhetoric Review,* vol. 11, no. 1, 1992, pp. 50–58.
Blackwell, Henry B. [H. B. B.] "Progress Involuntary." *The Woman's Journal,* vol. 4, no. 1, 4 Jan. 1873, pp. 4–5.
—. "Sex in Education." *The Woman's Journal,* vol. 3, no. 51, 21 Dec. 1872, p. 404.
Blair, Carole. "Contemporary US Memorial Sites as Exemplars of Rhetoric's Materiality." *Rhetorical Bodies,* edited by Jack Selzer and Sharon Crowley, U of Wisconsin P, 1999, pp. 16–57.
Blake, Lillie Devereux. "Sex in Education Reviewed." [New York] *Golden Age,* vol. 4, no. 13, 28 Mar. 1874, pp. 6–7.
Bledstein, Burton J. *The Culture of Professionalism: The Middle Class and the Development of Higher Education in America.* W. W. Norton, 1978.
Bodley, Rachel L. *Valedictory Address to the Twenty-Ninth Graduating Class of the Woman's Medical College of Pennsylvania.* Philadelphia, Grant, Faires & Rodgers, 1881.
Bohan, Janis S. "Contextual History: A Framework for Re-Placing Women in the History of Psychology." *Psychology of Women Quarterly,* vol. 14, 1990, pp. 213–27.
Brackett, Anna C. "Dr. Clark [sic] Reviewed." *Daily Missouri Democrat* [St. Louis], vol. 22, no. 71, 7 Dec. 1873, p. 2.
—. editor. *The Education of American Girls: Considered in a Series of Essays.* New York, G.P. Putnam's Sons, 1874.
Brandt, Deborah. *Literacy and Learning: Reflections on Writing, Reading, and Society.* Jossey-Bass, 2009.
"Brevities." *Christian Register,* vol. 52, no. 49, 6 Dec. 1873, p. 2.
Briggette, Lindy E. "Reading and Writing the Social Swirls of *The French Chef*: Social Circulation and the Fan Mail of Julia Child." *Peitho,* vol. 23, no. 3, 2021.
Briggs, Laura. "The Race of Hysteria: 'Overcivilization' and the 'Savage' Woman in Late Nineteenth-Century Obstetrics and Gynecology." *American Quarterly,* vol. 52, no. 2, June 2000, pp. 246–73.
Browdy, Ronisha. "Black Women's Rhetoric(s): A Conversation Starter for Naming and Claiming a Field of Study." *Peitho,* vol. 23, no. 4, 2021.
Brown, JoAnne. *The Definition of a Profession: The Authority of Metaphor in the History of Intelligence Testing, 1890–1930.* Princeton UP, 1992.
Browner, Stephanie P. *Profound Science and Elegant Literature: Imagining Doctors in Nineteenth-Century America.* U of Pennsylvania P, 2005.
Brumberg, Joan J. "'Something Happens to Girls': Menarche and the Emergence of the Modern American Hygienic Imperative." *Journal of the History of Sexuality,* vol. 4, no. 1, 1993, pp. 99–127.

Brumberg, Joan J., and Nancy Tomes. "Women in the Professions: A Research Agenda for American Historians." *Reviews in American History*, vol. 6, no. 2, 1982, pp. 275–96.

Bube, June J. "Prefiguring the New Woman: Frances Fuller Victor's Refashioning of Women and Marriage in 'The New Penelope.'" *Frontiers: A Journal of Women Studies*, vol. 18, no. 3, 1997, pp. 40–65.

Buchanan, Lindal. *Regendering Delivery: The Fifth Canon and Antebellum Women Rhetors*. Southern Illinois UP, 2005.

Buchanan, Lindal, and Kathleen J. Ryan. "Introduction: Walking and Talking through the Field of Feminist Rhetorics." *Walking and Talking Feminist Rhetorics: Landmark Essays and Controversies*, edited by Lindal Buchanan and Kathleen J. Ryan, Parlor P, 2010, pp. xiii–xx.

Bullough, Vern L. "An Early American Sex Manual, or, Aristotle Who?" *Early American Literature*, vol. 7, no. 3, 1973, pp. 236–46.

—. "Sex and the Medical Model." *The Journal of Sex Research*, vol. 11, no. 4, 1975, pp. 291–303.

Burstyn, Joan N. "Education and Sex: The Medical Case against Higher Education for Women in England, 1870–1900." *Proceedings of the American Philosophical Society*, vol. 117, no. 2, 1973, pp. 79–89.

—. *Victorian Education and the Ideal of Womanhood*. Routledge, 1980.

C. "VI." *Sex* and *Education: A Reply to Dr. E. H. Clarke's "Sex in Education,"* edited by Julia Ward Howe, Boston, Roberts Brothers, 1874, pp. 109–25.

Campbell, Karlyn Kohrs. *Man Cannot Speak for Her*. Vol. 1. Greenwood, 1989.

Cayleff, Susan E. "She Was Rendered Incapacitated by Menstrual Difficulties: Historical Perspectives on Perceived Intellectual and Physiological Impairment Among Menstruating Women." *Menstrual Health in Women's Lives*, edited by Alice J. Dan and Linda L. Lewis, U of Illinois P, 1992, pp. 229–34.

Cazden, Elizabeth. *Antoinette Brown Blackwell, a Biography*. Feminist P, 1983.

Charland, Maurice. "Constitutive Rhetoric: The Case of the *Peuple Québécois*." *Quarterly Journal of Speech*, vol. 73, no. 2, 1987, pp. 133–50.

Child, Lydia Maria. "Physical Strength of Women." *Woman's Journal*, vol, 4, no. 11, 15 Mar. 1873, p. 84.

Churchill, Alexandra. "9 Bizarre Facts About Your Period Nobody Ever Told You." *Your Tango*, 2021, https://www.yourtango.com/self/9-bizarre-facts-about-period-nobody-ever-told-you. Accessed 18 Aug. 2022.

Clancy, Kate. *Period: The Real Story of Menstruation*. Princeton UP, 2023.

Clark, Gregory, and S. Michael Halloran. "Introduction: Transformations of Public Discourse in Nineteenth-Century America." *Oratorical Culture in Nineteenth-Century America: Transformations in the Theory and Practice of Rhetoric*, edited by Gregory Clark and S. Michael Halloran, Southern Illinois UP, 1993, pp. 1–26.

Clark, Herbert H. *Arenas of Language Use*. U of Chicago P, 1992.

Clarke, Edward H. *The Building of a Brain*. Boston, James R. Osgood and Co., 1874.

—. "Medical Education of Women." *Boston Medical and Surgical Journal*, vol. 4, no. 24, 16 Dec. 1869, pp. 345–46.
—. *Sex in Education; or, a Fair Chance for the Girls*. Boston, James R. Osgood and Co., 1873.
Clifford, Geraldine Jonçich. *Those Good Gertrudes: A Social History of Women Teachers in America*. Johns Hopkins UP, 2014.
"Co-Education of the Sexes." *Zion's Herald*, vol. 50, no. 48, 27 Nov. 1873, p. 380.
"Collegiate Training of Women." *Medical Record*, vol. 6, no. 1, 2 July 1904, pp. 17–18.
Collins, Patricia Hill. "Moving Beyond Gender: Intersectionality and Scientific Knowledge." *Revisioning Gender*, edited by Myra Marx Ferree, Judith Lorber, and Beth B. Hess, Sage, 1999, pp. 261–84.
Collins, Vicki Tolar. "The Speaker Respoken: Material Rhetoric as Feminist Methodology." *Walking and Talking Feminist Rhetorics: Landmark Essays and Controversies*, edited by Lindal Buchanan and Kathleen J. Ryan, Parlor P, 2010, pp. 146–69.
Comfort, George F., and Anna Manning Comfort. *Woman's Education, and Woman's Health: Chiefly in Reply to "Sex in Education."* Syracuse, Thos. W. Durston & Co., 1874.
Commeyras, Michelle. "How Interested Are Literacy Educators in Gender Issues? Survey Results from the United States." *Journal of Adolescent & Adult Literacy*, vol. 42, no. 5, 1999, pp. 352–62.
Conable, Charlotte Williams. *Women at Cornell: The Myth of Equal Education*. Cornell UP, 1977.
Condit, Celeste M. *The Meanings of the Gene: Public Debates about Human Heredity*. U of Wisconsin P, 1999.
Cooper, Anna Julia. "The Higher Education of Women." *A Voice from the South*. Xenia, Aldine Printing House, 1892, pp. 48–80.
Costello, Karin Bergstrom. *Gendered Voices: Readings from the American Experience*. Harcourt Brace College Publishers, 1996.
Coughlin, Anne M. "Excusing Women." *California Law Review*, vol. 82, no. 1, 1994, pp. 1–93.
Craig, Mary. "Vassar and Beyond: Women and Baseball in the 1800s." *Beyond the Box Score*, 19 Sept. 2017, www.beyondtheboxscore.com/2017/9/19/16323942/women-baseball-history-vassar-suffrage-abolition. Accessed 11 Nov. 2022.
"Current Literature." *The New Church Magazine*, vol. 2, no. 2, 1 Dec. 1873, pp. 103–05.
"Current Notes." *Watchman and Reflector*, vol. 55, no. 3, 15 Jan. 1874, p. 2.
D. "Logical Deductions from 'Sex in Education.'" *Arthur's Illustrated Home Magazine*, vol. 42, no. 9, Sept. 1874, pp. 590–91.
Dall, Caroline H. *The College, the Market, and the Court, or, Woman's Relation to Education, Labor and Law*. Boston, Lee and Shepard, 1867.
—. "The Other Side." *The Education of American Girls: Considered in a Series of Essays*, edited by Anna C. Brackett, New York, G.P. Putnam's Sons, 1874, pp. 147–73.

—. "V." *Sex and Education: A Reply to Dr. E.H. Clarke's "Sex in Education,"* edited by Julia Ward Howe, Boston, Roberts Brothers, 1874, pp. 87–108.

—. *"Woman's Right to Labor": or, Low Wages and Hard Work*. Boston, Walker, Wise, and Company, 1860.

Dan, Alice J., and Linda L. Lewis, editors. *Menstrual Health in Women's Lives*. U of Illinois P, 1992.

D'Angelo, Frank J. "Tropics of Invention." *Rhetoric Review*, vol. 36, no. 3, 2017, pp. 200–13.

Darwin, Charles. *The Descent of Man, and Selection in Relation to Sex*. London, John Murray, 1871. 2 vols.

—. *On the Origin of Species by Means of Natural Selection, or the Preservation of Favoured Races in the Struggle for Life*. London, John Murray, 1859.

Deacon, Desley. "Bringing Social Science Back Home: Theory and Practice in the Life and Work of Elsie Clews Parsons." *Gender and American Social Science: The Formative Years*, edited by Helene Silverberg, Princeton UP, 1998, pp. 265–92.

Delgado, Richard. "The Imperial Scholar: Reflections on a Review of Civil Rights Literature." *University of Pennsylvania Law Review*, vol. 132, 1984, pp. 561–78.

DeLuzio, Crista. *Female Adolescence in American Scientific Thought, 1830–1930*. Johns Hopkins UP, 2007.

Dewey, John. "Health and Sex in Higher Education." *Popular Science Monthly*, vol. 28, Mar. 1886, pp. 606–14.

Diedrich, Maria I. *Cornelia James Cannon and the Future American Race*. U of Massachusetts P, 2011.

Dodd, Dianne, and Deborah Gorham. Introduction. *Caring and Curing: Historical Perspectives on Women and Healing in Canada*, U of Ottawa P, 1994, pp. 1–15.

Dorenkamp, Angela G, et al. *Images of Women in American Popular Culture*. Harcourt Brace Jovanovich, 1985.

Dorn, Charles. *For the Common Good: A New History of Higher Education in America*. Cornell UP, 2017.

Douglass, David Anderson. "Edward Clarke's *Sex in Education*: A Study in Rhetorical Form." Unpublished dissertation. Pennsylvania State University, 1992.

Dow, Bonnie J. "Feminism and Public Address Research: Television News and the Construction of Women's Liberation." *The Handbook of Rhetoric and Public Address*, edited by Shawn J. Parry-Giles and J. Michael Hogan, Wiley-Blackwell, 2010, pp. 345–72.

Drachman, Virginia G. *Hospital with a Heart: Women Doctors and the Paradox of Separatism at the New England Hospital, 1862–1969*. Cornell UP, 1984.

—. "The Limits of Progress: The Professional Lives of Women Doctors, 1881–1926." *Bulletin of the History of Medicine*, vol. 60, no. 1, 1986, pp. 58–72.

—. "Women Lawyers and the Quest for Professional Identity in Late Nineteenth-Century America." *Michigan Law Review*, vol. 88, no. 8, 1990, pp. 2414–443.

Duffey, Eliza Bisbee. *No Sex in Education: or, An Equal Chance for Both Boys and Girls*. Philadelphia, J.M. Stoddart & Company, 1874.

—. *What Women Should Know: A Woman's Book about Women*. Philadelphia, Fireside Publishing Company, 1882.

Duffy, Jennifer N. *Who's Your Paddy? Racial Expectations and the Struggle for Irish American Identity*. New York UP, 2013.

E.S.P. "Co-Education in 1789." *The Woman's Journal*, vol. 2, no. 2, 11 Jan. 1873, p. 13.

Ede, Lisa, Cheryl Glenn, and Andrea Lunsford. "Border Crossings: Intersections of Rhetoric and Feminism." *Rhetorica*, vol. 13, no. 4, 1995, pp. 401–41.

Ede, Lisa, and Andrea Lunsford. "Audience Addressed/Audience Invoked: The Role of Audience in Composition Theory and Pedagogy." *College Composition and Communication*, vol. 35, no. 2, 1984, pp. 155–71.

—. *Singular Texts/Plural Authors: Perspectives on Collaborative Writing*. Southern Illinois UP, 1990.

"Editorial Paragraphs." *Zion's Herald*, vol. 51, no. 9, 26 Feb. 1874, p. 68.

"Editor's Easy Chair." *Harper's New Monthly Magazine*, vol. 48, no. 285, Feb. 1874, pp. 441–46.

"Editor's Literary Record." *Harper's New Monthly Magazine*, vol. 49, no. 290, July 1874, pp. 287–90.

"Editor's Note-Book." *The Unitarian Review and Religious Magazine*, vol. 1, no. 2, Apr. 1874, pp. 163–65.

"Editor's Table." *Appletons' Journal of Literature, Science and Art*, vol. 10, no. 246, 6 Dec. 1873, pp. 729–31.

"Editor's Table." *Appletons' Journal of Literature, Science and Art*, vol. 10, no. 249, 27 Dec. 1873, pp. 825–27.

"The Education of American Girls," *The Galaxy: A Magazine of Entertaining Reading*, vol. 17, no. 5, May 1874, pp. 717–18.

"The Education of Girls." *Boston Daily Advertiser*, vol. 122, no. 104, 29 Oct. 1873, p. 2.

"Edward Hammond Clarke." *Proceedings of the American Academy of Arts and Sciences*, vol. 13, May 1877–May 1878, pp. 437–39.

Ehrenreich, Barbara. "Gender and Objectivity in Medicine." *International Journal of Health Services*, vol. 4, no. 4, 1974, pp. 617–23.

Ehrenreich, Barbara, and Deirdre English. *For Her Own Good: 150 Years of the Experts' Advice to Women*. Doubleday, 1979.

Elmore, Maria A. "XII." *Sex* and *Education. A Reply to Dr. E.H. Clarke's "Sex in Education,"* edited by Julia Ward Howe, Boston, Roberts Brothers, 1874, pp. 174–82.

Emmet, Thomas Addis. *The Principles and Practice of Gynæcology*. 2nd ed., Philadelphia, Henry C. Lea, 1880.

"The End of Dr. Clarke." *The Daily Graphic*, vol. 3, no. 227, 24 Nov. 1873, p. 154.

Enoch, Jessica. *Domestic Occupations*. Southern Illinois UP, 2019.

—. "Finding New Spaces for Feminist Research." *Rhetoric Review*, vol. 30, no. 2, 2011, pp. 115–16.

—. "Releasing Hold: Feminist Historiography without the Tradition." *Theorizing Histories of Rhetoric*, edited by Michelle Ballif, Southern Illinois UP, 2013, pp. 58–73.

Enoch, Jessica, and Jean Bessette. "Meaningful Engagements: Feminist Historiography and the Digital Humanities." *College Composition and Communication*, vol. 64, no. 4, 2013, pp. 634–60.

Erickson, Nancy S. "*Muller v. Oregon* Reconsidered: The Origins of a Sex-Based Doctrine of Liberty of Contract." *Labor History*, vol. 30, no. 2, 1989, pp. 228–50.

Eschbach, Elizabeth S. *The Higher Education of Women in England and America, 1865–1920*. Routledge, 1993.

Etter-Lewis, Gwendolyn. "Standing Up and Speaking Out: African American Women's Narrative Legacy." *Discourse & Society*, vol. 2, no. 4, 1991, pp. 425–37.

Fairchild, James H. "Experience of Oberlin—Letter from President Fairchild." *Woman's Journal*, vol. 4, no. 3, 18 Jan. 1873, p. 20.

Fehr, Carla. "Are Smart Men Smarter than Smart Women? The Epistemology of Ignorance, Women, and the Production of Knowledge." *The "Woman Question" and Higher Education: Perspectives on Gender and Knowledge Production in America*, edited by Ann Mari May, Edward Elgar, 2008, pp 102–16.

Fellman, Anita Clair, and Michael Fellman. *Making Sense of Self: Medical Advice Literature in Late Nineteenth-Century America*. U of Pennsylvania P, 1981.

Fillenwarth, Gracemarie Mike. "Contexts and Communities: Valuing Collectivity in Feminist Rhetorical Inquiry." *Ethics and Representation in Feminist Rhetorical Research*, edited by Amy E. Dayton and Jennie L. Vaughn, U of Pittsburgh P, 2021, pp. 160–74.

Fishbein, Morris. *A History of the American Medical Association, 1847–1947*. W.B. Saunders, 1947.

Fisher, Lydia. "American Reform Darwinism Meets Russian Mutual Aid: Utopian Feminism in Mary Bradley Lane's *Mizora*." *America's Darwin: Darwinian Theory and U.S. Literary Culture*, edited by Tina Gianquitto and Lydia Fisher, U of Georgia P, 2014, pp. 181–206.

Foner, Philip Sheldon, and Robert J. Branham. *Lift Every Voice: African American Oratory, 1787–1900*. U of Alabama P, 1998.

Foss, Sonja K., and Cindy L. Griffin. "Beyond Persuasion: A Proposal for an Invitational Rhetoric." *Communication Monographs*, vol. 62, no. 1, 1995, pp. 2–18.

Frankfort, Roberta. *Collegiate Women: Domesticity and Career in Turn-of-the-Century America*. New York UP, 1977.

Fredlund, Katherine, Kerri Hauman, and Jessica Ouellette, editors. *Feminist Connections: Rhetoric and Activism across Time, Space, and Place*. U of Alabama P, 2020.

Frow, John. "Afterlife: Texts as Usage." *Reception: Texts, Readers, Audiences, History*, vol. 1, no. 1, 2008, pp. 1–23.

Gage, Francis D. "Sex in Education." *The Woman's Journal*, vol. 4, no. 47, 22 Nov. 1873, p. 376.

—. "'Sex in Education' Once More." *The Woman's Journal*, vol. 5, no. 1, 3 Jan. 1874, p. 2.

Garvey, Ellen Gruber. *Writing with Scissors: American Scrapbooks from the Civil War to the Harlem Renaissance*. Oxford UP, 2012.

Gaynor, Gerren Keith. "Is the Anti-Abortion Movement Rooted in White Supremacy?" *Yahoo! News*, 12 July 2022, news.yahoo.com/anti-abortion-movement-rooted-white-130000079.html?guccounter=1. Accessed 4 Nov. 2022.

Gianquitto, Tina. "Botanical Smuts and Hermaphrodites: Lydia Becker, Darwin's Botany, and Education Reform." *Isis*, vol. 104, no. 2, 2013, pp. 250–77.

Gilb, Corinne Lathrop. *Hidden Hierarchies: The Professions and Government*. Greenwood P, 1976.

Ginsburg, Ruth Bader. *Justice, Justice Thou Shalt Pursue: A Life's Work Fighting for a More Perfect Union*. U of California P, 2021.

Glenn, Cheryl. *Rhetorical Feminism and This Thing Called Hope*. Southern Illinois UP, 2018.

—. *Unspoken: A Rhetoric of Silence*. Southern Illinois UP, 2004.

Goffman, Erving. *Forms of Talk*. U of Pennsylvania P, 1981.

Goodell, William. *Lessons in Gynecology*. 2nd ed., Philadelphia, D.G. Brinton, 1880.

Goodwin, Michele. "The Racist History of Abortion and Midwifery Bans." *ACLU News & Commentary*, 1 Jul. 2020. www.aclu.org/news/racial-justice/the-racist-history-of-abortion-and-midwifery-bans. Accessed 4 Nov. 2022.

Gordon, Lynn D. "From Seminary to University: An Overview of Women's Higher Education, 1870–1920." *The History of Higher Education*, 2nd ed., edited by Lester F. Goodchild and Harold S. Wechsler, Simon & Schuster, 1997, pp. 473–98.

—. *Gender and Higher Education in the Progressive Era*. Yale UP, 1990.

—. "The Gibson Girl Goes to College: Popular Culture and Women's Higher Education in the Progressive Era, 1890–1920." *American Quarterly*, vol. 39, no. 2, 1987, pp. 211–30.

Graban, Tarez Samra. *Women's Irony: Rewriting Feminist Rhetorical Histories*. Southern Illinois UP, 2015.

Greene, William B. *Critical Comments upon Certain Special Passages in the Introductory Portion of Dr. Edward H. Clarke's Book on "Sex in Education."* Boston, Lee and Shepard, 1874.

Griffin, Gail B. "Emancipated Spirits: Women's Education and the American Midwest." *Change*, vol. 16, no. 1, 1984, pp. 32–40.

Griffiths, Dorothy, and Esther Saraga. "Sex Differences in Cognitive Abilities: A Sterile Field of Enquiry?" *Sex-Role Stereotyping: Collected Papers*. edited by Oonagh Hartnett, et al., Tavistock, 1979, pp. 17–45.

Hall, G. Stanley. *Adolescence: Its Psychology and Its Relations to Physiology, Anthropology, Sociology, Sex, Crime, Religion and Education*. vol. 2. D. Appleton and Company, 1904.

Hallenbeck, Sarah. "Toward a Posthuman Perspective: Feminist Rhetorical Methodologies and Everyday Practices." *Advances in the History of Rhetoric*, vol. 15, no. 9, 2012, pp. 9–27.

—. "Resituating Rhetorical Failure: The Case of Nineteenth-Century Metallurgist Carrie Everson." *Women at Work: Rhetorics of Gender and Labor*, edited by David Gold and Jessica Enoch, U of Pittsburgh P, 2019, pp. 69–83.

Hallenbeck, Sarah, and Michelle Smith. "Mapping Topoi in the Rhetorical Gendering of Work." *Peitho*, vol. 17, no. 2, pp. 200–25.

Hallman, Dianne M. "'If We're So Smart, . . .': A Response to Trevor Gambell and Darryl Hunter." *Canadian Journal of Education/Revue Canadienne de L'éducation*, vol. 25, no. 1, 2000, pp. 62–67.

Hamlin, Kimberly A. *From Eve to Evolution: Darwin, Science, and Women's Rights in Gilded Age America*. U of Chicago P, 2014.

—. "Sex, Science, and Beards." *The Bearded Lady Project: Challenging the Face of Science*. Columbia UP, 2020, pp. 11–14.

Hansot, Elizabeth, and David Tyack. "Gender in American Public Schools: Thinking Institutionally." *Signs*, vol. 13, no. 4, 1988, pp. 741–60.

Harris, Randy Allen. "Reception Studies in the Rhetoric of Science." *Technical Communication Quarterly*, vol. 14, no. 3, 2005, pp. 249–55.

Hartmann, Thom. "The 'Browning' of America: Anti-Abortion Efforts Are Fundamentally about a Shortage of White Babies." *Milwaukee Independent*, 11 May 2022. www.milwaukeeindependent.com/thom-hartmann/browning-america-anti-abortion-efforts-fundamentally-shortage-white-babies/. Accessed 4 Nov. 2022.

Hawhee, Debra, and Christa J. Olson. "Pan-Historiography: The Challenges of Writing History across Time and Space." *Theorizing Histories of Rhetoric*, edited by Michelle Ballif, Southern Illinois UP, 2013, pp. 90–105.

Hayden, Wendy. *Evolutionary Rhetoric: Sex, Science, and Free Love in Nineteenth-Century Feminism*. Southern Illinois UP, 2013.

Haywood, Chanta M. *Prophesying Daughters: Black Women Preachers and the Word, 1823–1913*. U of Missouri P, 2003.

Hensley Owens, Kim. *Writing Childbirth: Women's Rhetorical Agency in Labor and Online*. Southern Illinois UP, 2015.

Herndl, Diane Price. *Invalid Women: Figuring Feminine Illness in American Fiction and Culture, 1840–1940*. U of North Carolina P, 1993.

Hickson, Ally. "8 of the Craziest Myths about Women's Bodies You Never Heard." *Refinery29*, 13 May 2016, www.refinery29.com/en-us/old-wives-tales-womens-health-bodies. Accessed 11 Nov. 2022.

Higginson, Thomas Wentworth. "II." *Sex and Education. A Reply to Dr. E.H. Clarke's "Sex in Education,"* edited by Julia Ward Howe, Boston, Roberts Brothers, 1874, pp. 32–51.

— [T. W. H.]. "Physician and Pedagogue." *The Woman's Journal*, vol. 4, no. 3, 18 Jan. 1873, p. 17.

—. "Sex in Education." *The Woman's Journal*, vol. 4, no. 45, 8 Nov. 1873, p. 353.

Higham, John. "The Matrix of Specialization." *The Organization of Knowledge in Modern America, 1860–1920*, edited by Alexandra Oleson and John Voss, Johns Hopkins UP, 1979, pp. 3–18.

Holmes, Oliver Wendell. "The Americanized European." *Milwaukee Daily Sentinel*, vol. 31, no. 288, 17 Dec. 1874, p. 7.

— [O.W.H.]. "Edward Hammond Clarke." *Boston Daily Advertiser*, 5 Dec. 1877, vol. 130, no. 134, p. 2.

Horowitz, Helen Lefkowitz. *Alma Mater: Design and Experience in the Women's Colleges from Their Nineteenth-Century Beginnings to the 1930s*. 2nd ed., U of Massachusetts P, 1993.

—. "The Body in the Library." *The "Woman Question" and Higher Education: Perspectives on Gender and Knowledge Production in America*, edited by Ann Mari May, Edward Elgar, 2008, pp. 11–31.

Howard, Edine T. "Mrs. Edine T. Howard." *The Lectures Read before the American Institute of Instruction*, Boston, American Institute of Instruction, 1879, pp. 41–49.

Howe, Julia Ward. "I." *Sex* and *Education: A Reply to Dr. E.H. Clarke's "Sex in Education,"* edited by Julia Ward Howe, Boston, Roberts Brothers, 1874, pp. 13–31.

Howell, Colin D. *Northern Sandlots: A Social History of Maritime Baseball*. U of Toronto P, 1995.

Hubbard, Ruth. "Feminism in Academia: Its Problematic and Problems." *Expanding the Role of Women in the Sciences*, edited by Anne M. Briscoe and Sheila M. Pfafflin, New York Academy of Sciences, 1979, pp. 249–56.

—. *The Politics of Women's Biology*. Rutgers UP, 1990.

Inness, Sherrie A. *Intimate Communities: Representation and Social Transformation in Women's College Fiction, 1895–1910*. Bowling Green State U Popular P, 1995.

Irving, Washington. "The Wife." *The Sketch-Book of Geoffrey Crayon, Gent.*, vol. 1, Philadelphia, Carey & Lea, 1831, pp. 33–43.

J.B.H. "Reviews and Notices." *Cincinnati Lancet and Observer*, vol. 16, no. 12, Dec. 1873, pp. 766–68.

Jack, Jordynn. "Acts of Institution: Embodying Feminist Rhetorical Methodologies in Space and Time." *Rhetoric Review*, vol. 28, no. 3, 2009, pp. 285–303.

—. *Science on the Home Front: American Women Scientists in World War II*. U of Illinois P, 2009.

Jackson, Mercy B. "Mercy B. Jackson." *Sex* and *Education: A Reply to Dr. E.H. Clarke's "Sex in Education,"* edited by Julia Ward Howe, Boston, Roberts Brothers, 1874, pp. 150–64.

Jacobi, Mary Putnam. "Mental Action and Physical Health." *The Education of American Girls: Considered in a Series of Essays*, edited by Anna C. Brackett, New York, G.P. Putnam's Sons, 1874, pp. 255–307.

—. "Shall Women Practice Medicine?" *North American Review*, vol. 134, no. 302, Jan. 1882, pp. 52–75.

—. *The Question of Rest for Women during Menstruation*. New York, G.P. Putnam's Sons, 1877.

Jasinski, James, and Jennifer R. Mercieca. "Analyzing Constitutive Rhetorics: The Virginia and Kentucky *Resolutions* and the 'Principles of '98.'" *The Handbook of Rhetoric and Public Address*, edited by Shawn J. Parry-Giles and J. Michael Hogan, Wiley-Blackwell, 2010, pp. 313–41.

K.N.D. "Education of American Girls." *Daily Inter Ocean*, vol. 2, no. 296, 3 Mar. 1874, p. 2.

—. Rev. of *Sex in Education*, by Edward H. Clarke. *United States Medical and Surgical Journal*, vol. 9, no. 34, Jan. 1874, pp. 235–41.

Kallendorf, Craig. "Introduction." *Classics from Papyrus to the Internet: An Introduction to Transmission and Reception*, edited by Jeffrey M. Hunt, R. Alden Smith, and Fabio Stok, U of Texas P, 2017, pp. 1–4.

Kates, Susan. *Activist Rhetorics and American Higher Education, 1885–1937*. Southern Illinois UP, 2001.

Kelly, Robert L. *The Lifeways of Hunter-Gatherers: The Foraging Spectrum*. Cambridge UP, 2013.

Kenschaft, Lori J. *Reinventing Marriage: The Love and Work of Alice Freeman Palmer and George Herbert Palmer*. U of Illinois P, 2005.

Kirschmann, Anne Taylor. *A Vital Force: Women in American Homeopathy*. Rutgers UP, 2004.

Kjeldsen, Jens E. "Audience Analysis and Reception Studies of Rhetoric." *Rhetorical Audience Studies and Reception of Rhetoric: Exploring Audiences Empirically*, edited by Jens E. Kjeldsen, Palgrave Macmillan, 2018, pp. 1–42.

Kjeldsen, Jens E., and Ida Andersen. "The Rhetorical Power of News Photographs: A Triangulatory Reception Approach to the Alan Kurdi Images." *Rhetorical Audience Studies and Reception of Rhetoric: Exploring Audiences Empirically*, edited by Jens E. Kjeldsen, Palgrave Macmillan, 2018, pp. 309–33.

La Vergata, Antonello. "Food, Nerves, and Fertility. Variations on the Moral Economy of the Body, 1700–1920." *History and Philosophy of the Life Sciences*, vol. 41, no. 4, 2019, pp. 1–30.

Lander, Louise. *Images of Bleeding: Menstruation as Ideology*. Orlando P, 1988.

"Liberal Learning and Long Life." *Medical Eclectic*, vol. 2, no. 2, 15 Mar. 1875, pp. 39–42.

Lindemann, Hilde. "The Woman Question in Medicine: An Update." *The Hastings Center Report*, vol. 42, no. 3, 2012, pp. 38–45.

"Literary." *Appletons' Journal of Literature, Science and Art*, vol. 11, no. 267, 2 May 1874, pp. 570–71.

"Literary News." *The Literary World; a Monthly Review of Current Literature*, vol. 4 no. 5, 1 Oct. 1873, pp. 77–80.

"Literary News." *The Literary World; a Monthly Review of Current Literature*, vol. 4, no. 8, 1 Jan. 1874, pp. 126–28.

"Literary Notes." *Boston Journal of Chemistry*, vol. 8, no. 6, 1 Dec. 1873, pp. 69–70.

"Literary Notices." *The Eclectic Magazine of Foreign Literature*, vol. 19, no. 3, Mar. 1874, pp. 373–76.

"Literary Notices." *The Eclectic Magazine of Foreign Literature*, vol. 20, no. 6, Dec. 1874, pp. 760–63.

"Literary Notices." *Popular Science Monthly*, vol. 4, 1 Jan. 1874, pp. 374–78.

"Literary Resume." [New York] *Daily Graphic*, vol. 3, no. 208, 1 Nov. 1873, p. 3.

"Literary Review." *Congregational Quarterly*, vol. 16, no. 3, Jul. 1874, pp. 478–89.

"Literary Review." *The Congregationalist*, vol. 25, no. 46, 13 Nov. 1873, p. 366.

"Literature of the Day." *The Jewish Messenger*, vol. 36, no. 16, 23 Oct. 1874, p. 4.

Logan, Shirley Wilson. *We are Coming: The Persuasive Discourse of Nineteenth-Century Black Women*. Southern Illinois UP, 1999.

Lowe, Margaret A. *Looking Good: College Women and Body Image, 1875–1930.* Johns Hopkins UP, 2003.
Lunsford, Andrea A., and Lisa Ede. "Among the Audience: On Audience in an Age of New Literacies." *Engaging Audience: Writing in an Age of New Literacies*, edited by M. Elizabeth Weiser, Brian M. Fehler, and Angela M. González, National Council of Teachers of English, 2009, pp. 42–69.
MacDonald, Victoria-Maria. "The Paradox of Bureaucratization: New Views on Progressive Era Teachers and the Development of a Woman's Profession." *History of Education Quarterly*, vol. 39, no. 4, 1999, p. 427–53.
"Magazine Notes." *Boston Daily Advertiser*, vol. 123, no. 152, 26 Jun. 1874, n.p.
Mann, Mrs. Horace [Mary Tyler Peabody]. "III." *Sex and Education. A Reply to Dr. E.H. Clarke's "Sex in Education,"* edited by Julia Ward Howe, Boston, Roberts Brothers, 1874, pp. 52–71.
Martin, Emily. "The Egg and the Sperm: How Science Has Constructed a Romance Based on Stereotypical Male-Female Roles." *Signs*, vol. 16, no. 3, 1991, pp. 485–501.
Martindale, Charles. "Thinking through Reception." *Classics and the Uses of Reception*, edited by Charles Martindale and Richard F. Thomas, Blackwell, 2006, pp. 1–13.
Mastrangelo, Lisa S. "Learning from the Past: Rhetoric, Composition, and Debate at Mount Holyoke College." *Rhetoric Review*, vol. 18, no. 1, 1999, pp. 46–64.
May, Ann Mari. "'Sweeping the Heavens for a Comet': Women, the Language of Political Economy, and Higher Education in the US." *Feminist Economics*, vol. 12, no. 4, 2006, pp. 625–40.
—. *The "Woman Question" and Higher Education: Perspectives on Gender and Knowledge Production in America.* Edward Elgar, 2008.
McAdam, Graham. "Dr. Clarke on 'Sex in Education.'" *Christian Leader*, vol. 44, no. 1, 3 Jan. 1874, p. 9.
McKerrow, Raymie E. "Critical Rhetoric." *Encyclopedia of Communication Theory*, edited by Stephen W. Littlejohn and Karen A. Foss, SAGE Publications, Inc., 2009, pp. 235–38.
Mckoy, Temptaous, et al. "Embodying Public Feminisms: Collaborative Intersectional Models for Engagement." *IEEE Transactions on Professional Communication*, vol. 65, no. 1, 2022, pp. 70–86.
McWilliam, Erica, and Jill Brannock. "The Way to a Boy's Heart? New Mechanisms for Making Boys Better." *Asia-Pacific Journal of Teacher Education*, vol. 9, no. 1, 2001, pp. 7–17.
Michaels, Rena S. "Woman's Education and Woman's Health." *The Ladies Repository; a Monthly Periodical, Devoted to Literature, Art and Religion*, vol. 34, Nov. 1874, pp, 349–53.
"Minor Book Notices." *Literary World*, vol. 4, no. 6, 1 Nov. 1873, pp. 90–92.
Mitchell, Koritha. *From Slave Cabins to the White House.* U of Illinois P, 2020.
Mitchell, Michele. "'Lower Orders,' Racial Hierarchies, and Rights Rhetoric: Evolutionary Echoes in Elizabeth Cady Stanton's Thought during the Late 1860s," *Elizabeth Cady Stanton, Feminist as Thinker: A Reader in Documents and Essays*,

edited by Ellen Carol DuBois and Richard Cándida Smith, New York UP, 2007, pp. 128–51.

Morantz-Sanchez, Regina. *Conduct Unbecoming a Woman: Medicine on Trial in Turn-of-the-Century Brooklyn*. Oxford UP, 1999.

—. *Sympathy and Science: Women Physicians in American Medicine*. 1985. U of North Carolina P, 2000.

Morton, Thomas. *Speed the Plough; A Comedy in Five Acts*. Philadelphia, Mathew Carey, 1807.

Mosher, Clelia D. "Normal Menstruation and Some of the Factors Modifying It." *The Johns Hopkins Hospital Bulletin*, vol. 12, nos. 121–123, Apr.–June 1901, pp. 178–79.

Myers, Christine D. *University Coeducation in the Victorian Era: Inclusion in the United States and the United Kingdom*. Palgrave Macmillan, 2010.

"New Publications." *Christian Watchman*, vol. 54, no. 48, 27 Nov. 1873, n.p.

"New Publications." [Boston] *Daily Evening Traveller*, vol. 30, no. 56, 5 Jun. 1874, p. 1.

"New Publications: Sex in Education." *Boston Daily Globe*, 28 Oct. 1873, p. 3.

Newman, Louise Michele. *Men's Ideas/Women's Realities:* Popular Science*, 1870–1915*. Pergamon P, 1985.

—. *White Women's Rights: The Racial Origins of Feminism in the United States*. Oxford UP, 1999.

Nguyen, Sophia. "Gymsuits, Pre-Spandex." *Harvard Magazine*, July–Aug. 2018, www.harvardmagazine.com/2018/07/gymsuits-pre-spandex. Accessed 6 Aug. 2022.

Nickliss, Alexandra M. *Phoebe Apperson Hearst: A Life of Power and Politics*. U of Nebraska P, 2018.

Nix, Elizabeth M. "Sweat Equity: Physical Education at The Bryn Mawr School for Girls." *Baltimore Sports: Stories from Charm City*, edited by Daniel A. Nathan, U of Arkansas P, 2016, pp. 59–71.

Noddings, Nel. "Feminist Critiques in the Professions." *Review of Research in Education*, vol. 16, 1990, pp. 393–424.

"Notes and News." *The Woman's Journal*, vol. 3, no. 42, 28 Dec. 1872, p. 413.

"Obituary Record." *Medical News*, vol. 36, no. 421, Jan. 1878, p. 11.

Ognibene, Elaine R. "Moving beyond 'True Woman' Myths: Women and Work." *Humboldt Journal of Social Relations*, vol. 10, no. 2, 1983, pp. 7–25.

Onion, Rebecca. "America Has Always Seen Ambitious Women as Unhealthy." *Slate*, 16 Sept. 2016, slate.com/news-and-politics/2016/09/hillary-clinton-is-just-the-latest-ambitious-american-woman-to-be-accused-of-ill-health.html. Accessed 6 Aug. 2022.

Oreskes, Naomi. *Why Trust Science?* Princeton UP, 2019.

Palmieri, Patricia A. "From Republican Motherhood to Race Suicide: Arguments on the Higher Education of Women in the United States, 1820–1920." *Educating Men and Women Together: Coeducation in a Changing World*, edited by Carol Lasser, U of Illinois P, 1987, pp. 49–64.

—. *In Adamless Eden: The Community of Women Faculty at Wellesley*. Yale UP, 1995.

Park, Roberta J. "Physiology and Anatomy are Destiny!?: Brains, Bodies and Exercise in Nineteenth Century American Thought." *Journal of Sport History*, vol. 18, no. 1, 1991 pp. 31–63.

—. "Sport, Gender and Society in a Transatlantic Victorian Perspective." *The International Journal of the History of Sport*, vol. 24, no. 12, 2007, pp. 1570–603.

Parvin, Theophilus. "The Inter-Dependence of Mind and Body." *Cincinnati Lancet and Clinic*, vol. 5, no. 24, 11 Dec. 1880, pp. 521–30.

Pau on Lau, Estelle. *Ellen C. Sabin: Proponent of Higher Education for Women, a Social History*. UP of America, 1978.

Paul, Danette, Davida Charney, and Aimee Kendall. "Moving beyond the Moment: Reception Studies in the Rhetoric of Science." *Journal of Business and Technical Communication*, vol. 15, no. 3, 2001, pp. 372–99.

Payne, R.L. "The Health of Our School-Girls." *North Carolina Medical Journal*, vol. 12, no. 3, Sept. 1883, pp. 121–30.

Peril, Lynn. *College Girls: Bluestockings, Sex Kittens, and Co-eds, Then and Now*. W.W. Norton & Company, 2006.

Perkins, Priscilla. "'A Little Body with a Very Large Head': Composition, Psychopathology, and the Making of Stein's Normal Self." *Modern Fiction Studies*, vol. 42, no. 3, 1996, pp. 528–46.

"Personal." *Galveston Daily News*, vol. 34, no. 29, 8 Feb. 1874, p. 2.

Petrina, Stephen. "The Medicalization of Education: A Historiographic Synthesis." *History of Education Quarterly*, vol. 46, no. 4, 2006, pp. 503–31.

Phelps, Elizabeth Stuart. "VII." *Sex* and *Education. A Reply to Dr. E.H. Clarke's "Sex in Education,"* edited by Julia Ward Howe, Boston, Roberts Brothers, 1874, pp. 126–38.

"The Physical Education of Female College Students." *Medical News*, vol. 41, no. 16, 14 Oct. 1882, pp. 437–38.

Picker, Les. "Human Sexuality Education: Implications for Biology Teaching." *The American Biology Teacher*, vol. 46, no. 2, Feb. 1984, pp. 92–98.

Poirot, Kristan. *A Question of Sex: Feminism, Rhetoric, and Differences That Matter*. U of Massachusetts P, 2014.

Pope, Emily F., Emma L. Call, and C. Augusta Pope. *The Practice of Medicine by Women in the United States*. Boston: Wright and Potter, 1881. Microform. *History of Women*, reel 943, no. 8551. Woodbridge: Research Publications, 1977.

Prescott, Heather M. "Sending Their Sons into Danger: Cornell University and the Ithaca Typhoid Epidemic of 1903." *New York History*, vol. 78, no. 3, July 1997, pp. 273–308.

"Problems and Their Solution." *Massachusetts Teacher*, vol. 27, no. 1, Jan. 1874, pp. 1–6.

Quintilian. *Institutio Oratoria*, edited by Harold Edgeworth Butler, Perseus Digital Library, www.perseus.tufts.edu/hopper/text?doc=urn:cts:latinLit:phi1002.phi0018.perseus-eng1:6. Accessed 3 Nov. 2022.

R.B. "Reviews." *The Clinic*, vol. 6, no. 1, 3 Jan. 1874, pp. 9–10.

Radke-Moss, Andrea G. *Bright Epoch: Women & Coeducation in the American West*. U of Nebraska P, 2008.

Ratcliffe, Krista. "A Rhetoric of Textual Feminism: (Re)Reading the Emotional in Virginia Woolf's *Three Guineas*." *Rhetoric Review*, vol. 11, no. 2, 1993, pp. 400–17.

—. *Rhetorical Listening: Identification, Gender, Whiteness*. Southern Illinois UP, 2005.

"The Replies to Dr. Clarke." *Nation*, vol. 18, no. 469, 25 Jun. 1874, pp. 408–09.

Report of the Commissioner of Education for the Year 1903. United States Bureau of Education, 1905.

"Reviews and Notices." *The Cincinnati Lancet and Observer*, vol. 17, no. 9, 1 Sept. 1874, pp. 566–76.

Rhode, Deborah L. "The 'No-Problem' Problem: Feminist Challenges and Cultural Change." *Yale Law Journal*, vol. 100, no. 6, 1991, pp. 1731–93.

Richardson, Angelique. *Love and Eugenics in the Late Nineteenth Century: Rational Reproduction and the New Woman*. Oxford UP, 2003.

Ritchie, Joy S., and Kate Ronald. "A Gathering of Rhetorics." Introduction. *Available Means: An Anthology of Women's Rhetoric(s)*, edited by Joy Ritchie and Kate Ronald, U of Pittsburgh P, 2001, pp. xv–xxxi.

Rosenberg, Charles E. "American Medicine in 1879." *"Send Us a Lady Physician": Women Doctors in America, 1835–1920*, edited by Ruth J. Abram, W.W. Norton & Company, 1985, pp. 21–34.

Rosenberg, Rosalind. *Beyond Separate Spheres: Intellectual Roots of Modern Feminism*. Yale UP, 1982.

Rossiter, Margaret W. *Women Scientists in America: Struggles and Strategies to 1940*. Vol. 1, Johns Hopkins UP, 1982.

Rothman, David J., et al. *Medicine and Western Civilization*. Rutgers UP, 1995.

Rowold, Katharina. *Gender and Science: Late Nineteenth-Century Debates on the Female Mind and Body*. Thoemmes P, 1996.

Royster, Jacqueline Jones. "'Ain't I a Woman': Using Feminist Rhetorical Practices to Re-set the Terms of Scholarly Engagement for an Iconic Text." *Peitho*, vol. 15, no. 1, 2012, pp. 30–64.

—. *Traces of a Stream: Literacy and Social Change Among African American Women*. U of Pittsburgh P, 2000.

Royster, Jacqueline Jones, and Gesa E. Kirsch. *Feminist Rhetorical Practices: New Horizons for Rhetoric, Composition, and Literacy Studies*. Southern Illinois UP, 2012.

Rury, John L. "'We Teach the Girl *Repression*, the Boy *Expression*': Sexuality, Sex Equity and Education in Historical Perspective." *Peabody Journal of Education*, vol. 64, no. 4, 1987, pp. 44–58.

Russett, Cynthia Eagle. *Sexual Science: The Victorian Construction of Womanhood*. Harvard UP, 1989.

S.W.M. "Sex in Education, or a Fair Chance for the Girls." *Philadelphia Medical Times*, vol. 4, no. 10, 6 Dec. 1873, pp. 156–57.

Salomone, Rosemary C. *Same, Different, Equal: Rethinking Single-Sex Schooling*. Yale UP, 2003.

Sax, Leonard. "Too Few Women—Figure It Out." *Los Angeles Times*, 23 Jan. 2005, https://www.latimes.com/archives/la-xpm-2005-jan-23-oe-sax23-story.html. Accessed 6 Aug. 2022.

Schiebinger, Londa. *The Mind Has No Sex? Women in the Origins of Modern Science*. Harvard UP, 1989.

Schuller, Kyla. *The Biopolitics of Feeling: Race, Sex, and Science in the Nineteenth Century*. Duke UP, 2018.

Schultz, Jaime. *Qualifying Times: Points of Change in U.S. Women's Sport*. U of Illinois P, 2014.

Schweickart, Patrocinio P. "Reading Ourselves: Toward a Feminist Theory of Reading." *Gender and Reading: Essays on Readers, Texts, and Contexts*, edited by Elizabeth A. Flynn and Patrocinio P. Schweickart, Johns Hopkins UP, 1986, pp. 31–62.

—. "Understanding an Other: Reading as a Receptive Form of Communicative Action." *New Directions in American Reception Study*, edited by Philip Goldstein and James L. Machor, Oxford UP, 2008, pp. 3–22.

Scott, Patricia Bell. "Schoolin' 'Respectable' Ladies of Color: Issues in the History of Black Women's Higher Education." *Journal of the National Association for Women Deans, Administrators & Counselors*, vol. 43, no. 2, 1980, pp. 22–28.

Sears, E.H. "Random Readings: The Co-Education of the Sexes." *The Religious Magazine and Monthly Review*, vol. 50, no. 6, Dec. 1873, pp. 567–68.

Seller, Maxine S. "Dr. Clarke vs. the 'Ladies': Coeducation and Women's Roles in the 1870s." Paper presented at the Annual Meeting of the American Educational Research Association (Montreal), April 1983.

"Sex in Education." *Chicago Daily Tribune*, vol. 28, no. 20, 12 Sept. 1874, p. 9.

"Sex in Education." *The Christian Union*, vol. 8, no. 26, 24 Dec. 1873, p. 522.

"Sex in Education." *Old and New*, vol. 9, no. 3, Mar. 1874, pp. 379–83.

"Sex in Education." *Quincy Daily Whig*, vol. 22, no. 208, 1 Apr. 1874, p. 2.

"Sex in Education." *The World*, vol. 14, no. 4608, 30 Mar. 1874, p. 2.

"Sex in Education." *Zion's Herald*, vol. 51, no. 13, 26 Mar. 1874, p. 100.

Sharer, Wendy B. "Venues and Voices: Welcoming Greater Participation in Feminist Rhetorical History and Inquiry." *Ethics and Representation in Feminist Rhetorical Research*, edited by Amy E. Dayton and Jennie L. Vaughn, U of Pittsburgh P, 2021, pp. 218–36.

Shattuck, Debra A. "Bats, Balls and Books: Baseball and Higher Education for Women at Three Eastern Women's Colleges, 1866–1891." *Journal of Sport History*, vol. 19, no. 2, 1992, pp. 91–109.

Shaw, Stephanie J. *What a Woman Ought to Be and to Do: Black Professional Women Workers During the Jim Crow Era*. U of Chicago P, 1996.

Showalter, Elaine. *The Civil Wars of Julia Ward Howe: A Biography*. Simon & Schuster, 2016.

Shure, Natalie. "Why Has It Taken the Menstrual Cup So Long to Go Mainstream?" *Pacific Standard*, 14 June 2017, https://psmag.com/news/why-has-it-taken-the-menstrual-cup-so-long-to-go-mainstream. Accessed 18 Aug. 2022.

Shuttleworth, Sally, et al. "Women, Science and Culture: Science in the Nineteenth-century Periodical." *Women: A Cultural Review*, vol. 12, no. 1, 2001, pp. 57–70.

Siegel, Reva. "Reasoning from the Body: A Historical Perspective on Abortion Regulation and Questions of Equal Protection." *Stanford Law Review*, vol. 44, no. 2, 1992, pp. 261–381.

Skinner, Carolyn. "'She Will Have Science': Ethos and Audience in Mary Gove's Lectures to Ladies," *Rhetoric Society Quarterly*, vol. 39, no. 3, 2009, pp. 240–59.

—. *Women Physicians and Professional Ethos in Nineteenth-Century America*. Southern Illinois UP, 2014.

Skinner, Ellen, editor. *Women and the National Experience: Primary Sources in American History*. 2nd ed., Longman, 2003.

Smith, Christi M. *Reparation and Reconciliation: The Rise and Fall of Integrated Higher Education*. U of North Carolina P, 2016.

Smith, Rogers M. *Civic Ideals: Conflicting Visions of Citizenship in U.S. History*. Yale UP, 1997.

Smothers, Hannah. "10 Bullsh*t Period Myths Women Were Told throughout History." *Cosmopolitan*, 20 July 2018, www.cosmopolitan.com/sex-love/a20963739/period-myths-lies/. Accessed 11 Nov. 2022.

Snowden, Monique L. "'Bettering Her Education and Widening Her Sphere': Betwixt and Between Coeducational Experiences." *Qualitative Inquiry*, vol. 17, no. 10, 2011, pp. 930–42.

"Social Life." *Cincinnati Commercial Tribune*, vol. 34, no. 158, 7 Feb. 1874, p. 12.

Solomon, Barbara Miller. *In the Company of Educated Women: A History of Women and Higher Education in America*. Yale UP, 1985.

Sorber, Nathan M. *Land-Grant Colleges and Popular Revolt: The Origins of the Morrill Act and the Reform of Higher Education*. Cornell UP, 2018.

Spears, Betty. *Leading the Way: Amy Morris Homans and the Beginnings of Professional Education for Women*. Greenwood, 1986.

Spencer, Herbert. *The Principles of Biology*. Appleton, 1864–67. 2 vols.

Stancliff, Michael. *Frances Ellen Watkins Harper: African American Reform Rhetoric and the Rise of a Modern Nation State*. Routledge, 2011.

Stanley, Gregory Kent. "'. . . And Not to Make Athletes of Them': Banning Women's Sports at the University of Kentucky, 1902–24." *The Register of the Kentucky Historical Society*, vol. 93, no. 4, 1995, pp. 422–45.

—. *The Rise and Fall of the Sportswoman: Women's Health, Fitness, and Athletics, 1860–1940*. Peter Lang, 1996.

Stanton, Elizabeth Cady. "An Old Story—Letter from Mrs. Stanton." *Woman's Journal*, vol. 4, no. 14, 5 Apr. 1873, pp. 108–09.

Stob, Paul. *William James and the Art of Popular Statement*. Michigan State UP, 2013.

Stone, Lucinda H. "Effects of Mental Growth." *The Education of American Girls: Considered in a Series of Essays*, edited by Anna C. Brackett, New York, G.P. Putnam's Sons, 1874, pp. 173–211.

Stone, Lucy [L.S.]. "Co-Education of the Sexes." *The Woman's Journal*, vol. 4, no. 1, 4 Jan. 1873, p. 4.
Strange, Julie-Marie. "Menstrual Fictions: Languages of Medicine and Menstruation, c. 1850–1930." *Women's History Review*, vol. 9, no. 3, 2000, pp. 607–28.
Strum, Philippa. "Women and Citizenship: The Virginia Military Institute Case." *Women and the United States Constitution: History, Interpretation, and Practice*, edited by Sibyl A. Schwarzenbach and Patricia Smith, Columbia UP, 2003, pp. 335–46.
"Submissions." *Literacy in Composition Studies*, licsjournal.org/index.php/LiCS/about/submissions. Accessed 4 Jan. 2023.
Swaby, Rachel. *Headstrong: 52 Women Who Changed Science—and the World*. Broadway Books, 2015.
Talbot, Marion, and Lois Kimball Mathews Rosenberry. *The History of the American Association of University Women, 1881–1931*. Houghton Mifflin, 1931.
Tavera, Stephanie Peebles. "Her Body, *Herland*: Reproductive Health and Dis/topian Satire in Charlotte Perkins Gilman." *Utopian Studies*, vol. 29, no. 1, 2018, pp. 1–20.
Thieme, Katja. "Constitutive Rhetoric as an Aspect of Audience Design: The Public Texts of Canadian Suffragists." *Written Communication*, vol. 27, no. 1, 2010, pp. 36–56.
Thomas, M. Carey. "Present Tendencies in Women's College and University Education." *Educational Review*, vol. 35, 1908, pp. 64–85.
—. "Should the Higher Education of Women Differ from that of Men?" *Educational Review*, vol. 21, 1901, pp. 1–10.
Thurs, Daniel P. *Science Talk: Changing Notions of Science in American Popular Culture*. Rutgers UP, 2007.
Tonkovich, Nicole. "Rhetorical Power in the Victorian Parlor: *Godey's Lady's Book* and the Gendering of Nineteenth-Century Rhetoric." *Oratorical Culture in Nineteenth-Century America: Transformation in the Theory and Practice of Rhetoric*, edited by Gregory Clark and S. Michael Halloran, Southern Illinois UP, 1993, pp. 158–83.
Trall, R.T. "Co-Education of the Sexes." *Phrenological Journal and Science of Health*, vol. 60, no. 1, Jan. 1875, pp. 32–33.
Trimbur, John. "Composition and the Circulation of Writing." *College Composition and Communication*, vol. 52, no. 2, 2000, pp. 188–219.
Tuchman, Arlene Marcia. *Science Has No Sex: The Life of Marie Zakrzewska, M.D.* U of North Carolina P, 2006.
Tuttle, Jennifer S. "Letters from Elizabeth Stuart Phelps (Ward) to S. Weir Mitchell, M.D., 1884–1897." *Legacy*, vol. 17, no. 1, 2000, pp. 83–94.
Tyack, David, and Elisabeth Hansot. *Learning Together: A History of Coeducation in American Schools*. Yale UP, 1990.
—. "Silence and Policy Talk: Historical Puzzles about Gender and Education." *Educational Researcher*, vol. 17, no. 3, 1988, pp. 33–41.
Vastal, Radha. "When Progress Ebbs: Career Women at the Turn of the 20th Century." *Los Angeles Review of Books*, 11 July 2017, lareviewofbooks.org/article/

when-progress-ebbs-career-women-at-the-turn-of-the-20th-century/. Accessed 6 Aug. 2022.

Vertinsky, Patricia. "Exercise, Physical Capability, and the Eternally Wounded Woman in Late Nineteenth Century North America." *Journal of Sport History*, vol. 14, no. 1, 1987, pp. 7–27.

—. *The Eternally Wounded Woman: Women, Doctors, and Exercise in the Late Nineteenth Century*. St. Martin's, 1990.

Vigoya, Mara Viveros. "Sex/Gender." *The Oxford Handbook of Feminist Theory*, edited by Lisa Disch and Mary Hawkesworth, Oxford UP, 2016, pp. 852–73.

Vostral, Sharra L. *Under Wraps: A History of Menstrual Hygiene Technology*. Lexington Books, 2008.

W.O.W. "Edward Hammond Clarke." *The Unitarian Review and Religious Magazine*, vol. 9, no. 1, Jan. 1878, pp. 62–69.

Walsh, Mary Roth. *"Doctors Wanted: No Women Need Apply": Sexual Barriers in the Medical Profession, 1835–1975*. Yale UP, 1977.

Ware, John Fothergill Waterhouse. *In Memoriam. Edward Hammond Clarke*. Address delivered in Arlington Street Church, 2 Dec. 1877.

Warren, James Perrin. *Culture of Eloquence: Oratory and Reform in Antebellum America*. Pennsylvania State UP, 1999.

Warren, Joyce W. *Women, Money, and the Law: Nineteenth-Century Fiction, Gender, and the Courts*. U of Iowa P, 2005.

Warsh, Cheryl K. *Prescribed Norms: Women and Health in Canada and the United States since 1880*. U of Toronto P, 2019.

Watson, Martha Solomon. "The Dynamics of Intertextuality: Re-Reading the Declaration of Independence." *Rhetoric and Political Culture in Nineteenth-Century America*, edited by Thomas W. Benson, Michigan State UP, 1997, pp. 91–111.

Weaver-Hightower, Marcus B. "An Ecology Metaphor for Educational Policy Analysis: A Call to Complexity." *Educational Researcher*, vol. 37, no. 3, 2008, pp. 153–67.

Weiler, Kathleen. "Hope and History: What do Future Teachers Need to Know?" *The Radical Teacher*, no. 65, 2002–2003, pp. 11–17.

Wein, Roberta. "Women's Colleges and Domesticity, 1875–1918." *History of Education Quarterly*, vol. 14, no. 1, 1974, pp. 31–47.

Wells, Susan. *Out of the Dead House: Nineteenth-Century Women Physicians and the Writing of Medicine*. U of Wisconsin P, 2001.

White, Hayden. *Tropics of Discourse: Essays in Cultural Criticism*. Johns Hopkins UP, 1978.

Widiss, Deborah A. "Re-viewing History: The Use of the Past as Negative Precedent in *United States v. Virginia*." *The Yale Law Journal*, vol. 108, no. 1, 1998, pp. 237–69.

Willard, Frances E., and Mary A. Livermore, editors. *A Woman of the Century: Fourteen Hundred-Seventy Biographical Sketches Accompanied by Portraits of Leading American Women in All Walks of Life*. Buffalo, Charles Wells Moulton, 1893.

Williams, Juliet. *The Separation Solution?: Single-Sex Education and the New Politics of Gender Equality.* U of California P, 2016.

Willis, Ika. *Reception.* Routledge, 2017.

Wood, Ann D. "'The Fashionable Diseases': Women's Complaints and Their Treatment in Nineteenth-Century America." *The Journal of Interdisciplinary History*, vol. 4, no. 1, 1973, pp. 25–52.

Yanni, Carla. "The Coed's Predicament: The Martha Cook Building at the University of Michigan." *Buildings & Landscapes: Journal of the Vernacular Architecture Forum*, vol. 24, no. 1, 2017, pp. 26–45.

Zakrzewska, M.E. "A Physician on the Other Side." *Woman's Journal*, vol. 5, no. 8, 21 Feb. 1874, p. 59.

Zieff, Susan G. "Leading the Way in Science, Medicine and Physical Training: Female Physicians in Academia, 1890–1930." *International Journal of the History of Sport*, vol. 27, no. 7, 2010, pp. 1219–36.

Zschoche, Sue. "Dr. Clarke Revisited: Science, True Womanhood, and Female Collegiate Education." *History of Education Quarterly*, vol. 29, no. 4, 1989, pp. 545–69.

Index

"9 Bizarre Facts About Your Period Nobody Ever Told You," 186
accretion, 10, 212
Adams, Tracey Lynn, 94, 96, 103
Adams, Bluford, 175
African American women, 130, 132, 134–140, 156, 161, 167, 202
African Americans, 43, 130, 134–141, 144, 161, 210
Agnew, Lois, 165
Ahmed, Sara, 188, 205
Althusser, Louis, 38
American Association of University Women (AAUW), 100, 118
American Eclipse: A Nation's Epic Race to Catch the Shadow of the Moon and Win the Glory of the World (Barton), 170
Ames, Jr., Azel, 147, 150–156, 160, 161
Andersen, Ida, 8, 26, 166, 188, 206
Anderson, Eric D., 46, 142
Anfara, Vincent, 184
Anthony, Dave, 186–187
Antonovich, Jacqueline, 180
Appel, Toby A, 179
Appletons' Journal of Literature, Science and Art, 63, 67, 78
Aristophanes, 49
Aristotle, 140

Arnold, Carrie, 195
Association of Collegiate Alumnæ, 100, 118, 178
Atchinson, Rena Michaels, 73
athletics, 176–177
Atlanta Baptist Female Seminary, 134
audience, 1, 4, 6–9, 11, 13–16, 22, 26–30, 32–34, 38–42, 49–61, 131, 166–167, 173, 179, 183, 185, 187–189, 193–195, 198–199, 203–207, 210–211
authority, 4, 6, 23–24, 33–34, 40–41, 63, 65, 68, 70–71, 77, 83–84, 89, 92–94, 106, 108–109, 111–112, 116, 123–128, 207
autonomy, 24, 70, 91, 94, 97, 112, 116, 121–124, 126, 149

Bacon, Jacqueline, 50
Badger, Ada Shepard, 86
Bain, Alexander, 37
Baker, Liva, 176, 179
Baker, Thomas Nelson, 136
Baron, David, 170, 174–175
Barreca, Regina, 168, 174, 184, 187
Bateman, Katharine Saunders, 20, 38
Batstone, William W., 10

Beedy, Mary E., 74
Bell, Richard C., 167, 174, 177
Bell, Susan Groag, 167, 174, 177
Bender, Bert, 174, 183–184
Bender, Leslie, 174, 183–184
Bennett College, 134
Bensaude-Vincent, 126
Bergland, Renée L., 173
Bessette, Jean, 17, 208
Biesecker, Barbara, 202
biology, 32, 37, 42, 59, 71, 95, 169
Bittel, Carla, 36, 104, 128, 179
Bizzell, Patricia, 210
Blackwell, Antoinette Brown, 35
Blackwell, Henry Browne, 21, 35–36
Blake, Lillie Devereux, 86–87
Bledstein, Burton J., 32, 93
Bodley, Rachel, 178
Boston Daily Advertiser, 35, 62, 72

235

236 *Index*

Boston Daily Globe, 88
Boston Journal of Chemistry, 1
Boston Medical and Surgical Journal, 34
Boylston Prize, 104–105
Brackett, Anna C., 53, 68–70, 73–74, 81, 84, 116
Brandt, Deborah, 205
Branham, Robert J., 130
Brooks, Phillips, 138
Browdy, Ronisha, 14
Brown, JoAnne, 35, 112
Brumberg, Joan Jacobs, 95–96, 112, 125, 179
Bryn Mawr, 119, 172, 176
Bube, June Johnson, 177
Buchanan, Lindal, 12, 15, 200
Building of a Brain, The (Clarke), 32, 37, 97, 107–109, 111, 127, 144
Burke, Kenneth, 38
Burstyn, Joan, 41, 43, 47, 174, 184
Burton (see Collins, Vicki Tolar)

Call, Emma L., 1, 178
Calvin, John, 38
Campbell, Karlyn Kohrs, 12, 189
Cannon, Cornelia James, 172–173
Cayleff, Susan E., 168, 174–175
Charité (Berlin), 103
Charland, Maurice, 29, 38–40, 56
Charney, Davida, 9
Chicago Daily Tribune, 62–63
Child, Lydia Maria, 36
Christian Union, The, 89
Christian Watchman, The, 68
Cincinnati Lancet and Observer, 93, 99
circulation, 13, 55, 177, 205, 212
citation practices, 205
Civil War, 32, 52, 134, 170, 174
Clark University, 120
Clarke, Edward H.: address to the National Education Association, 107–112; application of evolutionary theory, 20, 27, 131, 141–146;

audience constitution by, 27–28, 30, 37–41; biography, 30–32; commentary on working-class women, 146–148; gender construction by, 30, 41–50; lecture to the New England Woman's Club, 34–36; publication of *Sex in Education*, 1–5, 21–22, 36–37; reliance on physiology, 27–28, 37–38, 40–42, 44–45, 99, 110
Clarke, Mary Jones (Stimson), 30
Clarke, Pitt, 30
Clifford, Geraldine J., 113, 125
co-education, 2, 19, 24, 27, 31, 34–36, 38, 40, 48, 50, 54, 58, 65–66, 79, 81, 83, 99, 103, 106, 113, 119–121, 134, 142, 156, 164–165, 176, 181, 193, 195
Cole, Rebecca J., 202
Coleman, R. R., 172
Collins, Patricia Hill, 124
Collins, Vicki Tolar, 10, 189, 212
collaboration, 161, 205, 209–210
college education, 43, 84, 97, 105, 118, 120, 125, 127, 172, 176, 185
Collins, Patricia Hill, 124
Comfort, Anna Manning, 51–52, 69, 87–88, 103, 165
Comfort, George F., 51–52, 69, 87–88, 103, 165
Commeyras, Michelle, 181, 184
Commonwealth, The, 78, 84
Congregationalist, The, 68
conservation of energy, 37, 169
continuous education, 36, 48, 52–53, 67, 71, 84, 86, 102, 117
Cooper, Anna Julia, 135
Costello, Karin Bergstrom, 171, 175
Crumpler, Rebecca, 202

Daily Evening Traveller, 63
Daily Graphic, The, 82, 84
Daily Whig, 57
Dall, Caroline H., 52, 69–70, 74, 77, 84, 146–147

Darwin, Charles, 20, 27, 32, 37, 142, 169, 195; *The Descent of Man, 27; On the Origin of Species*, 27
Darwinism, 43, 105, 145, 162
Davenport, Charles B., 172
DeLuzio, Crista, 20, 37, 174–175, 179
Descent of Man, The (Darwin), 27
Desire and Imagination: Classic Essays in Sexuality (Barecca), 184
Dewey, John, 3, 118–119
Diedrich, Maria I., 172, 179
digital archives, 17, 207–208
Dillon, Halle Tanner, 202
Dodds, Susanna Way, 103
domesticity, 95, 149–150
Drachman, Virginia G., 175, 179, 185
Duffey, Eliza Bisbee, 53, 73, 85–87, 90, 146

E.S.P., 36
Eclectic Magazine, The, 51, 68, 75, 83
Ede, Lisa, 10, 12, 29, 188, 200, 205
education: female, 81; reform, 118
Education of American Girls, The (Brackett), 53, 68–69, 74, 116
"Effects of Mental Growth" (Stone), 116
Ehrenreich, Barbara, 179, 186–187
eloquence: culture of, 32–34, 46
Emmet, Thomas Addis, 106
emotion, 3, 198, 202–203
"End of Dr. Clarke, The" (news report), 84
England, 21, 34–35, 103, 136, 148
English, Deirdre, 27, 32, 35–36, 57, 109, 144, 186–187
Enoch, Jessica, 17, 28–29, 107, 198, 208
epistemology, 37, 45, 49, 53, 59, 78, 90–91, 94, 101, 123–124, 170; scientific, 27, 34, 41, 86
ethos, 19, 38, 64, 83, 86, 184, 187, 194

Europe, 37, 57, 103
evidence: scientific, 34, 71, 74, 79, 84, 126
evolution, 22, 32, 37, 44, 65–67, 76, 102, 129, 138, 141–142, 174
exigence, 145, 169
expertise, 6, 19, 23–24, 26, 33, 38, 53–54, 66–67, 70, 75, 77–78, 84, 89, 92, 95, 97–98, 101, 106–107, 112, 123–125, 127, 160, 185, 199; medical, 53, 69, 114, 150, 154

Fairchild, James H., 36
femininity, 8, 28, 41–43, 48–49, 55, 94, 97, 125, 127, 134, 149, 155, 183, 195
feminism, 1–2, 4–5, 7–16, 25–26, 53, 58–60, 92, 130–132, 167–168, 170, 173, 178, 188–189, 195, 197–198, 200, 202, 204–205, 207–212
feminization, 121
fertility, 36, 43, 48, 55, 105, 111, 121, 143, 174, 191–192
Foner, Philip Sheldon, 130
Fourteenth Amendment, 182
reproductive system: female, 2, 39, 43–44, 46, 111, 151
Frow, John, 9–10

Gage, Frances Dana, 62, 82
Galveston Daily News, 57
Garvey, Ellen Gruber, 205
gender, 10, 22, 27–30, 41–42, 44–45, 48–53, 55–60, 94–96, 103, 107, 111–112, 122–124, 126–128, 141–142, 181–184, 198–199; construction, 27–30, 50, 52, 56, 58–60, 183, 198–199; difference, 82, 141; ideology, 5, 15, 107, 134
gendered education, 45, 47, 52
gendering, 10, 22, 28–30, 97, 114, 127, 199

Gerritsen Women's History Collection (database), 17
Gilb, Corinne Lathrop, 93, 115
Ginsburg, Ruth Bader, 3, 181–184
"Girls and Women in England and America" (Beedy), 74
Glenn, Cheryl, ix, 10, 131, 133, 140, 161, 188, 202
Goodell, William, 100, 106
Graban, Tarez Samra, ix, 12–13
Greene, William B., 54, 57, 77
Griffin, Gail B., 12, 175, 177, 179, 200
Grundy, Madame, 82

Hall, G. Stanley, 3, 120–123, 126, 143
Hallenbeck, Sarah, ix, 12–13, 28, 96, 189, 201, 206, 211
Halloran, S. Michael, 66
Hamlin, Kimberly A., 171, 174–175, 178–179
Hammond, William, 30–31, 169, 193
Hansot, Elisabeth, 2, 112–114, 164, 174–175, 184
Harper's New Monthly Magazine, 68–69
Harris, Randy Allen, 9
Harvard Magazine, 176
Harvard Medical School, 31, 176
Harvard University, 30–31, 33, 35–36, 52, 104, 106, 121, 169, 172, 176, 181
Hawhee, Deborah, 209
"Health and Sex in Higher Education" (Dewey), 118
Helmholtz, Hermann von, 20, 37, 44
Hensley Owens, Kim, 12–13
Higginson, Thomas Wentworth, 30, 52, 77, 81–82, 84–85
higher education, 4, 21, 23, 35, 53, 59, 63, 66–69, 93, 113, 119–121, 131, 135, 137–138, 141, 156, 166, 172, 176, 182, 185–186

historiography, 16, 28, 170, 209
Holland, Sir Henry, 31
Hollingworth, Leta Stetter, 128
Holmes, Oliver Wendell, 2, 31, 62
Howard, Edine T., 115–116, 126–127
Howe, Julia Ward, 53, 55, 61, 80, 143–144, 165
Huxley, Thomas Henry, 38

infertility, 44, 46, 84, 90, 192
Irving, Washington, 85

Jack, Jordynn, 124, 198
Jacobi, Mary Putnam, 68, 75–77, 97, 103–106, 124–125, 150, 155–161, 165, 178
Jewish Messenger, The, 63
Jordan, David Starr, ix, 3
Justice, Justice (Ginsburg), 181

Kant, Immanuel, 38, 49
Kendall, Aimee, 9
Kirsch, Gesa E., 9, 12–13, 132, 140, 200, 203, 209
Kjeldsen, Jens E., 7–8, 26, 166, 188, 194, 206, 209

La Vergata, Antonello, 174
Learning Together (Tyack and Hansot), 112, 114, 164
"Liberal Learning and Long Life," (anonymous), 99
Lindemann, Hilde, 175
listening, 12, 16, 140, 209

Logan, Shirley Wilson, ix, 130, 135
logic, 23, 76, 85, 186, 202
Lunsford, Andrea A., 10, 12, 29, 188, 200, 205

MacDonald, Victoria-Maria, 125
Mann, Mary Tyler Peabody, 53, 55–57

marginalization, 2, 4, 16, 130–133, 200–202, 204, 206, 212
marriage, 55, 85, 114, 121, 125, 135
Martindale, Charles, 8, 10
masculinity, 8, 42, 94–96, 103, 106, 121, 123, 125, 127, 195
Massachusetts Bureau of Statistics of Labor, 150
Massachusetts Teacher, 114
Mastrangelo, Lisa, 175
Maudsley, Henry, 3, 37, 43, 169
McKerrow, Raymie E., 132
Mckoy, Temptaous, 205
McWilliam, Erica, 174, 184
Medical Eclectic (journal), 99
Medical News (journal), 100–101
Medical Record (journal), 106
menstruation, 41, 44, 46–48, 64, 87–88, 102, 104–106, 111, 124, 128, 152, 156–158, 160, 169, 178, 186
methodology, 197
Michaels, Rena, 73, 75
middle class, 106, 140, 142
misogyny, 25, 146, 162, 197
Mitchell, Koritha, 139, 142
Mitchell, Maria, 174
Mitchell, Silas Weir, 99, 120, 169
Morrill Land Grant Acts, 113, 164
Morton, Thomas, 82
Mosher, Clelia Duel, 128, 178

National American Woman Suffrage Association, 35
National Education Association (NEA), 97, 108–109, 112
New Church Magazine, 72
New England Hospital for Women and Children, 103
New York Academy of Medicine, 75
New York Infirmary for Women and Children, The, 75
New York Medical College for Women, 51

Newman, Louise Michele, 105, 141, 148–149
Nguyen, Sophia, 176, 179
No Sex in Education (Duffey), 53, 85
"Normal Menstruation and Some of the Factors Modifying It" (Mosher), 178
normal schools, 113, 116, 125
North American Review, 81
Northwestern University, 73

Oberlin College, 36, 134
objectivity, 23, 33, 38, 67, 70, 77, 85, 97, 103, 106, 124
Olson, Christa J., 209
Onion, Rebecca, 180, 184
Oreskes, Naomi, 171, 174–175, 185, 187
Other Side, The (Dall), 70

Park, Roberta J., 174, 176, 179
Patterson, Mary Jane, 134
Paul, Danette, 9
Peabody, George, 31, 55
Peril, Lynn, 171, 175
periodicity, 2, 35, 44, 46, 49–50, 72, 142, 148
persistence, 2, 44, 126–128, 145, 191
persuasion, 4, 9, 11, 38–39, 59, 64, 83, 92, 203, 205
Phelps, Elizabeth Stuart, 53–54, 56, 69
Philadelphia Medical Times, 99
physicians, 46–48, 53–54, 69–70, 84, 93–109, 111–112, 114, 123–126, 177–178,
physiological education, 82
physiology (and physicians), 2–4, 27, 34, 36–40, 43, 49, 52–54, 67–72, 76–83, 98–99, 102, 104, 110–111, 154, 156, 179, 184–186, ; female, 2–4, 27, 34, 36–40, 43, 49, 52–54, 67–72, 76–83, 98–99, 102, 104, 110–111, 154, 156, 179, 184–186,
Poirot, Kristan, 95

240 *Index*

Pope, C. Augusta, 178
Pope, Emily F., 178
Popular Science, 3, 65, 78, 118
positionality, 10, 12, 130, 193, 198, 202–203
power, 4, 6, 8, 13–14, 16, 25–26, 28, 41–42, 44–45, 49, 88–89, 94–95, 102–103, 111, 121, 129, 132, 166, 170, 180, 183, 188, 190, 192, 194–195, 200–201, 211

Principles and Practice of Gynæcology, The (Emmet), 106
Principles of Biology (Spencer), 27
privilege, 18, 55, 88, 149, 212
"Problems and Their Solution" (editorial), 114–115
professionalism, 4–5, 22, 24, 26, 33–34, 65, 93–96, 103, 106–108, 112–114, 116–117, 119–128, 130, 189, 198, 204; culture of, 32–34, 38, 40, 46, 93
professionalization, 24, 64, 93, 95–97, 103, 106–107, 112, 114, 116–117, 122, 125, 127–128, 134, 202
Progressive Era, 112, 125
public discourse, 3, 64–65, 71–72, 75–77, 80, 83, 88–89, 91–92, 202

Question of Rest for Women During Menstruation, The (Jacobi), 97, 104, 155, 157, 159, 165, 178
Quintilian, 168

race, 1–2, 43, 45, 49, 51, 65, 67, 90, 94–95, 106, 109, 111, 131, 135–138, 142–146, 156, 167, 172, 191–192
race suicide, 43, 90, 172
racism, 20, 25, 133, 139, 141–143, 146, 161–162, 170, 192, 198, 205
Ratcliffe, Krista, 7, 12, 203
reception: direct, ix, 1–2, 4–30, 34, 39, 50, 54, 57–66, 71–72, 75, 77–78, 83–84, 89–93, 96–97, 100, 105–107, 109, 111–112, 114, 122–123, 125–134, 137–143, 146, 148–150, 154–155, 157, 160–167, 171, 173, 176, 178, 180, 182–183, 185–212; history, 7; indirect, 24, 131–133, 154, 160–162, 200; rhetoric, 20, 28, 89, 128, 132, 146, 181, 195, 199, 201, 204, 209–210; silences, 17, 132–133, 162, 209; text-to-text, 16, 203–204; theory, 7–8
reception studies, 5, 7–8, 12–15, 58, 130, 165–166, 197; feminist rhetorical, 4–5, 8, 15–16, 26, 92, 197, 207, 210
recovery, 9–10, 12, 25, 212
reproduction, 95, 99, 105, 138, 178, 185, 190–191
reproductive functions, 3, 37, 43–44, 46, 110, 125, 182
reproductive health, 44, 63, 150–151, 154–156, 186
reproductive physiology, 4, 24, 28, 41–42, 45, 49–51, 63, 77, 80, 88, 93, 99, 102, 117, 141, 148, 153–154, 165, 178, 186
Republican Motherhood, 136
repurposing, 13, 166, 181, 184, 187, 194
research methods, 17, 61, 64, 70, 89, 92, 103, 106, 123–124, 127, 197, 209, 211
resistance, 24, 144, 189–190, 192, 201, 205, 207, 210
Reynolds, Gareth, 186–187
rhetoric, 2–3, 5, 7–11, 13, 15, 17–18, 22, 25–26, 30, 38, 46, 59–60, 64–65, 87, 92, 101, 129–132, 161, 165–167, 188–189, 191–192, 194, 198, 201–202, 205–212
rhetorical action: collective, 26, 161, 189, 198–201
rhetorical analysis, 1, 5–6, 26, 166–167, 212

Rhetorical Feminism (Glenn), 202–203
rhetorical reception, 1, 5, 16–17, 58, 161, 164, 187–188, 194–195, 197, 206–207, 209–210, 212
rhetorical silence, 24, 130, 133
rhetorical theory: feminist, 197, 204
Rice, Rebecca S., 74
Riesman, David, 182
Roosevelt, Theodore, 179
Rosenberg, Charles E., 97–98
Rosenberg, Rosalind, 20, 37, 114, 174–175, 179
Rosenberry, Lois Kimball Mathews, 100, 118
Royster, Jaqueline Jones, 9, 12–13, 62, 130, 132, 134, 137–138, 140, 200, 203, 209
Ryan, Kathleen J., 15

Sax, Leonard, 181, 184
Schiebinger, Londa, 3
Schweickart, Patrocinio, 9, 11
scientific method, 33, 52, 65, 178
scientific values, 52
Scott, Patricia Bell, 167, 174, 177
Sears, E. H., 80
second-wave feminism, 25, 165
Seller, Maxine, 2
Sex in Education: popularity of, 50, 61–63, 66, 171; publication history, 1–5, 21-22, 26, 34–37, 61–63;
Sex in Industry: A Plea for the Working-Girl (Ames), 150
sexism, 20, 180–183, 187, 191, 194, 205
Sharer, Wendy, 200
Shaw, Stephanie J., 137–139
Shiebinger, Londa, 3
Shure, Natalie, 186–187
Shuttleworth, Sally, 65–66
silence, 5, 16, 20, 24, 54, 57, 130–134, 140, 142, 144, 146, 148–150, 152, 154, 160–162, 200–201, 209–210

Skinner, Carolyn, 70, 99, 103, 187, 202
Skinner, Ellen, 185
Slate (magazine), 3, 180
Smith, Cándida, 174–175
Smith, Michelle, 96
Smith, Rogers M., 174
Snowden, Monique L., 193–194
social change, 2, 8, 12, 14–15, 17, 26, 59, 129, 189, 201, 204, 206
social circulation, 13, 200
social Darwinism, 3, 27, 37, 140–141, 147, 197
social institutions, 192, 199
social media, 11, 201, 206
Sojourner Truth, 62
Somerville, Mary, 35
specialization, 33

Spelman College, 134
Spencer, Herbert, 3, 20, 27, 37, 43, 147, 169

Stanton, Elizabeth Cady, 36
statistics, 104–105, 118, 150, 158, 178
Stob, Paul, 32–33, 38, 61
Stone, Lucinda H., 116–117
Stone, Lucy, 35–36
subjectivity, 124, 167, 188, 195
Summers, Lawrence H., 181
Supreme Court, 3, 17, 181
Swaby, Rachel, 186–187
synecdoche, 25, 166, 168–171, 173–175, 182–183, 187

Talbot, Marion, 100, 118
teachers, 23–24, 30, 46–48, 50–51, 58, 80–81, 92–93, 96–97, 105, 107–118, 120–123, 125–127, 135, 137, 143, 155, 157, 164, 204
teaching (as a profession), 111, 114–115

thermodynamics, 32, 37, 44, 169, 174, 185
Thieme, Katja, 39, 59
Thomas, M. Carey, 3, 119–120, 122–123, 127, 185
Tomes, Nancy, 95–96, 112, 125
Trall, Russell, 99
Trimbur, John, 205
Tyack, David, 2, 112–114, 164, 174–175, 184

Unitarian Review and Religious Magazine, The, 74
United States v. Virginia, 181
University of Michigan, 116, 171, 176
Unspoken: A Rhetoric of Silence (Glenn), 131–132

values (rhetorical), 4, 12, 14, 20, 23–24, 34, 66, 71, 83, 85, 88–89, 91–92, 97, 124, 127, 161, 198–199, 202–204
Vassar College, 69, 84, 100–101
Vigoya, Mara Viveros, 95
Virginia Military Institute (VMI), 3, 182
Vostral, Sharra L., 71, 169, 174

Walsh, Mary Roth, 50, 175, 179
Ware, John Fothergill Waterhouse, 31
Warren, J.W., 175
Warren, James Perrin, 32
What Women Should Know: A Woman's Book about Women (Duffey), 85
white women, 43, 63, 65, 134–138, 140–143, 145–146, 148–149, 156, 168–169, 174
White, Hayden, 141, 148–149, 170, 205
Whitney, Adaline S., ix, 100
Widiss, Deborah A., 182, 184
Willis, Ika, 7–8, 16, 203–204
Woman of the Century: Fourteen Hundred-Seventy Biographical Sketches Accompanied by Portraits of Leading American Women in All Walks of Life, A (Livermore), 51
Women Physicians and Professional Ethos in Nineteenth-Century America (Skinner), 99, 103, 202
working women, 53, 108, 146–152, 154–156, 160

Yanni, Carla, 177, 179
Youmans, Edward L., 3

Zakrzewska, Marie, 103

About the Author

Carolyn Skinner is Associate Professor of English at The Ohio State University at Newark. She has taught courses on histories of rhetoric, women's rhetoric, health and medical rhetoric, and technical writing. Her research examines the development of professional and scientific rhetoric in the nineteenth-century United States, especially medical rhetoric written by or about women; historical women's rhetorical theory; and rhetorical reception. Skinner's work has appeared in *College English, Advances in the History of Rhetoric, Technical Communication Quarterly, Rhetoric Society Quarterly,* and *Rhetoric Review.* Her earlier book, *Women Physicians & Professional Ethos in Nineteenth-Century America* (Southern Illinois University Press), examines the rhetorical practices of early women medical professionals.

Photograph of the author by Chris Dawson.
Used by permission.

www.ingramcontent.com/pod-product-compliance
Lightning Source LLC
Chambersburg PA
CBHW030824230426
43667CB00008B/1369